WITHDRAWN

SYNGMAN RHEE:

THE MAN BEHIND THE MYTH

BOOKS BY ROBERT T. OLIVER

Syngman Rhee: The Man Behind the Myth

Verdict in Korea (1952)

The Truth About Korea (1951)

Why War Came in Korea (1950)

Korea: Forgotten Nation (1944)

Four Who Spoke Out: Burke, Fox, Sheridan and Pitt (1946)

Training for Effective Speech (1939)

Psychology of Persuasive Speech (1942)

Developing Ideas (1943)
(With H. L. Robbins)

Effective Speech Notebook (1945)

The New Training for Effective Speech (1946, 1951)
(With Rupert L. Cortright)

Essentials of Communicative Speech (1949)
(With H. P. Zelko and D. C. Dickey)

Persuasive Speaking: Principles and Methods (1950)

Korea, My Country, by Yung Tai Pyun (1953). *Editor*

An "official" photograph distributed by the Republic of Korea Office of Public Information in 1952.

SYNGMAN RHEE

The Man Behind the Myth

By ROBERT T. OLIVER

ILLUSTRATED

DODD MEAD AND COMPANY

NEW YORK · 1954

For Mary
Who else could it be?

PREFACE

Biography is a challenge no one should face lightly. A life is too sacred to be carelessly reviewed. No one should attempt to chronicle the strengths and the weaknesses, the character and the temperament, the achievements and the failures, the ideals and the ambitions of one of his fellows without giving the effort long and careful thought. The *outwardness* of a man worth writing about is a living portion of the history of the race, and unless he is portrayed rightly the blemish is suffered by us all. The outward life of Syngman Rhee is built closely into the fabric of the new Korea that fell to the imperialism which punctured the old civilization of North Asia at the turn of the twentieth century but that held onto its integrity through a generation while awaiting an opportunity to arise again. In its rising the conflict between the Soviet imperialism and the democratic will to live in freedom came to painful focus and Rhee was in the center of the whirlwind, unable to control it but successfully surmounting its storms. His life story, then, is a vital part of the history of the most colossal struggle of our times. He represents a rare stabilizing force in an age and in an area of disintegration. If stability in his part of the world is to be restored it will develop around the program and upon a foundation of the ideals for which he is not alone the spokesman but also in essence the architect.

The *inwardness* of such a man is especially difficult to penetrate. The feelings, the motives, the convictions of a public man are so distorted and concealed by the cause he represents that few can expect to penetrate behind the veil.

Since he lives in the center of international controversies, all that is written about him in the daily press tends more to obscure than to reveal the intrinsic nature of the man himself. To only a few can he truly be known and those few, in the nature of things, must be his friends. The intimacies which portray the real personality occur only in the unguarded relaxation of genuine comradeship. Those who understand Syngman Rhee best can only be those who have known him with affection and admiration across a lengthy span of years.

While the life of Syngman Rhee is complex (like all lives) and unique in its essence and achievements (so that his equal is not likely to appear in Korea soon, if ever again), the general pattern of his development adheres to a simple and vital formula. He is an archtype of that new man who has begun to appear in our century: an integration of the cultures of the East and the West. One of his greatest values and perhaps the chief foundation of his effective leadership is that he successfully synthesized his excellent education in the ancient culture of the Orient with his advanced studies in American and European history and philosophy. At a time when the two disparate hemispheres have been united in a common destiny, he has stood in the center, able with equal ease to see the central meanings of both. One of the keys to the nature of the man is that he speaks with equal facility in Korean and in English, but with different styles and emphases in the two languages. He knows how to talk to his own people as well as to ours. And he does not make the mistake of thinking that the two audiences have as yet become one. The synthesis which he exemplifies is one the peoples of the Orient and the Occident are just now beginning to approach. That is one major reason why we need to listen to what he says and to seek to interpret the manner of his speech.

It has been my fortunate opportunity to work with him in

Washington before the liberation of Korea from the Japanese, frequently in Korea during the years since 1945, and in Washington and at the United Nations as a counsellor and as manager of the Washington Office of the Korean Pacific Press. It has also been my good fortune to have the active assistance in the preparation of this book of those who have known and worked with him for many years. To make suitable acknowledgement to all of them would be impossible. Very special appreciation must be extended, however, to Ambassador Ben C. Limb, Pyo Wook and Chungnim Han, Yung Tai Pyun, Hugh Cynn, John W. Staggers and Jay Jerome Williams, Walter Jhung, Peter S. Hyun, Sr., Mrs. Ethel B. Kamp, Henry Chung DeYoung, Sae Sun Kim, Won Soon Lee, Young Han Choo, Maurice William, Frederick Brown Harris, M. Preston Goodfellow, Kyung Ho Lee, Louise Yim, Ambassador You Chan Yang, Philip Jaisohn, Kimm Kiusic, George Paik, Horace Underwood, Merritt Earl, Homer B. Hulbert, John Orr, Arthur I. Andrews, O. R. Avison, Won Soon Lee, Young-shik Kim, Tayson Jhung, Soon Ju Chey and Nod-hi Sohn. Without the living recollections of such people as these, this account could not have been rounded out or rendered reasonably complete.

Foremost among those who have been gracious and helpful in assembling this record are President and Mrs. Syngman Rhee. During twelve years of intimate association with them, I have been privileged to learn of many of their thoughts and plans, both in personal talks and through a large accumulation of correspondence. President Rhee has also kindly turned over for my use many documents, letters and diary notes covering the major portions of his life. Without this whole-hearted cooperation the story of his life would necessarily have been meager indeed.

In the actual writing I have benefited much from the patient and critical reading of the manuscript by my brother, Egbert S. Oliver, and by Raymond T. Bond, Consul General

Young Han Choo and Philip (Pyo Wook) Han. Far beyond these others I owe a tremendous debt of appreciation to the devoted assistance of my wife, who has shared fully with me the experience of our work together on the Korean question and who has carefully assisted in my reconsideration of all the facts and judgments which are interwoven in the attempt to delineate accurately the life and character of Syngman Rhee.

Finally, I send this work to press with a full realization that much more remains to be said about its subject and with the confident expectation that time will clarify some of the problems that are now confused in the maze of contemporary disagreements. The real significance of Syngman Rhee will emerge only in the future when time will provide the perspective on which all ultimate judgments must be based. I am confident that in the long view his stature and importance will continue to grow. Meanwhile, the facts set forth in the following pages will speak for themselves.

ROBERT T. OLIVER
State College, Penna.

January 11, 1954

CONTENTS

CONTENTS

ILLUSTRATIONS

SYNGMAN RHEE:

THE MAN BEHIND THE MYTH

Chapter I

CHILDHOOD—
OUT OF MEDIEVALISM

THE ODDS were all against the birth of Syngman Rhee. For five preceding generations his paternal family line had produced only one surviving son in each generation—a slender thread on which to hang a chance for life. His own mother was forty years of age and had borne two daughters and a sickly son who failed to survive boyhood. The period of her fertility was drawing to an end when, one night, she dreamed that a dragon flew down from heaven and entered into her bosom. She awoke in a transport of joy and told the story to her husband and daughters, for in the Orient the dragon is as much revered as it has been dreaded in the West. Her dream was nothing uncommon among pregnant women of the East, who are steeped in Buddhist lore and in supernatural folk tales. But in this instance the portent proved to be well founded. On March 26, 1875, a healthy son was born.

When his elder brother died, this new babe was given the stately title of *Yukdai Dokja,* or the last of six successive only sons. Because of the dragon dream, his boyhood name was *Yongi,* the Korean term for dragon. He was wept over

1

with joy and watched over with care, for in the Yi family *
he was a precious treasure. All Korean children are given
an amount of personal attention rare in any other country.
They are carried about strapped to the back of mother, father, nurse or older brother or sister, with their legs clasped
around the carrier's thighs. Always they feel the warmth of
the bodily contact, and always a protective custody is in-
sured. When they cry, comfort is close at hand. As infants,
they are shifted around on their mother's hip to feed from
her breast. Even from the first weeks of life, they are taken
out on the streets, into the fields for work, or on social calls,
wherever their bearer may go. Loneliness is something they
never experience. The sense of belonging is early inbred.
When, as in the case of this *Yukdai Dokja,* the child is especially valued, he is entertained, played with, babied and
lionized almost constantly. Not many specific details of
Rhee's youth have been preserved, but we can be certain
that his childhood was a happy one.

The official Rhee family genealogy extends backward for
seventeen generations, but when the boy Syngman was
born, nature had played out its game. Neither of his sisters
lived to marry. His father had no brothers or surviving sister, and he has no living relations on his maternal side. For
six generations the family had barely survived on the doubtful thread of a single son in each. In the seventh it is dying
out. Syngman Rhee, too, fathered an only son; but in childhood this boy died, and the ancestral line is drawing to an
end.

Yi Kyung-sun, the boy's father, was a member of the

---

* The baptismal name given to this boy amid suitable ceremonies at the
Buddhist Temple was Yi Seung-man. Since he is known around the world
as Syngman Rhee, this is the name by which he will henceforth be identified, although he did not adopt it until 1905, when he was thirty years
old. During his youth he became known to the missionaries as Yi or Lee
Seung-man. In Korea (because of the difficulty of transliterating from the
Korean to the English alphabet) Yi is often spelled Ri, Lee, Li, Rhee, Ryee
or even Ni.

scholarly *Yangban* * class. He was reared in wealth, and educated for nonproductive scholarship. Although he lost his wealth long before Syngman's birth, to the end of his life he always dressed in the formal gowns of the scholar, cultivated a flowing beard and comported himself with careful dignity. Neighbors used to say, "Sain-Nim (an honorific term for scholar) is a gentleman to his fingertips." A fine-looking man, he was warm-hearted, generous, convivial—and improvident. As was common in upper-class Korean families (even when they are poor) the father lived a life of restrained dignity in his family relationships, and his son had little real companionship with him except for a brief period when Rhee was in his forties. In his character and temperament he belongs to Korea's ancient past—separated from Syngman Rhee by a vast gulf.

Syngman's mother, Kim-Hai Kimsio, who was his closest companion through his childhood, used to tell him, "Your father has never had any interest in women or gambling, but he would give the world for friends and convivial parties." In Korean homes of that period, even the poorest had one reception room that belonged specifically to the husband, and there he would entertain male guests, while his family remained out of sight. In Yi Kyung-sun's home, this room was small—probably not more than ten feet square in size—and, as was the Korean custom, almost completely unfurnished. Small black-lacquered tables, about eighteen inches high, would be brought in for the guests—one in front of each—who would sit cross-legged on the floor while sipping their rice wine or tea and telling stories. Such parties were the solace of Master Yi's life, and when he was entertaining a party of friends, nothing else seemed important.

Yi Kyung-sun's very genuine scholarship was largely devoted to genealogy, as was generally true of the intellectual

* In the Confucian system this was accounted the highest social class, followed in order by the farmers, industrialists, merchants and soldiers.

aristocracy of his time. He would spend hours studying from twenty-four large volumes which he kept in a beautiful bookcase, learning by heart all the main lines and branches of the Yi family and of other noted Korean families. Many a time he would draw his young son up beside him and recite stories of their ancestors. When Syngman proved to be uninterested in these past glories, his father would sigh with exasperation and send him out to play. The old scholar finally copied out the main lines of the family ancestry in a small notebook and charged Syngman always to keep it safe. This advice the son observed, and the old notebook is still preserved among his papers. Yi Kyung-sun also used to recite many old classical poems, tales and essays to Syngman, and taught many of them to the boy. On occasion he would ask Syngman to recite them to him; and when the boy forgot a line, he would shake his head disapprovingly and then give him a cue.

Syngman's mother worked very hard at her household tasks, but seemed never too busy to teach him or read to him. She, too, was distinctly a product of the old, conservative Korean culture, and her thinking was devoted to preserving and passing on the values of the past. His first idea of poetry came from a verse she read to him in his early childhood. For years it stayed in his mind and became a model and inspiration for his own poetry:

> The wind has no hands but it shakes all the trees;
> The moon has no feet, but travels across the sky.

During Syngman's early boyhood (until he was seven) Korea was so tightly closed to the outside world that it was known as "The Hermit Kingdom." Foreigners were not permitted in the country, and no Koreans traveled abroad, except a few officials who made annual trips to Peking and Tokyo. Social life was strictly governed by the Confucian codes of behavior, which emphasized courtesy and rigidity of conformance to prescribed etiquette devised for all manner of relationships and for all probable situations. Education consisted largely of learning what was right and proper to be done. Ideas of change and progress were unthought of. Stability and decorum were the ideals. Conformity to established standards of thought and behavior demanded the learning of extensive and complex rules. Otherwise, life at that time in Korea was the essence of simplicity.

The houses were small, one-storied, and made of easily available materials. The great bulk of the homes were straw-thatched huts with walls of mud plastered on a woven willow or bamboo frame, without windows and with only one outer door. Typically the houses were shaped like an L or a U, with a work-yard surrounded by a high brush fence. Except in the entertainment room, the floors were of dirt. Cooking was done on a small hearth fire, and the dishes were as few as the diet was unvaried—consisting of rice gruel for breakfast, rice and *kim-che* (a mixture of pickled vegetables) for lunch and more rice and *kim-che*, with perhaps a bit of meat or fish added, and, on fortunate days, rice-flour cakes for dessert, at the evening meal. Furnishings consisted chiefly of a few small tables and one or two chests which contained clothing and the bedding that was spread on the floor at night.

Toys were almost nonexistent except those the children made for themselves. Flying kites was a traditional exercise at New Year's and was frequently enjoyed all through the spring. Homemade ice skates (consisting of a thin piece of wood fastened on each shoe) and sleds were frequently used during the cold winters. Most of the games were highly social, such as hide-and-seek, hopscotch and contests of strength, fleetness or agility. Many kinds of simple and not-so-sweet candies were sold by hawkers along the streets. The children enjoyed one another and had a good time. They learned to get along together, to be self-reliant, and to develop their wits. In summer, family picnics or picnic groups of youngsters were common, with the abundant hills and streams of Korea providing excellent picnic spots. Traveling storytellers would be sure to arrive in the neighborhood at least two or three times each month, and crowds of children would gather around them to hear their dramatized song-recitals of old legends. It was a simple but far from barren life.

During his childhood, Syngman observed many of his father's friends fondling their ancestral books and reciting genealogies. He noted that few of them did anything to support their families or to serve their country, but that they took it for granted that respect and subsistence were owed by the populace to the twentieth or thirtieth generation of some notable line. This same disease of ancestor-reverence spread all the way down through the society, even to the poorest share-crop rice paddy farmers. The Koreans of seventy-five years ago spent so much time extolling the glories of their forebears that they let their own and their country's welfare degenerate into a deplorable state of disorder and inefficiency. The boy Syngman hated it! Even though he was part and parcel of this social system, somehow at a very early age he sensed its weaknesses and understood some of its defects.

While he was a child someone told him a story which made such a deep impress on his imagination that he never forgot it. A certain Korean died and his soul followed a celestial guide who showed him all through a palace in the Great Beyond. (The native Korean religion was based on the worship of a single god, *Hananim*, and a belief in personal immortality.) When they reached the richly decorated quarters of the aristocratic *Yangbans*, the newcomer discovered that all the men therein were so emaciated that there seemed hardly any flesh on their bones. These men all crowded him and urged him to return to earth to advise their descendants to make their own way in the world, instead of living on the memories of their ancestors. "Our offspring," they cried, "are living on us to such an extent that we are eternally consumed." It is interesting and fortunate that somehow, in the early, formative years of his childhood, Syngman encountered some influences that impelled him to look toward the future rather than to the past.

For many years Syngman Rhee's own ancestry was an irritation and in some respects a handicap to him. In the seventeenth generation preceding his birth, his paternal ancestor, Prince Yi Yang Yung, who was the grandson of the founder of the Yi dynasty, was persuaded by his father to renounce his own right of succession to the throne to make way for a younger brother. Rhee's ancestral record was well-known among educated Koreans, and his political enemies long tried to submerge him with the charge that he was trying to re-establish the monarchy and make himself king.

Syngman's great-grandfather, Yi Hwang, had moved from the ancestral home in Seoul to the Haiju District in Whang-Hai Province, among the low mountains on the west coast, just above the 38th parallel and at the top of the Ongjin Peninsula. Before Syngman's birth, his parents were forced by their diminishing income to move to a small house in Nung-an-gol, in the Pyungsan District, where he was born. Still further reduction in the family circumstances forced another move, when the boy was three, to Seoul, and later to Do-dong (Peach Village), in the southern outskirts of Seoul. Here, in a small hut on a barren hillside, Syngman lived until 1895. Despite his aristocratic lineage, he grew up with Korea's poor and learned to think as they think and feel as they feel. Along with his first flickering sparks of childhood progressiveness, democracy rooted in the welfare of the masses of the people was inbred in his earliest experience.

One of the stories told to Syngman by his father related

to an ancestral shrine on a hillside in Do-dong, which was
watched over by poor descendants of the famous *Yangban*
in whose honor it had been erected. The small temple, hous-
ing ancestral tablets commemorating some of Syngman's
ancestors, was hidden by the branches of a big juniper tree.
One freezing morning a mendicant Buddhist priest stopped
to ask at the door of the caretakers for alms. He was told
the family was so poor it did not even have firewood with
which to cook rice. "How, then, can we give alms?" the
priest was asked. Either his hunger or his theological liberalism provided an answer, and he advised them to cut down
the tree which sheltered the family shrine. With some re-
luctance his suggestion was followed, and the family was
warm again.

On the opposite side of the valley rose a great temple
called *Kwan Je Myo,* where the King himself came at times
to worship. One day when the King was leaving this temple, his eye was caught by the poor shrine across the valley,
which formerly had been hidden by the tree. He inquired
and found it housed ancestral tablets of some of the descendants of Prince Yang Yung. He ordered the building to be
replaced by a much finer shrine, and appointed another de-
scendant of Prince Yang to watch over it. His bounty did
not, however, stretch far enough to result in any benefits
for Syngman's poor relatives, who for so long had attended
to this family duty. The point of this story, as Yi Kyung-sun
carefully pointed out, was not that the King was unjust, but
that fortune is fickle and may bring good or ill, without system or reason, like the random gusts of the March wind. Do
not count upon what may never come to pass, Syngman was
taught, for—in the words of an old Korean proverb—"What
looked like blossoms on the dead tree turned out to be only
the white mold of decay."

The learning of proverbs, indeed, was an essential part
of the boy's education, for every household treasured a store

of old folk sayings that served as a practical balance for the unreality of the classical Chinese volumes that were learned by heart. One of the proverbs which Rhee has often quoted in later life as an apt description of Korea's plight among the surrounding powers warns, "A shrimp is crushed in the battles of the whales." Others of these old proverbs illustrate the varied teachings which helped to form the characters of Syngman and his playmates:

Pinch yourself and you will know the pain another feels when pinched.

Where there are no tigers, wildcats will be very self-important.

To make a mountain, you must carry every load of earth.

Blame yourself, not the stream, when you fall in the water.

Be shrewd in making a bargain and a gentleman in abiding by it.

A virtuous character is necessary even in driving a cow.

A room easily warmed is also easily cooled.

A finger prick will demand attention, though the worms be eating the heart unknown.

You cannot carry a stone up the mountain without getting red in the face.

You cannot eat the picture of a loaf of bread.

The water downstream will not be clear if the water upstream is muddied.

Don't kill a bullock for a feast when a hen would suffice.

You cannot sit in the valley and see the new moon set.

From the vast store of Korean proverbs, from the many folk tales which Syngman heard from his mother, from the mothers of his comrades and from strolling storytellers, and from the lyric poems that through eight hundred years were written in Korea in celebration of nature, of yearning and striving, and of loyalty and love, the young Syngman gathered into his own character some of the strands of the sturdy optimism and the hardy endurance of his countrymen's traditions. The love of his native land became a living part of his being and shaped in his mind and in his heart a flaming devotion that no hardship has ever been able to dim.

Another heritage from his youth is a strong body and a love of outdoor exercise. The home of Syngman's youth was a small shelter that offered him little inducement to stay inside except for eating, studying and sleeping. On the other hand, for three months in the spring and another three months in the autumn, the climate around Seoul is almost ideal. The hot weather and abundant rains of midsummer invite swimming in the streams, and winter provides its own opportunities for vigorous sport. There is no evidence that Syngman's childhood was different from that of his friends, and there is ample evidence from his mature tastes that as a youth he must have spent a great many hours in vigorous outdoor activities.

When Syngman was nine years old an epidemic of small-pox swept through the country and the boy became blinded in both eyes. With no idea of what the cause might be, his parents were perplexed as well as sadly worried. Syngman felt as though red hot irons were being pushed into both his eyes. He screamed and jumped until the *ondol* * floor in their home was partly broken through. The old man and his wife who served the Yi family took turns carrying him on their backs, completely wrapped in thick quilts so no light could penetrate. His father and mother prayed every day that their *Yukdai Dokja* might be restored to sight. They called upon herb doctors and all their friends, to find every possible medicine. At least one hundred different remedies were tried. At last a relative advised Syngman's father to

* The room for entertaining guests in a Korean home has an *ondol* floor covering of oiled paper, somewhat like linoleum. Underneath are flues leading from the kitchen stove, or (in better houses) from a special heating fireplace, providing a radiant form of heating which has been in use in Korea for many centuries. At night during the winter months the family spread out quilts on the pleasantly warmed floor and thus remained comfortable with the minimum use of fuel, even in the coldest weather.

take him to a foreign doctor, Horace Allen, a Presbyterian missionary, who had arrived in Seoul in July, 1884, and who had accomplished remarkable feats. When Syngman was taken from the house in a closed sedan chair, with his eyes tightly bound, his mother cried as though he were being taken to the burial grounds. To a woman of her devout Buddhist convictions, entrusting her son to a foreign doctor was degrading as well as dangerous. The fact that she would let him go at all was an indication of her desperation.

After the examination, Dr. Allen gave Yi Kyung-sun some liquid medicine, to be dropped into Syngman's eyes three times daily. He advised them to watch for effects on the third day—which, as it happened, was Syngman's tenth birthday. At first the medicine had no more results than had the remedies of the herb doctors. But on the third morning, while Mrs. Yi was in the kitchen preparing breakfast, Syngman sat on the floor with his back to the window. His father sat near the window, writing a letter. Mrs. Yi brought in Syngman's breakfast and placed it on a small table in front of him. Then she placed a spoon in his hand, showed him where to find the plate, and went back to the kitchen. While Syngman was eating, he was suddenly startled by the awareness that he was seeing the lines of the pattern of the straw matting upon which he sat. Trembling with eagerness and anxiety, he reached out his hand. Sure enough, there were the lines! Several times he looked for a line and then traced it out to be sure; then he sprawled across the floor toward his father, crying, "I can see the lines!"

His father, who was deeply intent upon his letter, at first brushed the boy aside. But as soon as he understood, he held up his inkstone and asked, "What have I here?" When Syngman replied, "An inkstone," Yi Kyung-sun called huskily to his wife, "Our son's eyes are opened. He can see!" Mrs. Yi came quickly to the door, hesitated a moment, then kicked off her shoe and, pointing toward it with her foot, asked, "What is that?" When Syngman replied, "Your shoe," she ran to embrace him, shaking with sobs. Yi Kyung-sun took Syngman back to Dr. Allen, to thank him, and offered a straw bundle of ten eggs as a token of appreciation. This Dr. Allen refused, saying, "Your boy needs them more than I do." This was Syngman Rhee's first experience with any foreigner. He was to have many more—including another, much less happy, with Dr. Horace Allen, after another decade had passed.

The turning to a Christian doctor to cure Syngman's blindness made no lasting ripple in the religious observances of the Yi household. Like most other Korean families of the period, they devotedly practiced both Buddhism and Confucianism. There was no conflict between these two faiths, for Buddhism pays scant attention to this life and Confucianism ignores the next. To the parents of Syngman Rhee—and to the boy as he grew into an awareness of life's intangible values—these two complementary religions were fully satisfying. Had they desired further religious guidance, or solace, or discipline, the world in which they lived had much more to offer. The Shamanistic cult of Taoism filled their woods and streams and the dark recesses of the night with gods evil and good, foreboding and fun-loving. The recently founded Chuntokyo Cult promised a heavenly way to immortality based on the kindly intercession of a personalized God. Most housewives and all children of the period were believers in auguries, crystal-gazers, sorcery and superstition. As a household of unusual educational achievement, the Yi family was tolerant of the varied beliefs of the community but remained faithful to its own creeds. Syngman's mother taught him the elementary Confucian principles and sent him each year on his birthday to the Buddhist temple to offer sacrifices and prayers. The spiritual atmosphere of these early years sank into his temperament and became a part of him which has continued to guide his thinking through all the years since.

In later life Syngman Rhee recalled that he had never forgotten his first impression of the beautiful Buddhist monastery isolated on the high slopes of *Pook Han* Mountain. In the exalted and ascetic environment, everything appeared so unearthly to his child's eyes that he felt as though he were in the Lotus Heaven with the five hundred La Hans, the idols with varying dresses and hats, sitting side by side along the walls of an immense hall, with pictures of heaven and hell gorgeously painted behind them. In the summer of 1946, Dr. and Mrs. Rhee went on a Sunday afternoon for a visit to that same Buddhist temple, and he stood in the entranceway looking into it while he said softly, again and again, "Beautiful! Beautiful!" Many a time in conversation he has reflected that if the peacefulness and serene self-forgetfulness of Buddhism could effectively be joined to the Christian spirit of brotherhood and mutual helpfulness, the benefits to millions of troubled and uneasy people would be immense.

His mother, who was in many ways a remarkable woman—far advanced for her time and of far more than average intelligence—was his first teacher. His first book was the Chinese basic reader, incorporating one thousand ideographic characters. By the time he was six, he had them all memorized. Neighbors were invited to a feast to celebrate this triumph, and his parents were the proudest in Peach Village. Such a feat as he had mastered might be roughly compared to learning to read, write and spell an English vocabulary of ten thousand words—supplemented by considerable skill in artistic drawing. From this beginning he went on to the *Dong Mong Sun Sup,* or Second Reader, consisting of introductory Chinese and Korean history and elementary rules of conduct. In his seventh year he proceeded to the *Tonggam* book of history, and before his eighteenth birthday he had memorized the remainder of the indispensable seven Chinese classics: The Doctrine of Means, the Analects of

Confucius, The Teachings of Mencius, the Confucian Books of History and of Poetry, and The Book of Changes.

In the Korea of that day there were no schools. A family would engage a tutor for its own children and those of relatives or friends. Syngman studied with Yi Pyung Joo, Choi Eul Yong, and the two older brothers of Hugh Heung-woo Cynn—the man whom he later appointed as ambassador to Japan, and who became one of his rivals for the presidency in the election of 1952.

Thus passed Syngman's youth, until, in the late fall of 1894, when he was nineteen years of age, the Sino-Japanese War commenced. Syngman was rereading the Book of Poetry (*Si-jun*) in an intensive review for the annual civil service examinations. Keung-woo Cynn, one of his classmates and closest friends, entered the Pai Jai Middle School, which had been established in September of that year by Methodist missionaries. He urged Syngman to join him and study the modern world (interest in which was greatly stimulated by the exciting war between China and Japan) instead of concentrating upon the memorization of ancient classics. One day, with several other curious friends, young Rhee slipped into a back seat in the Pai Jai chapel, intending to scoff at the "foreign devils" who had come to upset the old learning and undermine the old religions. After a few days he began to think it would be worth while to learn English, and he had complete confidence in his ability to listen to whatever was said without letting it affect his religious or social beliefs.

When Keung-woo first talked to him about attending Pai Jai, young Rhee replied loftily, "Let them change the order of heaven and earth, but I never shall give up my mother's religion." It should be noted that here, as in other instances, it was his mother rather than his father, whom he regarded as his guiding influence. She it was who did more than any other individual to mold his evolving personality. To her he was the sun and center of her universe, her dragon child,

Syngman Rhee in his teens (standing, right) shown with his father and a cousin (*courtesy, Peter S. Hyun, Sr.*); and at Princeton in 1910 (*courtesy, Dr. John Orr*).

her crowning achievement, her pride, her hope for an earthly immortality. Upon him she lavished affection and, as his remarkable intellectual powers became evident, near veneration. From his father he experienced occasional bursts of discipline, but his mother wrapped him in a pervasive and continuous attention which, without any of the physical manifestations of authority, actually shaped and directed his thoughts and feelings with the steady pressure of commanding devotion. All his life Syngman Rhee has been more intimately influenced by women than by men. From them he has acquired something of the yielding toughness and soft perseverance which makes of womankind the stronger of the sexes while seeming, deceptively, to be the weaker. It is not that Rhee became in any way effeminate, but it may not be fanciful to see in the succession of female followers and counselors a key to his ability to maintain a chosen course of action against all manner of opposition, without bluster or apparent strain. It is also probably because of this influence that he fostered and led the first significant movement for feminist rights in the Orient. Despite all these considerations, his announced determination to remain steadfast in his mother's faith proved to be one of his least durable predilections.

His decision to become a regular student in the Pai Jai school was not an easy one to make. His parents' opposition would have been so strong that he dared not discuss the question with them. Every morning he slipped out of the house to attend classes without telling them where he was going. He was almost twenty years of age and his mother used to sigh as she thought her son was falling into habits of idleness and perhaps worse. But his father indulgently insisted that the boy be left alone, and not be questioned too closely about how he was spending his time, while he found his own way across the threshold from youth to manhood.

Foreigners had only been allowed in Korea for thirteen years. Their number was still few, and all of them (but especially the missionaries) were objects of suspicion and considerable dislike. There was much gossip and many rumors about their strange customs. Their dress was queer, and they wore their hair ludicrously cropped close to their heads. The foreign women walked brazenly out in the streets in open daylight without a covering for their faces and even apparently without concern for the glances that were openly cast at them. What they ate nobody knew, but there were many knowing looks and sly remarks about their probable diet. Their eyes and complexions were strange, and their hairy faces seemed outlandish. Hair also grew on their arms, and some spoke of seeing hair on the chests and the legs of the men as well. Obviously these strangers were lacking in the niceties of good breeding and did many things which violated the most lax rules of courtesy. Most of the Koreans were at first a little afraid of them, and everyone held them in a degree of contempt. But there was no denying that they had a kind of cleverness and certain types of startling ingenuity. They talked of utterly fascinating (if often unbelievable) things about the land from which they had come, and the Koreans who mingled with them found much in their behavior to arouse wonder and a growing admiration.

The world the missionaries talked about and the world the Koreans knew were separated not only by thousands of miles but, figuratively, by hundreds of years. When Commodore Robert Schufeldt in 1882 persuaded the wily Korean king to accept a treaty of mutual commerce and friendship, Korea was a hermit kingdom nestled in the twin protection of strict isolationism and regimented reaction. Life in the Seoul of Syngman Rhee's childhood was not greatly different from life in the Paris of 1400. The streets were narrow lanes, wandering almost at random among rows of mud-walled, straw-thatched huts. Sanitary practices recalled the old medieval European merry madcap custom of dumping the contents of chamber pots out of upper windows onto the heads of passers-by. An absolute monarchy, flanked by a hereditary aristocracy, dealt with the people with an unpredictable mixture of indolent indifference and uncomprehending cruelty. Lines of stakes bounding the bridge across the majestic Han River were seldom without fresh adornments of the heads of some of His Majesty's subjects who had broken one or another of the multiple laws enforced by capital punishment.

In the streets no one was to be seen but Koreans, for the hated Japanese were not tolerated, and the Chinese cannily wooed Korean friendship by maintaining a buffer strip north of the Yalu River, and by executing any Chinese who dared to cross it. As a matter of fact, few were seen in the streets except Korean men, for by immemorial custom the women stayed in their homes until after dark; or, if they had to venture out, they were accompanied by a husband, father or brother. Not lacking, however, were the solid and chunky Korean oxen, pulling their two-wheeled carts, or the small but sturdy Korean horses—in size and disposition like American burros, but in appearance a smaller edition of the wild Mongolian ponies.

Few of the Koreans crowding the streets of Seoul in Syngman's youth had ever been outside of Kyonggi Province, and scarcely one of them had been outside Korea. Then, into their midst, had come the missionaries, miners and businessmen from some fabulous and splendid land across the endless waters—*Megooks*, the Koreans called them, or "splendid people." They told tales that seemed scarcely believable, of wide streets and big houses (some of them with rooms piled on top of one another); of steel tracks that ran for thousands of miles, with puffing trains rolling along them at speeds that carried their passengers more miles in an hour than Koreans could traverse in an entire day; of huge factories where men went to work for money, and then bought the many things made in other factories by other men.

The missionaries talked of a new religion that seemed strangely like Confucianism in some respects, and strangely unlike Buddhism in others. Many Koreans were drawn to it, however, because of its similarities to their own native Chuntokyo Cult, or the "Doctrine of the Heavenly Way"— a religion with perhaps two million followers, which proclaimed the existence of one God, of an immortal life, and of eternal reward or punishment to be determined by the righteousness of an individual's life and the soundness of his beliefs. Could this Christianity of the missionaries, some Koreans wondered, be a foreign variation of their own faith? At least it was worth a hearing. From this foundation Christianity spread so widely in Korea that the peninsula came to be known among the missionaries as "the most Christian land in the Orient."

Aside from religion, the missionaries talked of schools and of printing presses, and of a curious kind of politics called democracy—in which people expressed their own ideas, and elected their own governors by making marks on paper, and decided for themselves what taxes they should pay and what laws they should obey. To the Koreans of that time it all seemed impractical and, indeed, highly imaginative. But they listened to the foreigners with the same attentiveness we might accord the tales of a traveler back from a fabulous journey of discovery to an unknown civilization cradled in the wilds of the Amazon valley. What was said might or might not be true, and it surely had little relevance or significance for them, but to listen did no harm and in its own way was an interesting method of passing the time.

Syngman Rhee's first teacher at Pai Jai was Dr. W. A. Noble. The first English sentence which Noble taught to the boys in the class Syngman joined was, "His father told him to go to Pai Jai and study chemistry." Years later, in

1912, while Rhee was attending an international Methodist convention in Minneapolis, he asked Noble why he ever thought the boys could profit by starting their study of English in such an unusual way. Noble laughed and replied, "I was just starting a course in chemistry and wanted to get some students!" From Noble Rhee learned the English alphabet, and to Noble's gentleness, patience, and strength of character he has never ceased to pay tribute. Dr. Noble's son Harold was to have a considerable influence in the later life of Syngman Rhee and a part in the tangled diplomacy which eventuated in the establishment in 1948 of the Republic of Korea.

The superintendent of Pai Jai was Henry Appenzeller, a man of enormous energy, who, in addition to his teaching, helped edit the *Korean Repository*, a primary source for the events of that time, published monthly at the Methodist Printing and Publishing House adjoining the school. Appenzeller encouraged the students to start a school newspaper, as an aid to their mastery of English, and Rhee became the chief editorial writer. Appenzeller edited all the text submitted for the paper, both to correct the English and to censor any statements that might prove embarrassing to the school. Out of this came Syngman's first venture in leadership.

After a time Rhee called a private meeting of the student editors and harangued them, saying, "We are cowards to publish under the protection of the missionaries!" As a result, the boys arranged to secure the use of a printing press which had been purchased in Japan ten years earlier by the uncle of Kimm Kiusic, whose life was destined to be closely intertwined with that of Rhee. Under the purchase agreement they hired the Japanese printer for a term of ten years. Thus Syngman Rhee became the first editor of a daily newspaper in Korea, under the auspices of the uncle of a man who was to become one of his closest associates and eventually his most troublesome opponent, and with the technical supervision of a Japanese, whose homeland was to be Rhee's lifelong *bête noire*.

As the editor of the *Maiyil Shinmun,* or *Daily News,* published partly in English and partly in Korean, Syngman Rhee commenced what turned out to be a long life devoted to reform and agitation. As has proved to be true during his entire life, he addressed himself in part to Korean and in part to American readers. His theme was an ardent and repetitive demand for governmental and social reform. Here in this little newspaper was the real birth of the new Korea —the true beginning of Rhee's career of statesmanship.

Even before the start of the *Maiyil Shinmun* newspaper, Rhee found still another outlet for his energies and another means of broadening his experience. A new missionary teacher, Miss Georgiana Whiting, arrived at Che-joong Won; and because Syngman's knowledge of English was greater than that of his fellows he was hired to teach her the Korean language. His first salary, consisting of twenty silver dollars, frightened his mother (who could not imagine he could honestly earn so much) when he took it home. By this time Syngman had confessed to his parents that he was studying at Pai Jai, and they had reluctantly agreed to let him continue. Six months after he enrolled in the school he was hired to teach English to a new class of boys.

Other Pai Jai teachers included Mr. D. A. Bunker, Dr. F. Ohlinger, who founded the *Korean Repository,* and Dr. Homer B. Hulbert, who managed the Tri-Lingual Press and who became the most famous and able American interpreter of Korean culture. Because of Rhee's liberal ideas, active intelligence, and intense interest in expressing himself in English speech and writing, he became friends with these men and spent countless hours in their company. Rhee had many talks with Hulbert while the latter was writing his two-volume *History of Korea.* Hulbert's later book, *The*

Passing of Korea, became for Rhee, as for other Koreans, the most valuable record of the last days of the monarchy. The friendship between these two continued until, in 1949, Hulbert returned to Korea to die in the land that had always held his heart.

During Syngman's enrollment at Pai Jai, his father was away from home a great deal, traveling and visiting with friends. His mother remained very apprehensive about his association with the foreigners, but Syngman comforted her with repeated assurances of his loyalty to the Confucian and Buddhist doctrines. She gradually came to take pride in his mastery of English, as she had in his primacy in the Chinese classics. She listened with fascinated interest to his stories of the Western world far beyond the seas. Someday, he told her, he hoped to visit these strange lands and see some of the wonders for himself. When he said that she would weep, but she never asked him to abandon his plans. Perhaps she thought they were too fantastic ever to come true.

Rhee became increasingly interested in the ideas of American democracy and in the theory that all people should have equal rights and opportunities. He became an avid reader, and a fair selection of Western books and magazines (including *McClure's, The Nineteenth Century and After,* and *The Outlook*) were supplied to him by the missionaries. By this time there was considerable travel between Korea and Japan, and a number of Koreans of his acquaintance had made trips to America. The world outside was becoming more real to him, and the medievalism of Korea's political and social system became increasingly unbearable.

Syngman Rhee's involvement in the stirring changes taking place in his country was personal and deep-seated. As the only son in an ancient and conservative family, he was deeply rooted to the Korean past and (through the Chinese classics) to Oriental religion, philosophy and traditions. But temperamentally he was a rebel and intellectually he was becoming firmly convinced that the old society had to be remade into a new. Seoul was astir like an anthill disturbed by a stick. The king abolished the centuries-old civil service examinations, based on the old learning, and instituted new ones covering modern foreign languages and Western administrative methods. The life for which Rhee had been so successfully educating himself was vanishing. For the first time women were beginning to appear on the streets without veils. New ideas of every kind were taking form. One of them caused a crisis in the Rhee household which can scarcely be appreciated at this distance but was very real and serious at the time.

Like all other Korean males, young Rhee wore his hair long and gathered into a tightly rolled knot on the top of his head. So characteristic was this hair style for men that one of the earliest American missionaries, Mrs. L. H. Underwood, entitled her book on Korea, *Fifteen Years among the Topknots*. Violation of the topknot style was considered as much an act of sacrilege as would be neglect or degradation of the family ancestor-shrine. Yet Rhee became deeply troubled about the topknot and came to regard it as a symbol of the old conservative past from which Korea must be divorced. He discussed the problem for many hours with Dr. O. R. Avison, a medical missionary who remained one of his lifelong friends. Finally, one afternoon at home, when his father was away, Syngman Rhee walked over to the family shrine, took out the ancestral tablets, and holding them respectfully before him on the palms of his hands he told his mother that in accordance with the changing customs of the times he was going to have his topknot cut off. He then bowed respectfully to his mother, replaced the tablets, and told her he would be away for a few days. His mother wept, but without trying to dissuade him she bade him good-by. Going to the Avison home, Rhee then had his topknot removed by the doctor, in a solemn ceremony which they both recognized as a decisive repudiation by Rhee of the old classic pattern into which his parents had sought so devotedly to mold his life, and for which they had made many sacrifices. It was several days before young Rhee could gather courage enough to return home. When he did so he found that sorrowful as his mother was, she accepted better than he had expected the fact that he would have to chart for himself the course of his own life. This acceptance was in itself a significant indication of how greatly the times were changing in Korea. No one should think that either the older or the younger generation was having an easy time. The oldsters were seeing everything they had treasured slipping from them. The youngsters were shyly entering into a new world without guidance and with inevitable feelings of guilt as they turned their backs on the standards of their forebears.

Syngman Rhee was caught in the middle of the first decades of this drastic change in Korea's modernization. From the serene and untroubled happiness of his youth, his normal disturbances of adolescence were intensified and sharpened by the revolutionary convulsions which penetrated so deeply into his own life. But the great overriding fact is that whatever the problems may have been, he did surmount them and arrived at the threshold of maturity with at least a significantly successful beginning of an integration in his thinking and feeling of the values and standards of the East and the West. By the time he was twenty Rhee was already becoming a complete man, rounded with the civilizing influences of both the world's hemispheres. Born in medievalism, he had grown into modern times. Confined to the city of Seoul, whose environs he had never left, he was already becoming a creature of both the old world and the new. He was ready for new duties, and the opportunities were not delayed.

Chapter II

YOUTH—
LEADERSHIP IN REFORM

SYNGMAN RHEE's transition from childhood to manhood was abrupt. Leadership was thrust upon him at an age when he should have had time and leisure for study and meditation on the vast world of new ideas from the West with which he was becoming acquainted. He needed a chance to read Locke and Jefferson, Emerson and Carlyle—to study the evolution of democracy in England and the American and French revolutions—to evaluate the growth of the new nationalism in Italy and Germany—to analyze the nature of the Western colonialism in Asia. All of this was to come later, but before he had time to acquire such breadth of background or to formulate his own philosophy of government, he was thrust pell-mell into the midst of the searing problems of a disintegrating society. For Seoul was the heart of Korea; Pai Jai was the modernizing yeast in the ferment of Seoul politics; and Rhee was early marked among the Pai Jai students as a natural leader. In order to understand the crucial next stages in his development it is necessary to look first at the situation unfolding in the Pai Jai school, and next at the swift succession of crises that were hammering down the shaky Korean state.

At about the end of Rhee's first year at Pai Jai, in 1895, there arrived at the school a young Korean named Soh Jai

24

Pil, who had been to America to study, and who had already had a noted career as a reformer and political radical. Befriended by the powerful Kim Ok-kiun and other strong leaders of the court circle, he was made an adviser to the king's Privy Council and enjoyed general prestige as the first Korean to receive higher education in the United States. Early in 1896 he founded a thrice-weekly newspaper called *Independence* and filled its columns with accounts of the Western world. Half-jokingly, he asked Rhee to discontinue the *Maiyil Shinmun*, to avoid competing for circulation, but Rhee declined with a firm—if smiling—"No!" Using the anglicized name of Philip Jaisohn, he taught a class at Pai Jai in Western history, in which Syngman Rhee was one of the students. He also founded a debating society, *Hyupsung Hoi*, or "The Mutual Friendship Society," for the purpose of studying and practicing parliamentary law. This was something entirely new. There were not even words in the Korean language for the parliamentary terms. There were scarcely even thoughts in the Korean minds for such ideas as amending a motion, or referring a disputed point to a committee, or rising to a point of personal privilege, or appealing from the decision of the chair. Rhee and his friends were deeply interested in this new method of developing democratic participation in solving problems and in arriving at majority-approved agreements. At first the topics discussed were carefully noncontroversial, but gradually basic questions of the nature and rights of man and the organization of society were introduced.

Although the society was organized for students, the meetings were opened to the public and soon were attended by many government officials, writers, and publicists. The intellectual circles in Seoul were astir with a restive desire to burst out of the ancient bonds of reactionary customs, and this new society proved to have a catalytic effect. Since the school authorities frowned on discussion of any subjects which might cause trouble for their work, the society moved to quarters away from Pai Jai and was renamed The Independence Club. This event took place on June 7, 1896—a notable day in Korean history. The first president was Mr. Ahn Kyong Soo, a large and portly man, who was Minister of War in the king's Privy Council, and whose interest in modern weapons (which were displayed so impressively in the Sino-Japanese War) led him on to further inquiries concerning other innovations of the Western nations. The government of Korea had entered a near hiatus, for the weak king, fearful of Japanese intrigue, had fled to the Russian Embassy, where he remained under the close influence and surveillance of Ambassador Waeber for a year. As a result of this situation, the discussions in the club centered largely upon the dangers to Korean independence from Russia and Japan. Although the club members did not then know it, Japanese and Russian representatives were at that very time attempting to work out an agreement for a division of Korea between their two countries along the 38th parallel. Their failure to do so was not from fear of Korea but from concern about the effects of such a move upon the British and Americans, who were much interested in the potential mineral, railway and industrial resources of Manchuria.

Meanwhile, an ambitious and able American named Horace Allen (who had cured Rhee's blindness ten years earlier) was laboring almost alone to interest his government and also American businessmen in the resources and strategic importance of Korea. A missionary turned business agent, diplomat and court politician, Allen was determined to help modernize Korea. When he found the United States did not intend to burden itself with this responsibility he turned to the Japanese and helped actively in placing control of the Korean government in their hands. Rhee knew him only from a distance, for Allen was far too discreet to get involved personally with a young man who was showing distinct evidence of rebellion. When Rhee did finally approach Allen to discuss his reform movement, he got a cold rebuff. Like Philip Jaisohn, Allen was too much concentrated upon his own approach to the problems of Korea to permit himself to be diverted by any other program.

Unlike these two men, Rhee had not a program but only an attitude, an urge toward improvement of social and political conditions. From earliest days he was by nature a politician. That is to say, he saw the problems of people around him as something more than merely personal to themselves. With an alert mind, a retentive memory and a remarkably sympathetic nature, he could not avoid noting inequalities and injustices on every side, nor could he abstain from identifying himself with the victims of oppression. A man in trouble was a man to be helped; many men in trouble meant a society diseased and in urgent need of remedial care. Thus, on the one hand, Rhee would turn from the suffering or struggling individual to look at the nature of his problem in the broad social context and to look for a generalized solution that would not only serve him but would also help others in a like state. However, on the other hand, Rhee has always tended to personalize politics intensely and vividly—often to his sorrow and sometimes to the detriment of the ends he has sought to serve. When social ills are present, he cannot forbear to look for villains who cause them in order to profit by them. When crises arise, he is liable to see in them the scheming hand of some genie of ill-will.

To a large degree this personalization of politics has derived from the nature of the Seoul in which he grew to manhood. A small and closely knit political community which subsisted upon the favors and waxed or waned according to the whims of the king, every participant knew (and hated or loved) all the others. Even in the midst of the zealousness of the reformers, personalities counted fully as much as principles. Tea houses were the caucus rooms. Sociability was inseparable from political maneuvering. Seated on the floor around low tea tables, with heads bent together while the young men discussed plans or listened to the counsels of the elders, the political gatherings took on the characteristics of clannish meetings. Disagreements among the members of the group were few and minor, for the very nature of the Independence Club brought together only those of like mind. On the other hand, the constant intrigues of the court encouraged a certain amount of spying and the betrayal of some of the king's ministers by others or by the agents of other ministers. Loyalty became the cardinal test of worthiness and suspicion became a normal mark of reasonable astuteness. Revolution was in the air, and as Rhee breathed deep of its heady fumes he became addicted to its mannerisms and characteristics. Many times after his election to the presidency of the Korean Republic he has remarked, "I know I should be more careful of what I say in public, but you know I have been an agitator all my life and I cannot change now."

The early twenties are a time of exhilaration for all spirited youths, and Rhee and his associates, for all their seriousness of purpose, were having the time of their lives. They could not fail to know that their education had unveiled before their eyes a higher vision than any of their forebears had ever known. Their minds were bursting with ideas for the improvement of the state, and they were idealists enough and impatient enough to want to rush immediately to the task of reform. If they were troubled from time to time, as Syngman was when he faced his mother with the news that he was cutting his topknot, their predominant mood was one of enthusiasm and unquestioning certainty. Like Hamlet, they were born in a time that was out of joint, but unlike Hamlet, the youthful Rhee was thrilled and stimulated by the assurance that he would play a leading role in setting conditions aright.

The placid contentment and acceptance which, in retrospect, we ascribe to the Victorian Age in England, was completely lacking in the Korea in which Syngman Rhee grew to manhood. The Korean-American Treaty of 1882 ushered Korea into the modern world at a time when the imperialistic nations were all scrambling for positions of privilege and power in North Asia. Russia had pushed to the Pacific a generation earlier and was eagerly reaching southward, toward warm water ports. Japan's Emperor Meiji was skillfully guiding his nation into a robust industrialism and was ambitious to secure bases and resources on the continent. Germany, England, France, and some Americans were casting greedy eyes at the coal and iron of Manchuria and were trying to insure primacy in the expected huge revenues that could be derived from developing favorable trade relations with the masses of China. Among all these rivals, only the Russians and the Japanese realized the primary value of securing Korea, as the heart of the strategic triangle of North Asia, but they made up in the intensity of their rivalry for the relative quiescence of the others. And in the midst of this struggle, the Korean monarchy had degenerated into slothfulness, intrigue, corruption, and almost moronic inefficiency. To understand what next befell Syngman Rhee, it is necessary to consider the main outlines of Korea's situation at that time.

When King Chul-Jong had died in 1864, he had no sons and his widow, Queen Cho, violently seized the seals of office and nominated for the kingship the twelve-year-old son of Prince Heung-sung, who is much better known by his later title, Taiwunkun. Taiwunkun was the last strong man in Korea's monarchial tradition, and the strongest and most ruthless who had appeared in Korean public life for many generations. In an effort to consolidate his power, he had himself named as regent until his son should come of age, and he married the boy to a daughter of the Min family, who was several years older than her child-husband. This proved to be his great mistake, for Queen Min was a woman of great intellect and of even stronger will. The next thirty years of Korean history were marked by the struggle between the regent and the young queen, with the king simply a weak pawn between them.

At first, of course, Taiwunkun was in complete control. He at once set about destroying the foreign influences which were beginning to penetrate into the fringes of Korean life. In this effort he was only following the tradition of isolationism which had been handed down ever since the virtual destruction of the country by the Hideyoshi-led Japanese invasion of 1592-98. In January, 1866, a Russian gunboat had dropped anchor briefly in Wonsan harbor and sent a message to the king asking the right of trade with Korea. The Koreans were alarmed by the steady pressures exerted by the West upon China and Japan, and Taiwunkun took advantage of the uneasiness caused by the Russian mission to order the arrest and execution of eleven French Catholic priests who several years earlier had entered Korea from China. Eight of them were killed, three went into hiding, and one of them (Father Ridel) later escaped into China to tell the story of what happened. Thousands of Korean converts were put to death in as bloody a pogrom as recent history had witnessed. The savagery of the attacks on the Christians stemmed from the fact that Japan had sent into Korea large numbers of Buddhist priests, who had been discovered to be spies preparing for a renewed Japanese invasion. The Catholics were confidently believed by the Koreans to be preparing the way in Korea for the same kind of inroads which had become familiar in China. The antiforeignism of the massacre of 1866 was a Korean forerunner of the later Boxer uprisings in China.

Meanwhile, while this antiforeign agitation was at white heat, an American sailing vessel, *The Surprise*, was wrecked off the coast of Whang-hai Province. The crew was treated kindly, for even that early the Koreans distinguished the Americans from the European imperialists, and were escorted across the Yalu River into China. Several months later, in September, 1866, another American vessel, *The General Sherman*, defied warnings and sailed up the Taidong River to Pyengyang. Reports spread through Korea that this ship had come to break up the burial mounds of the Silla dynasty and to seize the buried treasures. Unfamiliar with the tides, the vessel ran aground, and when a boatload of Korean officials approached the ship, a sailor on *The General Sherman* fired a pistol at them. The Koreans organized an attack with fire-rafts, with the result that the ship was destroyed and the sailors killed.

In October of that same year seven French men-of-war attacked Inchon harbor (then called Chemulpo) and besieged Kang-wha Island. Taiwunkun ordered Korean vessels to be sunk in the mouth of the Han River, to protect the approaches to Seoul, and sent a force of 5,000 men—tiger hunters and other sturdy fighters, armed with flintlocks and bows and arrows—to hold off the invasion. They established themselves in a strongly fortified Buddhist monastery on the south side of the island, some twelve miles from where the French fleet was anchored. The French admiral sent a strongly armed force of 160 men to attack this fortress. The Korean defenders felled almost half of them in the first volley, and the French fled in confusion, with the Koreans in close pursuit. The French admiral hastily sailed away, confessing failure.

Taiwunkun and the Korean populace were intoxicated with victory. They had defeated the great Western power which had invested Peking, humbled the mighty emperor of China, and with two gunboats in Yokohama harbor had bullied the Japanese. From this time until 1870 the persecution of the Catholic converts in Korea persisted unrelentingly, until as many as twenty thousand were slain and this foreign sect seemed to be completely eliminated.

In 1871 a force of five American gunboats entered Inchon harbor, commanded by Admiral Rogers and accompanied by Frederick F. Low, the American minister to Peking. While a mission was en route to Seoul with a message to the king, Admiral Rogers sent two small vessels up the Han River to take soundings. They were fired upon from a small Korean fort on an island in the estuary of the Han, and, to protect the honor of the American flag, the vessels attacked the fort. The Korean garrison fought till their ammunition and arrows were exhausted, and then threw gravel in the faces of the attackers. None surrendered, and at last the defenders were all killed. However, Rogers and Low realized they could not conquer Korea and, having lost any chance of a peaceful agreement, they withdrew.

By 1875 the king had come of age, the regency was dissolved, and Taiwunkun found himself outmaneuvered in court politics by Queen Min. He grandiloquently resigned all his appointments and retired in disgust to a rural estate. Queen Min was approached by the Japanese, who were flushed with the wondrous success of the modernization of their country. The queen stood solidly for what she conceived as progress, and worked to turn the destiny of Korea toward the new day that seemed to be dawning in the Orient. Followers of Taiwunkun murdered her father and sought to intimidate her, but to no avail. In 1876 she sponsored a treaty with Japan—the first in Korean history with a foreign power—and Japanese traders were admitted under carefully restricted conditions to Pusan harbor.

The year 1880 (when Syngman Rhee was five years old) proved to be crucial in Korean history, for during that year Queen Min became embittered against the Japanese, who were intriguing to gain control of Korea. At this time a small group of genuinely patriotic and far-seeing liberals were striving earnestly to find some means of modernizing Korea without surrendering it to Japanese overlordship. When it appeared they could not succeed through political means, Queen Min organized a reactionary movement of gradual withdrawal from Japanese and Western contacts.

In 1882 a scandalous mistreatment of Korean troops by their corrupt and inefficient officers led to a revolt against Queen Min and the Japanese advisers who still clustered about her court. The Japanese legation in Seoul was burned and the Japanese were driven to Inchon, from where they withdrew to Japan. Taiwunkun was briefly brought back into power by the rebellious troops. The Chinese emperor sent to Korea his outstanding diplomat and politician, Yuan Shih-kai, and with his astute assistance Queen Min was restored to a dominant position. Chinese soldiers were brought in to maintain order and Yuan Shih-kai set about reorienting Korea away from Japan and toward China.

In May, 1882, Commodore R. W. Schufeldt of the American navy sailed into Inchon harbor with messages from the court of Peking. With the help of the politician Yuan, he accomplished through diplomacy what others had failed to achieve by force. He proposed a treaty between the United States and Korea which provided in its first article: "If other powers deal unjustly or oppressively with either government, the other will exert their good offices, on being informed of the case, to bring about an amicable arrangement, thus showing their friendly feelings." The king's advisers candidly told Schufeldt of their mistrust of the Western imperialist powers, but said their chief fear was encroachment by the Japanese. They insisted they could never undertake to allow foreigners to enter Korea unless the treaty would serve as an absolute bar to aggression. Schufeldt assured them that was the purpose of the treaty, and his sentiments were reaffirmed during the subsequent debate on it in the United States Senate. Following ratification of this treaty in 1883, similar treaties were signed by Korea with England, France, and other nations. Korea thus entered into a new era in its long history, and although many had misgivings none could foresee how utterly disastrous the results would be.

In December, 1894, while Syngman Rhee was first being teased by some of his friends to enter the Pai Jai mission school, the Japanese launched an undeclared war against China and within a few months completely defeated the unorganized and dispirited Chinese. On June 6, 1895, under the guidance of Japanese advisers who had replaced the Chinese lately established in the court by Yuan Shih-kai, a great celebration was held in Korea, on the occasion of the renewed pledges made by Japan and other powers guaranteeing Korea's complete independence. A prominent Korean named Yun Chi-ho had recently returned from many years of sojourn abroad, alive with new ideas of reform and modernization, and the intellectuals in Seoul genuinely expected that a new era was beginning. Under the leadership of Philip Jaisohn the Independence Club solicited funds and erected in Seoul an Independence Arch which still stands, though now surrounded by scores of acres of war-devastated ruins.

Syngman Rhee had already begun to exercise leadership within the Independence Club and was in frequent demand as a speaker before groups interested in liberalism. Despite all the difficulties of the time, he, along with his associates, was hopeful that real progress was being made.

Then, in October, 1895, occurred one of the most horrible events in modern Korean history—an event which set back the cause of progress and foreshadowed evil times to come. Viscount Miura had arrived in Seoul on September 1, as the new Japanese envoy, specifically charged to create conditions which would be more favorable to the advancement of Japanese interests in Korea. He entered into an alliance with the aged Taiwunkun and was soon deeply involved in the intrigues of the court. Min Yong-whan, the queen's most powerful friend, was dispatched as minister to the United States. With the queen's personal status thus weakened, the plot was ready to unfold. Viscount Miura prepared plans to capture the palace, murder the queen, and hold the king under Japanese control.

At 3:00 A.M. on October 8, a large party of Japanese gathered at the home of Taiwunkun near the Han River, then proceeded with him to the king's palace. About dawn they entered the palace through the Kwang-wha Gate and went at once to the royal apartments. All of these facts were later certified by the Japanese Court of Preliminary Inquiry, which sat at Hiroshima in January, 1896, to examine the case. The court then concluded that what happened thereafter was so confused that it felt unable to establish further facts or to adjudge anyone's guilt. What the Japanese court discreetly sought to veil from view and to preserve from punishment was this:

The invading rabble rushed into the king's quarters and brandished weapons around him and the crown prince, but did them no physical harm. Another portion of the attacking crowd went into the queen's apartments, seized the palace women, and demanded of them the whereabouts of the queen. When they came upon Yi Kyung-jik, the Minister of the Household, they slashed him down. He managed to crawl into the presence of the king, where the Japanese murdered him. Finally Queen Min was located in one of the rooms of her suite and was stabbed several times with swords. Then her bleeding body was wrapped in quilts, saturated with petroleum, and burned at the edge of a grove of pine trees on the eastern edge of the pond in the palace grounds. While Queen Min was being murdered, Taiwunkun came into the presence of the king and roughly assumed direction of affairs.

Later that same day Mr. Waeber, the Russian chargé d'affaires, and Dr. Horace Allen, who was then serving as the king's personal physician, insisted upon seeing the king. They were not, however, successful in releasing him from his captors. Through the following months the court was in chaos. Taiwunkun had an order issued reducing the murdered queen to the rank of the lowest order of citizens. Japanese officials assumed virtual control, though they were careful to remain behind the scene. The amount of intrigue that went on within the court and political circles can scarcely be imagined. An ambitious and capable *yangban*, Yi Choong-ku, plotted to overthrow the pro-Japanese government and liberate the king, but his *coup d'état* failed and he was arrested and tortured to death. Since Syngman Rhee had also taken part in this plot, he, too, was marked for arrest. However, when Yi Choong-ku was seized, Rhee's body servant, Bok Ney, came running to inform him of the failure of the plan, and Rhee escaped to a hiding place in Pyongsan, on the outskirts of Seoul. Finally, on the night of February 11, 1896, with the assistance of Waeber and Dr. Allen, the king and the crown prince, disguised as court ladies, were taken out of the palace in sedan chairs and hurried to the Russian legation. From this refuge, the king announced the formation of a new cabinet which resumed control of the government. At this time, some three months after the failure of the *coup*, Rhee was enabled to return to Seoul to resume his studies and political activities.

It was in the midst of these conditions that the Independence Club was formed and undertook the arduous task of preserving Korea for Koreans. Philip Jaisohn's newspaper angered the king, who sent him the remainder of his three years' salary, under his contract as adviser to the Privy Council, and, through the American minister, commanded him to leave the country. This he did, returning to the United States, where he took part in the Spanish-American War as a physician, and then settled down in Philadelphia, determined to live as an American citizen and to forget Korea. In 1919-1920, following the *Mansei* Revolution, Jaisohn once again for a brief time entered into agitation for the restoration of Korean independence. When he became convinced that the cause was hopeless, he washed his hands of it completely.

When Jaisohn left Korea for the United States, and Rhee returned to Seoul from his hideout at Pyongsan, the Independence Club was confronted with a crisis. The departure of its founder and moving spirit led many of the members to feel that the club had best be dissolved. The aroused anger of the king, in that land of autocracy, was not to be lightly ignored. Rhee himself had come near to being captured and was certain to be closely watched. The temptation confronting all the reformers was strong to drop their program and drift with the current. On the other hand, the current obviously was washing Korea toward the falls of oblivion as a nation and unless the Independence Club continued its own efforts there was no force in Korea that would even attempt to check the trend.

Rhee didn't even hesitate. Immediately upon his return to Seoul he called a meeting of the Independence Club members in their headquarters near the West Gate and proposed that their work be intensified and expanded. His newspaper, the *Maiyil Sinmun,* had suspended publication while Rhee was in hiding in Pyongsan and its resumption under the circumstances would be difficult. Hence the group decided to turn their major attention toward organization of street meetings, in which Rhee was a popular and dynamic speaker. Marching demonstrations were organized, and many of these dissolved into mobs and riots. As in London around 1780, Seoul for a time was characterized if not dominated by mobs. The king was helpless either to rescue himself from the Russo-Japanese intrigues or from the popular pressures arising among his own people.

Superficially—judging merely from the noise made by the surging mobs in the streets of Seoul—the reformist movement appeared to be rising to a new height of influence. However, the ingredients for real success were all absent. Neither Rhee nor any of his associates dreamed or planned of trying to unseat the king, much less to end the monarchy. They had no effective friends in the inner circle of the court to help them inject more liberal ideals into the ruling clique. With no publication and no organized means of communication, they could do little more with public opinion than to keep it aroused in the large metropolitan centers.

When the king, in 1897, attempted to reassert his own independence from foreign control and his own mastery over the domestic situation by assuming the title of emperor, they hoped briefly that this might mark the beginning of a real change. However, the new title could not add an iota to the king's intelligence nor increase the strength of will which he so notably lacked. Caught between the claimant powers of Russia and Japan, he could only draw away from one by yielding more power to the other. Reform of his own corrupt and inefficient government never proved appealing to the unhappy monarch, nor does it appear in retrospect that the onward rush of events would have left him time to achieve much in that direction. Yet his situation was so bad that action of some sort to escape from his dilemma was obviously necessary. Naturally, some of his advisers urged that the first thing he should do was to destroy the clamoring critics who were threatening to smother orderly government beneath a chaotic upsurge of mob rule.

The emperor soon yielded to the intrigues around him and the word went through the court circles that the Independence Club was to be broken up. Its first President, the

portly Ahn Kyong Soo, escaped to Japan, viciously charged
with complicity in the murder of Queen Min. Yi Wan Young,
who replaced him in the presidency, was very soon bought
off with an appointment as a provincial governor and resigned from the club. Yun Chi Ho, who became the third
(and last) president of the club was awakened in the middle
of the night by a police detective who came to arrest him.
Pleading for a few moments of privacy in which to dress, he
escaped and fled to Pai Jai school, where he was safe under
the protection of the American flag. Seventeen of the other
leaders of the club were arrested. The streets were crowded
with police and soldiers with drawn bayonets. Edicts were
posted branding the nationalist-reform leaders as traitors.

Syngman Rhee went to Dr. Appenzeller's house and there
found Yun Chi Ho and others of the membership in hiding.
They begged him to hide with them, but he refused. Instead,
Rhee went straight to the police headquarters, followed by a
gathering crowd that soon numbered in the thousands. They
demanded that the police release the seventeen men who
had been arrested. Rhee organized a mass meeting before
the police commissioner's office, which resembled in some
ways an American sitdown strike. There they remained
through the rest of that night, all the next day, and through
the following night. Syngman's father came and pleaded
with him to come home, reminding him with tears in his
eyes that he was *Yukdai Dokja*—the last of the six only-sons
representing six consecutive generations of the family. To
refuse his father's request was agony, but young Rhee could
not desert what he felt was clearly his duty. Dr. Appenzeller
came to watch, and, though he said nothing, Rhee felt he
was proud that so many Pai Jai students were taking the lead
in this great mass movement.

Rumors swept back and forth through the crowd. One
was that the emperor had ordered his soldiers to charge upon
the demonstrators and shoot them down. Another rumor

was that Rhee was to be bribed with an offer of a high government post. In fact, two court favorites, Ko Yung-kun and Kim Chong-han, came to Syngman and intimated such a position was his for the asking. Of course it never occurred to him to abandon his stand or his imprisoned comrades. All during the night they kept bonfires burning, and young Rhee spoke to the crowd almost continually, holding them together, for if the mass dispersed the soldiers could easily arrest the leaders.

The hardest time came at dawn after the second night. The ranks of the demonstrators had thinned considerably and those who remained were cold, hungry and sleepy. Then a band of soldiers appeared, marching toward them, preceded by a drum and bugle corps. Some of the demonstrators quickly slipped away. Rhee ran to meet the band and commenced kicking at the drummers to make them turn aside. Apparently they were under orders to use no actual violence, for they turned about and the entire band marched off, leaving the agitators unmolested. Morning editions of the newspapers appeared with stories describing the scene, and picturing Rhee as a radical and fire-eater.

That morning Syngman's father again came out to him, weeping, taking him by the hand, and begging him not to betray his family by his actions. Finally, word was brought by a scowling policeman that the seventeen men had been released. Rhee long recalled the event as the proudest and happiest in his life. All the club's leaders felt that a great victory had been won for democracy and liberalism.

Disorders continued for several days. The Independence Club members organized mass meetings in the great square before the ancient Big Bell, which had been erected in 1486 —and which still stands, in a new pagoda built by American soldiers to commemorate the recapture of Seoul from the communists in 1951. Continuous mass meetings were held, day and night, before the *Duk Soo* Palace Gates. The pro-

Russian group in the government hastily organized the *Po Whang Hoi Club* (Supporters of the Emperor) and employed hoodlums and members of the Peddlers Guild (*Pu Sang Pai*) to attack the Independence Club demonstrators and to break up the meetings. Rhee was a particular target of their attacks. On one occasion he escaped with his life only by vaulting the low walls of the German legation, which then stood on the present site of the Seoul Courthouse, near the *Duk Soo* Palace, and from there slipped into the grounds of Pai Jai school. Syngman long remembered the evil looks of the peddlers and the stout clubs they carried, longer and thicker than ordinary broomsticks. When the peddlers charged into a crowd, they wielded these clubs with a savage, unrestrained frenzy.

The numbers of the demonstrators were so great, and the feeling aroused was so genuine and widespread that the emperor called in the liberal-minded Prince Min and his friend General Hahn and asked them to do all they could to quiet the clamor. They appeared at the mass meetings and urged the agitators to disperse, promising that the emperor would introduce a real reform program in the government. However, Rhee and his associates were adamant. They had been fooled before and now they demanded real action, not empty promises.

After this refusal of the shadow peace, the Peddlers Guild again descended on them. At this time their meeting was being held before the gates of the improvised royal palace in the foreign sector of Seoul, where the emperor was living adjacent to the Russian legation, into which he might escape in case of danger to his person. Rhee was standing on a small keg in the middle of *Chungdong* Square, before this *Chungdong* palace, exhorting the crowd. As the peddlers charged upon them, many of the demonstrators fled for their lives. Rhee was doing his best to rally and hold them, when he saw Kil Yung-soo, one of the most vociferous royalists, advancing in front of the peddlers. In a sudden rush of unreasoning rage, Rhee ran toward Kil and began kicking at him madly. Suddenly, he felt strong arms reach around him from behind, pinioning his arms and squeezing the breath from him, while a voice whispered urgently in his ear "Yi Seung Man, Sir, calm yourself and get out quick!" As Rhee looked about he saw that he was surrounded by the peddlers and that all his friends had gone.

Then he was seized by a strong inspiration. He felt as though it were an inner voice speaking to him, as he believes it has in other moments of crisis, telling him without fail what to do. If he had turned to run from the mobsters, he would surely have been killed. Instead, he slipped quickly and quietly into their very midst, and began shouldering his way carelessly through them back toward the Pai Jai school. In all the excitement he was not recognized and walked through the mob to the gates of the Pai Jai compound, unharmed. The last thing the peddlers expected was to find the leader of the Independence Club calmly pushing his way deeper into their gang. When Rhee entered the Pai Jai entrance, he found many of his associates pouring into the school grounds through a back gate. Kim Won Kun, one of his dearest Pai Jai friends, was running into the school yard, with tears streaming down his cheeks, shouting that Yi Seung Man had been killed by Kil Yung-soo. When Syngman walked up to him, he was transformed into a vision of happiness. The afternoon newspapers also reported that Rhee had attacked Kil Yung-soo and had been killed in the melee.

Crowds followed Rhee as he left the Pai Jai compound and went to Chongno, where the earlier meetings had been held. It was already getting dark, and as Rhee rose to address the crowd they could not believe it was he. Some yelled out, "It is Yi Seung Man coming alive!" Many pressed forward to touch him and to see how badly he had been wounded.

In the clashes of that night and the next day, one of the

most popular Independence Club members, Kim Duk-ku,
was killed near Yongsan. A massive funeral procession was
formed, with thousands marching behind his bier. The
emperor feared that a national revolution was brewing, and,
as usual, sought to evade trouble by a weak compromise. He
called together leaders of the Independence Club and of the
new *Po Whang Hoi* for a meeting in the open *Wha Moon*
Square, in front of his palace, where an impromptu audience
hall was erected. In the presence of all the foreign am-
bassadors and missionaries, the king called Yun Chi Ho and
Kil Yung-soo, the presidents of the two clubs, before him.
He promised that he would reform the government and
would not arrest any of the leaders of the demonstration.
He called upon the foreigners to be witnesses of his sincerity.

The heart of the emperor's proposal was the formation of
a Privy Council, which he declared would have real legislative powers. He proposed election to it of twenty-five
members from each of the opposing clubs. Rhee was one of
the Independence Club members and Yun Chi Ho was
chosen Speaker of the Privy Council. Once again they hoped
that through orderly means real reforms could be accomplished.

The amount of undercover intrigue in that period passes
belief. The Japanese were especially active. Using the reformist Korean nationalists who had sought refuge in Japan,
they undertook to make friends with the Independence Club
members in the new Privy Council. They posed as the real
champions of Korean independence, warning that Japanese
help was needed against Russia, China, and the Western
imperialists. A number of the expatriates returned from
Japan to Seoul and commenced spending money freely to
entertain the Privy Council members. Rhee was too young
and inexperienced to be wholly aware of their aims or of
the source of their funds. He had many secret talks with
these men concerning the formation of a *Dai Dong Hap*

Bang—a Confederation of all the Peoples of the Great East. The program was an early forerunner of Japan's later plan for an All-Asian Co-Prosperity Sphere. Gradually the expatriates revealed that their plans called first for *Il Lo Chun Chaing*—a war between Japan and Russia; and then for *Il Mi Chun Chaing*—a war between Japan and the United States. Japan, they argued, was doing all it could to protect the Far East against Western encroachment. China and Korea must join with them in this holy cause. They showed Rhee extensive manuscripts, mapping out detailed plans for these two wars. He was deeply impressed by the motives they professed, for it was all too clear that the East was indeed being inundated by the West. Many years later he realized that what he was then shown was an early draft of what became the Tanaka Memorial. In his book, *Japan Inside Out,* published in 1941 (months before Pearl Harbor) Rhee wrote: "As early as 1895, soon after Japan's victory over China, I heard the Japanese talking about *Dai Dong Hap Bang* (The United States of the Great East), under the hegemony of Japan, of course. And later I read a book under the title of *Il Mi Chun Chaing Mi Rai Ki* (Japanese-American War of the Future). I have in my possession now a book written in Japanese by a high Japanese naval authority, predicting a war between the United States and Japan."

When the Privy Council held its first meeting, Rhee arose and proposed that all the political exiles in Japan be pardoned, and that Prince Park Yung-ho be named as chairman of the Privy Council. When this proposal was made known to the emperor he became furious and instantly dissolved the newly formed Privy Council. The instant arrest of its Independence Club members was ordered. The members scattered and took refuge in foreign compounds. Rhee went into the American Methodist Hospital compound, just inside the South Gate, where the Methodist School (*Joon Ang Hokko*) and Church are now located, and just across the street from the present location of the Bankers Club (which was used as an officers' club during the period of American Military Government in South Korea, 1945-48).

Here the American adviser to the police department and several missionaries came to see him every day, to make sure he was safe, for they felt bound by the promise the emperor had made in their names. Rhee resented such a necessity, for he felt it violated the spirit of Korean independence. He wanted to go out and start the mass movement all over again. Choo Sang-ho, one of his Independence Club friends, came to tell him that thousands of people were simply waiting for a leader to direct and organize them in renewed demonstrations.

One day Dr. Harry C. Sherman, an American Methodist doctor, asked Rhee if he would like to go out with him to call on a patient who lived near by. Rhee was extremely restive under his confinement and eagerly went with him. They had walked only as far as the vicinity of the near-by Japanese consulate, on the Square of the Bank of Chosen, when several plainclothes policemen rushed up, arrested Rhee, and took him off to jail.

Dr. Sherman immediately went to the American legation and, together with Dr. Horace Allen, the U.S. minister, called at the Korean Foreign Office to protest Rhee's arrest. They demanded his release on the grounds that he was serving as a temporary interpreter for an American physician, and according to existing agreements could not be arrested without previous notice being given. Negotiations proceeded for several weeks. To make sure that Rhee was not tortured in the jail, Mr. Stripling, the American adviser to the police department, made frequent visits to see him. It is possible that the efforts in his behalf might shortly have secured his release, but the Pai Jai students became impatient.

Word was smuggled in to Rhee that a vast crowd of his

followers would be assembled in Chongno Square, waiting for him to appear to speak to them and resume the planned agitation. Rhee communicated this information to Choi Chung Sik and Suh Sang Dai, fellow club members who had been arrested before him, and who were in the same cell with him.

Choi Chung Sik was a fiery orator, about four years Rhee's senior. He was marked by the government for specially severe treatment because, at the meeting in Wha Moon Square in which the emperor had decreed the re-establishment of the Privy Council, Choi had cried out in a loud voice, "If the emperor does not keep his word, how can we enforce it?"

On one of Mr. Stripling's visits he was accompanied by Choo Sang-ho, another club member, who secretly slipped a pistol to Rhee. After these visitors left, Rhee and his two jail mates soon found an opportunity to break out of their cell, and, brandishing his pistol to intimidate the guards, Rhee led them in a rush out into the street. When they reached Chongno Square, they were aghast to find no crowd assembled. Choi and Suh fled on and entered the safety of the Methodist compound, but Rhee simply collapsed with disappointment and a sense of betrayal. He later learned that the failure resulted from a misunderstanding as to the time of escape. No shot was fired from his pistol, and this fact, too, he attributed to an inner guidance, for later the evidence that his pistol was unused saved his life.

Choi and Suh, following their escape, took refuge in the home of an Englishman named Emberly, who lived in the Pai Jai compound. They stayed with him about a month, then dressed in Western style women's clothes and, with Emberly walking between them, they left his home on a dark night and passed out of Seoul through the West Gate. Suh escaped to Manchuria. Choi got as far as Chinnampo, the port of Pyengyang, where he took refuge in the Japanese

Inn, expecting to take ship to Japan. The innkeeper, however, betrayed him to the police. Choi was brought back to the jail where Rhee was held in Seoul, and they were tried together.

The court sentenced Choi to death and he was carried from the cell loudly crying Rhee's name, over and over again. Wretched though Choi's fate was, in the months and the years ahead Syngman Rhee often prayed that he, too, might have been meted out that same sentence of death—which at least was merciful in that the end came quickly.

Chapter III

A NEW LIFE
BEGINS IN PRISON

As Syngman Rhee collapsed in Chongno Square he was surrounded by a body of soldiers with drawn bayonets and was marched off in their midst to the army headquarters. While he was being held there in the front office, with officers buzzing around excitedly waiting for the arrival of their chief who would tell them what to do with this key prisoner, one of the soldiers quietly and unobtrusively brought Rhee a cup of water, accompanying it with encouraging glances. For his own part, Rhee was unable to think of his own plight but was lost in disappointment over the expected opportunity to resume the demonstrations, which somehow had failed to develop. Then an order was brought in by a scurrying messenger, and he was led off to Seoul Prison, *Hahn-sung Gahm-ok,* there to be turned over to the police.

The first man young Rhee saw when he was ushered into the police office was Park Dul Puk, one of the reactionary royalists, who was among his bitterest enemies from *Po Whang Hoi,* the Society of Supporters of the Emperor. Park was impatiently awaiting his coming and leered at him with a mixture of triumph and venomous hatred. At the first word of Rhee's capture, he had hurried to the emperor and received permission to put him to the torture. As soon as the

48

prisoner was transferred from the soldiery to the police, Park had him dragged at once into the dark inner room from which screams of the tortured wretches were muffled by heavy stone walls.

What Syngman Rhee endured during the next several days at the hands of Park Dul Puk surpasses twentieth-century comprehension. It must be recalled that in its penal system Korea had not yet advanced far beyond medievalism, and it should be remembered that this brash revolutionary had gone to extreme lengths in incurring the hatred of the emperor and his servile brood. Park was particularly vindictive, for his officiousness was sharpened by the acid of personal hatred. Deep behind those heavy stone walls, shut off from all his friends, unreported to the public, and beyond the succor of the missionaries, who had done so much for him, Syngman Rhee learned to pray for death with a passionate ardor. His arms were bound tightly behind his back with ropes of silk which cut into the flesh. Two sticks were placed between his legs, which were then bound tightly together at the knees and ankles, after which two policemen twisted the sticks. Triangular pieces of bamboo were tied between his fingers, which then were drawn so tightly together that the flesh sheared off from the bones. Each day he was pulled out flat on the floor, spread-eagled, and beaten with whiplash rods of bamboo until his flesh was raw. Were it not for Rhee's extraordinary vitality, he never could have survived. Each night he was dragged from the torture cell and thrown into a dark underground dungeon, and each day he was taken out for more tortures. Mercifully his mind became dulled with suffering and in retrospect those awful days became veiled in a deep mist of half-forgetfulness. However, in a note written during his seventy-seventh year, he said, "Often I find myself in prison in my dreams." On one occasion, when asked to tell something about those days, he replied with a look of physical pain, "Won't you let me try to forget?"

After the first few days, Park Dul Puk left the daily torture to his agents and the worst extremities were given up. Each night Rhee's feet were placed in stocks and his hands were handcuffed. A twenty-pound cangue of heavy wood was placed around his neck, so that he could neither stand, sit, nor lie down, but could only crouch in a half-sitting posture. A daze descended over him and his fearful anxiety faded into stoic acceptance. Memory fled from him, even as hope was dead. One day the Seoul newspapers carried word of his death, and his weeping father came to the prison to claim his body, only to discover that the rumor was false.

For seven months he continued in solitary confinement, with the cangue, a three-foot-long wooden collar, about his neck and with his hands and feet shackled. He was released from these manacles for only five minutes each day. Then, as he sat dully in his cell, with his chin drooped upon the heavy cangue, he commenced dimly to recall the preaching he had heard in Pai Jai chapel. With a sudden inrushing vision of a new life, he bent his head and prayed, "Oh God, save my country and save my soul." A puzzling kind of peacefulness descended upon him, when all his reason told him he was the most miserable wretch alive.

All his torture occurred before his trial. Finally, after seven months, the shackles were struck from him, and he was given a few days of respite to regain some strength, and then was led into the courtroom to face trial. There on the bench before him sat another implacable political enemy, Hong Jong Wo, to serve as his judge. Rhee's servant, Bok Nye, stood at the gate of the prison as he was brought out and accompanied him to the courtroom. His father, also, was present. His mother had died before his arrest and thus was spared the knowledge of his suffering. This phase of his life is so painful to Syngman Rhee that he has never been willing to discuss it.*

Brought to trial with him was his comrade, Choi Chung Sik, who had been returned to Seoul after his capture in the Japan Inn at Pyengyang. In the first day of the trial Choi amazed Rhee by trying with all his eloquence to ascribe all the political crimes to Rhee. Young Syngman himself was too weak from his ordeal and too battered in spirit to utter a word in his own defense. Choi, however, was caught in a number of contradictions and discrepancies in his testimony. Rhee's pistol was brought into court, and it was shown that it had not been fired. When Judge Hong rendered his verdict, Choi Chung Sik was sentenced to death, and Rhee was given a sentence of life imprisonment.

In addition to the sentence of life imprisonment, Syngman was to receive one hundred blows from a bamboo rod. However, Rhee's father appealed to the *Ap-noi,* or prison guard, who was to administer the blows, saying, "*Yeung Nam* (meaning His Honor) in his weakened state cannot survive the blows." This *Ap-noi* was a guard who had been shot in the leg eight months previously, during the attempted escape of Rhee and his two companions. As it turned out, however, he bore them no ill will, and he knew what Rhee had already had to endure. The Judge, Hong Jong Wo, as was the custom, came to watch the beating being administered, but as the first blow was about to fall, he left the room, shutting the door behind him. The *Ap-noi* raised his rod and brought it down, time after time, till the hundred blows were counted. When it was over, there was not a mark on Rhee's body.

After this merciful reprieve, Rhee was led into the prison cell which for the next six and a half years was to be his home. It was a huge converted rice storehouse with a wooden floor—and with the thick, tiled roof supported at in-

* His mother died on July 26, 1896, after a prolonged and painful illness.

tervals by heavy wooden pillars. This room was partitioned
into four large cells, each of about thirty square feet, with
a narrow aisle down the center. There was no heat in the
prison, and each inmate had to provide his own bed-cloth-
ing. On the floor were some thick rice straw mats. A single
kerosene lamp hung in the aisle, well out of reach of the
inmates. The families of the prisoners were permitted to
visit them at long intervals to bring food and other small
comforts.

From this time on Syngman Rhee's prison life was marked
by a succession of kindnesses. Both Kim Yung Sun, the warden, and his deputy, Lee Choong Chin, sympathized with
his political endeavors, and used to visit with him whenever
they could—standing in the aisle and talking to him through
the bars. The hard labor which was supposed to be part of
Rhee's sentence was remitted or forgotten. Dr. D. A. Bunker,
one of the Pai Jai teacher-missionaries, sent him a Christmas
basket. The famous Presbyterian educator, Dr. Horace Underwood, came to the prison to visit with him and to discuss
his newfound faith. Dr. O. R. Avison, who had removed his
topknot, sent him medicine. Rhee's family brought him
more comforts than their circumstances could afford.

There is another facet to this period of Syngman Rhee's
life, which is little known and is wrapped in general obscurity. Some two years before his capture in Chongno
Square his parents had arranged his marriage (in accordance
with the Korean custom of that time) to a somewhat older
woman who was distinguished by unusual strength of intellect and character. To them was born a son, who survived
infancy and was about eight years of age when Rhee's imprisonment finally ended in 1904. What happened to his
wife remains uncertain. She apparently lived on in obscurity for some years. The son was later sent to America,
while Syngman Rhee was studying in Washington, D.C.,
and died in Philadelphia in 1908. What is of chief import

in the biography of Rhee is that he did have a son—the seventh solitary son in seven successive generations—but lost him at an early age. Since then he has been childless, and when he passes on he will leave no descendants to carry on his name or his work. As for Rhee himself, the marriage was not of his own choice, and the fate of his wife and his son were a part of the general suffering of his prison ordeal.

In the prison with Rhee were seven of his old Independence Club friends, including his childhood study companion, Hugh Heung-woo Cynn, and another man, Park Youngman, who was to mean much in his later life. A Miss Harroyd, a newly-arrived missionary from Nova Scotia, brought a New Testament into the prison, and Rhee used to read aloud from it, while one of his companions turned the leaves, for it was several years before his fingers healed sufficiently to make it possible for him to use them without pain. Even in his latter years, whenever emotionally upset or agitated, he unconsciously blows upon the tips of his fingers, a habit developed during the time of pain.

Gradually, Rhee learned the fate of other leaders of the reform movement. Kim Ok Pyun escaped to Shanghai, where he was assassinated. Hong Yung Sik, who had become the vice-prime minister, was murdered in the presence of the emperor. Park Yong Hyo and Suh Kwang Bun escaped with Philip Jaisohn to Japan. The former accompanied Jaisohn to America and the latter was named Korean minister to Washington. All of them followed some path that led them from their work as reformist agitators, and Rhee—who had been one leader among many in the formative years of the movement—was the one principal leader left.

Thanks to the friendship of Warden Kim and his deputy, Lee, Rhee's prison life became a period of mental and spiritual growth. Books and magazines were brought in and a prison library was started. Rhee had a pocket English dictionary to aid him in his reading, and he tried to memorize every word. He also memorized many passages from the magazines, and years afterward used to surprise his friends by his ability to repeat such passages word for word. Through the intensive nature of this study he greatly extended his mastery of English and molded his English style. Appenzeller and Bunker regularly brought him copies of the American periodicals, *The Outlook* and *The Independent.* Lyman Abbot was editor of *The Outlook,* in which he conducted an editorial campaign of support and praise for the "liberalism" and modernization of Japan. Rhee read these articles with distaste but learned much from the pieces on social and political conditions and theories.

Prison rules forbade any light except the single kerosene lamp and it was always turned out early in the evening. Each cell, however, was allowed to have an empty kerosene can. Tallow candles were smuggled into the cell, and Rhee used to place a candle inside the can, which he turned down on its side, and with its mouth a few feet from the wall. In this way, by lying with his face close to the mouth of the can, he could read very well. Fellow prisoners always warned him when a guard was approaching, so that he could pull the can against the wall, thus concealing the light. Doubtless the guards became aware of what he was doing, but through the kindness of the warden he was not disturbed.

Writing implements, too, were forbidden. However, Rhee made ink from dyes that were smuggled in, and practiced writing on used copies of the magazines. After a time he commenced writing editorials for his daily newspaper, the *Maiyil Sinmun,* which once again was being published. These were smuggled out and printed, unsigned, of course, but the fact of his authorship gradually became well known. One of Rhee's companions in the prison was Lee Yo In, a noted poet and scholar. Yu Sung Joon, another prisoner, who was a brother of a former prime minister, was also

proud of his poetry-writing ability. The three of them vied
in the writing of poetry. One of Rhee's poems, published
in the newspaper—*Sarip Bong In Ku Mien So*—became well
known. It read, in part: *Chul sa gyul ban shin jung mil;*
sarip bong in ku mien so, which may be translated as, "Tied
together in chains men develop new intimacies; moving
about in politics, one finds old friends estranged." In ways
such as this the tedium of prison life was lightened, and the
stultifying effects of confinement were partially transmitted
into intellectual development.

Yu Sung Joon encouraged Rhee to write a book setting
forth the principles of the independence movement. All previous movements, he urged, had failed because the leaders
neglected to educate the public and their cause was soon
forgotten. Yu assured Rhee that his brother, then in exile
in Japan, would one day return to political favor and would
then use government funds to have the book printed and
distributed for the education of the people. With this encouragement, Rhee made notes and gathered ideas for a
political treatise called, *Dong-nip Jung Shin,* or *The Spirit*
of Independence, which he finally commenced to put into
final form on February 19, 1904—near the end of his imprisonment—and of which 34 chapters were completed before
his release. It became the political bible of the Korean people. As a matter of fact, during the political reversals which
preceded the Russo-Japanese War, Yu's brother, Yu Kil Joon,
did return to office. However, the government was strongly
influenced by the Japanese, who had no intention of permitting (let alone assisting) the publication of a book designed
to arouse the nationalistic zeal of the Korean people.

The manuscript was smuggled out of the prison and later
Park Youngman took it out of Korea, concealed in the false
bottom of his trunk, to evade detection by Japanese customs
officials. It was taken to Los Angeles where an edition of
one thousand copies, well bound and illustrated, was printed

in 1906, through the endeavors of several devoted Korean exiles. Upon the liberation of Korea in 1945, many Koreans brought out of hiding separated pages of this book, which they had torn apart to keep it concealed from the Japanese. In 1920 it was reprinted in Honolulu by the Korean community there, and following the liberation of Korea in 1945 it has been reprinted several times. This book has served much the same purpose for the Koreans that the writings of Tom Paine and Thomas Jefferson have served for Americans.

The Spirit of Independence consists of forty-seven chapters, in addition to an Appendix on "Essential Conditions of Independence." Since the book has never been translated into English, and since its contents reveal the consistency with which Syngman Rhee has maintained his fundamental political views for more than half a century, there may be interest in noting its subject matter. Of the thirty-four original, prison-written chapters, five dealt with the necessity of individual duty, loyalty and responsibility. Two more stressed the value of education. Chapters seven and eight were an introduction to Korea's international complications and ten chapters discussed the political aspirations of key nations. Eleven chapters dealt with democratic government, including discussions of the American and French revolutions, and the American political principles and institutions. One brief chapter traced the short and turbulent history of the Korean reform movement.

This much of the book was written in prison; the remaining thirteen chapters were written afterward and relate to the background, development, progress and results of the Russo-Japanese War. These first thirty-four chapters show clearly the pragmatic character of Syngman Rhee's mind— the tendency to formulate his thinking around the principles and the problems of most genuine importance to his country and people. The book sought to serve as a general introduction to a new way of life, to the modern world and to the democratic ideals which Rhee believed would have to be adopted in Korea if his people were to be led from their condition of backwardness and impotency into a fruitful era of individual and national liberty. The latter chapters deal with the passionate crusade for liberation from the gathering tentacles of Japan, which belongs to the next period of his life.

The general tone of the book, the nature of its appeal, and the revelation of the sentiments of the writer may best be illustrated by a selection of brief excerpts, offered in translation. Stressing the need for a sense of personal responsibility, he wrote: "My dear Korean friends, regardless of your age, sex or position, you all belong to Korea and are part of its total population. Upon the shoulders of each of you there rests the responsibility for establishing a nation. . .

"The main reason why the people do not work together is that they do not know to whom the nation belongs. People often think that to work for their country is to work for others. They do not realize that what they do for others is most truly working for themselves. Hence, they wait for others to do what must be done. Will you not hasten to extinguish the fire in your own house even if others ignore it? Isn't it much better to plunge into the fire to save what you can, whether others assist you or not? . . .

"If your own heart," he wrote, "is without patriotism, your heart is your enemy. You must struggle against your own feelings if they urge you to forgo the struggle for the common cause. Let us examine our hearts now, at this moment. If you find within yourself any single thought of abandoning the welfare of your country, tear it out. Do not wait for others to lead or to do what must be done, but arouse yourself. If you do not do it, it will never be done.

"Let us gather all our powers and make our nation like the nations of wealthy, powerful and civilized people. Keep independence in your own hearts. The most important part

is to cast out hopelessness. We must become diligent workers. Our own individual dedication is the seed from which
will grow the harvest of a sound nation."

In a rare passage of personal revelation, he wrote: "For
my oppressed fellowmen I stood up against the cruel enemy.
Even though my life can be erased by the evil forces in the
world, such a death is not destruction but is eternal life.
May each of you, my fellow countrymen, be enabled to realize your own responsibility and perform it, whether others
do or not. Avoid any act of shame or blemish."

Explaining the nature of democracy—a new concept—he
said: "Generally speaking, a nation is analogous to an assembly in which many gather to discuss various matters. In a
nation many people unite together to survive. The officials
of a nation are those charged to carry on the business of its
organization. The people are the members of the assembly.
Without the assistance of the people, the officials have no
source of strength. Where the people are not attentive, vice
enters in."

Always, all through the book, he returned again and again
to the central theme—that a nation is what its individual
citizens make it.

"As I have indicated before, to live in this nation is comparable to being a passenger on a ship in a cruel sea. How
can you be so indifferent as not to be concerned with the
affairs of your own nation, but to insist they are the business
of high officials? The ship may be wrecked if you try to help
yourself alone or are concerned only to save the captain of
the ship. . .

"No matter how wise a ruler may be, he cannot administer
the state without the help of the people. Therefore, the responsibility of the subject is great. It is dangerous to make
subjects the slaves of the ruler. Subjects must serve the ruler
with reverence and according to right principles, and advise

him with wise words. The ruler must edify the people with
virtue so the people will obey him from their hearts.

"In a civilized nation each subject has his own responsibility, and to carry out this responsibility is his solemn duty.
When a nation is governed in this manner, the people cannot rebel against their ruler, for all of them join in ruling one
another."

Judged as the prison production of a young man who had
never been out of the country, and who had received but a
few glimmerings of elementary education beyond the old
conservative culture of essential feudalism in which he was
reared, this book must rank as a remarkable example of lib-
ertarian inspiration. But, despite its crudities and limitations,
the insistence upon the responsibility of every individual—
man, woman, or child—to make his own utmost contribution
to the welfare of the nation, and the concurrent emphasis
upon the fact that the nation exists for the benefit of its individual members, make this book a genuine, if not a strik-
ingly original, contribution to the philosophy of democratic
government. There are few countries at any time in which
it would not be appropriate to address such an appeal as:
"The relationship between you and your nation may seem
so remote that you have little reason to love it or to make
efforts to save it. Therefore, two enemies must be guarded
against: first, the people who try to destroy the nation; and
second, those who sit passively by, being without any hope
or sense of responsibility." This was the heart of Syngman
Rhee's *Spirit of Independence*, as it has proved to be the
heart of his lifelong endeavors, ever since.

The fact that Rhee was enabled to write his book in prison,
while supposedly denied the use of writing materials, was
due in great part to Lady Um, consort of the king and
mother of the Prince Lee who still lives in Tokyo under the
patronage of the Japanese (raising orchids as a hobby and
striving to forget the great days of the Yi dynasty, of which

he is the remnant but no longer heir). Lady Um was a regular reader of Rhee's newspaper editorials and in a languid and dilettantish way a supporter of the reform movement. She was a friend of Warden Kim and encouraged him to be lenient to Rhee and his associates. Enough has already been written of the situation then existing in Seoul to indicate that everything political in the Korea of that day was dependent upon favoritism at court. When a man's friends were in power, he prospered. When they lost favor, he was ruined. But always there were many cross-currents, with some political figures at court wielding a measure of influence counter to that of the ruling clique. Thus it was that Rhee and his fellows of the Independence Club had friends powerful enough to lighten their imprisonment, but powerless to have them released.

A different kind of release, however, did come to Rhee—and that was his conversion in prison to Christianity. In 1904, with the help of a Presbyterian minister, James S. Gale, he wrote out a brief sketch of his early life, as a background for his conversion. In it he wrote:

"The strangest thing to me was the idea that a man who died 1900 years ago could save my soul. 'Is it possible,' I asked myself, 'that the people who are doing all these marvelous things we are told about can really believe in such a foolish doctrine as this? Perhaps they have come here only to induce our ignorant people to believe what they cannot believe themselves. No wonder only the poor and ignorant are going to Church. An educated scholar who has the knowledge of the great Buddha and the wisdom of Confucius would never be led to believe such a teaching.'

"Having come to this conclusion, I rested my mind more or less at ease, and told my mother all about my attendance at Pai Jai. She took me by the hand and said, 'My child,' (such a loving mother was she that she continued to call me *Ahgah* or child until I was nineteen years old) 'you are going

to become a *Chunchuhak Koon* (God-cult fanatic), are you
not?' 'No, mother,' I assured her, 'I am too wise to believe
what they say. Have you ever known a scholar to become a
believer of that religion?' These remarks relieved her a little,
but did not entirely free her mind from anxiety. She was
soon to find that her son was changing rapidly under the
transforming influence of Western civilization. . . .

"It must be remembered that the great ambition which
led me to the mission school was to learn English, and English only. This ambition I quickly achieved, but I soon discovered I was learning something of far greater importance
than the English language. I was imbibing ideas of political
equality and liberty. Those who know anything about the
political oppressions to which the masses of the Korean people were subject can imagine what a revolution took place
in the heart of a young Korean *Yangban* when he learned
for the first time that people in Christian lands were protected against the tyranny of rulers. I said to myself, 'It
would be a great blessing to my downtrodden fellow men
if only we could adopt such a political principle.'

"Then I began to understand that political changes do not
come by themselves and are not only a question of laws and
regulations. There must also come deep and abiding changes
within the hearts and minds of the people—and particularly
in the ruling class. I began to listen a little bit to the morning services in the chapel and when I listened I heard that
Jesus was more than a symbol of salvation in afterlife. He
was also a Great Teacher who brought a gospel of brotherly
love and service. I began to have more respect for these
foreign religious teachings and in my own private mind I
began to consider that maybe Jesus deserved to rank some-
where near Confucius. But further than this I could not or
would not go."

This account probably represents pretty accurately his
feelings about the Christian religion in the period of his

political agitation leading up to his imprisonment. In those days, because of his spiritual and intellectual immaturity, he was far more certain of what he was against than of what he was for. The old tyranny must be broken down! Of that he was sure. But he might have been very much embarrassed if he had been given responsibility at that time for building something new to take its place.

Through his torturous imprisonment, however, maturity was thrust upon him apace. It was in prison that there burst upon him an enveloping vision of faith in God and in his fellow men as a foundation upon which his philosophy of government and of life itself was gradually established. Like Thomas Jefferson, he began to see religion and politics as inseparable. He felt that the political and social reform articles he was reading in the American magazines did not make sense except as they were interpreted in the light of the Christian faith. Without such faith he could not envisage any effective answer to the doctrine of "every man for himself." With such a faith, he could see that true believers could never rest content while they saw their fellows in misery and suffering from injustice. His mind was so rigidly trained in logic that he argued himself into the inevitable necessity of adopting this line of thinking.

His conversion to Christianity, however, was much more profound than a mere intellectual agreement with its principles. The figure of Jesus became for him a living inspiration. A feeling of the infinite compassion of Christ entered into his soul and gave him a positive and unquestioning assurance that he, too, was under the care of God and that his life, however roughly it was ordered, was a part of God's plan for humanity. He learned the humility of acceptance of whatever might be dealt out to him, and this acceptance became integrated with a fierce driving sense of personal mission to do and to be more for God than he ever could expect to do or be for himself. It was in those days that Rhee began to picture himself as an instrument which must be always ready and willing to be used as God's will might direct. More than ever before in his life, Syngman felt both helpless and powerful—helpless to guide his own destiny or to seek his own ease, but imbued with a power never before suspected to help in some manner to carry out God's great design. This feeling gave him a sense of release and peace. He felt able for the first time to view his own personality objectively. He could ask himself what were his own weaknesses and wherein lay his strength. He felt impelled to wrestle with his shortcomings and to do his best to improve them in every way, the better to carry on whatever responsibilities should be laid upon him.

The very fact that this conversion occurred in prison gave it an immediate and practical character. Crowded into the cell with him were other human beings representing every kind of misery. Some of them were really desperate criminals who had committed all the evil that lay within their power. Others were vibrant with idealism and, like himself, had been condemned for sincere efforts to erase the bitter wrongs of the corrupt monarchy. Very few of them had ever learned anything of Christianity and many of the rest had only endured a superficial acquaintance with it as the necessary price of acquiring some Western learning.

Rhee began to read to as many as would listen while he intoned chapters from the Scriptures—and since their confinement needed every possible means of lightening the oppressive boredom of the passing months, he found that even the most skeptical would listen. Prayer became a natural means of communion for him, and he acquired a habit that has persisted all his later life of opening and closing the day with prayer. He found that this communion with God was the most refreshing experience both for his body and for his spirit that he had ever known. All through the remainder of his life, during the years of painful exile and hopeless

agitation and under the burdens of the presidency, he has
found that his troubles would flow away from him and become a part of the infinite burden of God when he turned
to Him to seek reassurance that the ordeals of the day were
but an infinitely small portion of His great plan.

During his six years in prison more than forty inmates
were converted as a result of his readings and meditation
with them. Years later he would occasionally be brought to
a warm recollection of some of them and would recall vividly
how their miseries and cares lightened as they, too, accepted
the Christian faith. Several of the *Ap-nois,* or prison guards,
who were charged to prevent the prisoners from holding
any services or reading any books (let alone to engage in the
study of a foreign sect) began to gather at the bars of the cell
to listen to Rhee's stumbling efforts to preach. Some of
them, too, became converts and the leniency of their supervision derived in part from the fact that the prison cell was
recast into a kind of sanctuary.

From the teaching of religion, Rhee and some of his better-
educated associates gradually commenced to develop a regular school in the prison. Mr. Bunker, who, in addition to
his teaching duties at Pai Jai, was director of the Religious
Tract Society, sent in to them 150 copies of religious books.
With these and other secular volumes a circulating library
was established among the four large cells, with the tacit
consent of Warden Kim. There were children as well as
adults in the prison, and the classes were organized at first
to teach them. Rhee was elected as the spokesman to persuade the jailers to accede to this plan, which, with the approval of Lady Um, they did. Soon regular classes were
organized for adults as well as children. Chinese calligraphy,
arithmetic, geography, the Japanese language, and history
were taught by several of the prisoners. Rhee lectured from
time to time on a variety of subjects, chiefly on political
democracy as he was learning it from American periodicals

and expounding it in his *Spirit of Independence*. There were about fifteen boys in the classes, though of course the number and personnel varied through the years. Some went out of the prison to lives of prominence and usefulness and some returned to lives of crime.

During these prison years (1897-1904) affairs in Korea continued their dismal course. The Independence Club was completely broken up. Efforts toward reform were sporadic and ineffectual. The old Taiwunkun died peacefully in his bed in February, 1898, and for all his cruelty and ambition, his loss to the nation was keenly felt. There remained no single man of stature great enough or purpose strong enough to save the nation from the ruin that was hastening upon it. Japan continued her efforts to entrench herself ineradicably upon Korean soil. Russia was making similar efforts and for a time they appeared to be equally effective. In 1898 and again in 1900 envoys of Russia and Japan met secretly and agreed to a dividing line on or close to the 38th parallel, in order to mark off between themselves their areas of special interest in the Orient. Only their fear of Great Britain and the United States prevented them from formalizing these understandings into public pronouncements. Meanwhile the Russo-Japanese rivalry for control in Manchuria continued and after both the United States and Great Britain withdrew from that area, the way was left open for their clash of interests to develop. Korea, caught squarely in the middle, and with corroding corruption and inefficiency in the decaying monarchy, was helpless.

The news the prisoners were receiving from the outside was matched in tragic gloom by an epidemic of cholera which swept through the jail in March, 1903. Forty prisoners were carried off by this dreadful disease in the space of two days. In the close confinement and lack of sanitation within the cells, there seemed no hope for any of them to escape. Rhee sent an urgent appeal to Dr. O. R. Avison, who made an attempt to visit them but was refused admittance. However, he did succeed in sending medicine to Rhee, who administered it to the patients according to Avison's directions. In some manner, the remnants of the prisoners survived.

In the rapid succession of political changes which accompanied the attack by Japan against Russia, on February 9, 1904, the political prisoners began to hope for release. Korea, as "the shrimp caught between two whales," was desperately seeking for any means of saving herself. At the very beginning of that year the emperor sought the favor of the Russians by granting them the timber-cutting concession in the northeastern mountains, with access to the port of Yongnampo. Although the port was never transferred to their jurisdiction, the Russians immediately changed its name to Port Nicholas. The emperor then made a quick about-face and began to deal with Japan. A treaty was signed granting the Japanese the right to land troops in Korea and to cross Korean territory as necessitated by the war. This treaty strongly reaffirmed Japan's recognition of Korea's complete sovereignty and independence and the hapless emperor interpreted these pledges as being more than mere form and symbol.

With these tumultuous changes occurring in court, Rhee's friends made every effort to secure his release. Unfortunately the breakup of the Independence Club left him without any powerful friends within the court circle. One painful blow came in the form of a letter which he received on March 20, 1903. It was signed by George Heber Jones, one of Rhee's missionary friends, and read as follows:

Last Sunday I heard from your father that the emperor had not included you in the amnesty recently proclaimed. I am more sorry than I can tell you for this. I write to express my sorrow to you. However, do not give way to despair. Trust God and He will help you. I hope and pray that the emperor will grant you a full pardon and you will come out to help us in making Korea a Christian land.

It was hard in that spring and summer of 1904 to see the prison doors open and so many of his friends and companions walking out to freedom, while he remained behind. It was disheartening to think that not all the efforts of his friends had succeeded in having his name placed on the rolls of an amnesty so sweeping that almost every prisoner classified as political was let out. The fear seeped into his soul that he might have to remain in that noisome prison for the remainder of his days. Once again the temptation was great to pray for death. This was the hardest blow his faith had yet had to endure.

It was not until almost six months after the discouraging letter from Jones that Warden Kim came running to him on August 9 to announce that he had an order for his release. All Rhee could feel was a great emptiness in his heart as he rose tremblingly to his feet, unbelieving, trying to understand what this news could mean. Then at Warden Kim's order an *Ap-noi* swung open the door of the cell and motioned him to come out. For a few moments young Rhee stood unsteadily, staring about at the cell walls, at the familiar ceiling and the matted floor. Even this place where so much misery and degradation had been suffered he could not leave quickly, for too many memories would have to be left behind.

As he glanced once more around the gloomy walls he seemed to see in the shadows the faces of many companions who had been led out to be beheaded in the courtyard behind the jail. In his ears there rang again the echoes of their cries. He could feel with heightened emotion the tremor of their bodies when the saber cut down into their flesh. Particularly he recalled the great patriot Chang Ho Yik who was beheaded behind the jail, crying out *"Mansei!"* (May Korea live ten thousand years!) until the third blow of the saber silenced him forever. This and many another experience remained in his mind to trouble and torture him for many years.

It seemed unreal that after having hovered so close to death from torture, from privation, from cholera, from execution, and from sheer lethargy, he now at last should be free. Free to walk out and leave it all behind! (But how could he leave behind experiences that were eaten into his sinews and bones and the very fabric of his mind?)

He gazed deep into Warden Kim's eyes, and these two men wept unashamed. Then, staggering with weakness and blinking his eyes at unaccustomed daylight, he walked out through the prison doors.

Chapter IV

A WORLD
TUMBLES DOWN

FOLLOWING SYNGMAN RHEE's release from prison he had little leisure or inclination for rejoicing. His father's happiness moreover soon changed to pathos, when he discovered that his son—far from having learned his lesson—was all the more determined to devote himself to political reform. As for Rhee's own feelings, it never occurred to him that he had any choice in the matter. Bad as the Korean situation had been when he entered prison, it had steadily deteriorated during the seven intervening years. The near-chaos of 1897 was succeeded by a pattern, but it was clearly a pattern of destruction.

Everywhere, in the streets, in the offices, and in the government buildings, Rhee saw the busy and officious Japanese civil and military officers, scurrying around with the deceptively random purposiveness of ants, gesticulating earnestly, staring solemnly through oversized spectacles, and speaking (always speaking) with insistent authority. The war between Japan and Russia was already clearly nearing an end. And equally clearly, Japan was entrenching its own power more and more firmly in every cranny of Korean life.

Rhee's old friends of the liberal movement were widely scattered, subdued, confused or converted. The Independence Club had fought against the inefficiency and corruption of the court; and now Japanese officials were proving themselves both efficient and personally honest. (The fundamental dishonesty with which the Japanese government was cold-bloodedly planning to undermine Korean independence while pledging through treaties to uphold and insure it was hidden from all but a few eyes.) Harsh treatment had broken the spirit of some of the old reformists. Hopelessness overwhelmed others when it became evident that the democratic United States, which the Korean liberals had enthusiastically adopted as the very model of a modern idealistic state, was not going to play the Confucian role of "big brother" to Korea. Meanwhile, the Japanese imperialists were buying support in every conceivable quarter by granting special trading privileges to those Koreans whose motives were governed by cupidity, and by openly paying homage to those who were moved largely by vanity. Bribery and open venality of every sort had become commonplaces of the court circle. Yet over this cesspool of intrigue and vice was laid a deceptive covering of modernization and progressiveness of a new Japan rapidly taking its place among the leading nations of the world.

President Theodore Roosevelt, who admired strength and aggressive energy above all else, frankly showed his friendly support of Japanese ambitions. His friend D. W. Stevens (who had been serving as an employee of the Japanese Foreign Office) went to Korea to play the dual role of advisor to the Korean Foreign Ministry and critic of Korea in articles written for American journals. Another old friend of Roosevelt's, Mr. George Kennan, persuaded him that the Koreans were unfit for self-government. Roosevelt sent his Secretary of War, William Howard Taft, to Tokyo, where on July 29, 1905 he signed a secret executive agreement with Katsura, the Japanese prime minister, agreeing to support Japan's claims of a special interest in Korea and Manchuria in return for a promise not to attack the Philippine Islands. Some years afterward Roosevelt gave his own explanation for this agreement, as follows:

To be sure, by treaty it was solemnly covenanted that Korea should remain independent. But Korea itself was helpless to enforce the treaty, and it was out of the question to suppose that any other nation, with no interests of its own at stake, would do for the Koreans what they were utterly unable to do for themselves.

England, meanwhile, had signed a treaty with Japan in 1903, in effect recognizing Japan's preponderant interests in northern Asia. The opportunistic ambitions of Russia's Czar Nicholas, both in eastern Europe and in Asia, were disturbing both London and Washington. Anglo-American interests alike seemed to require the development of counter-forces to oppose the beginnings of a new Russian aggressiveness. A practical means to that end appeared to be the establishment of Japanese power on the mainland of northern Asia— to wit, on the Korean peninsula. Japan was so firmly committed to the development of Westernization and seemed so friendly to the United States and Great Britain that such an encouragement to Japanese expansion appeared to offer dividends in checking Russia without creating any new threat. The feelings and the welfare of Korea were belittled or ignored.

It was a strange and disheartening world for a Korean patriot to re-enter. Of course Rhee did not know all that was happening. (The Taft-Katsura agreement was not revealed until 1922.) But there was ample evidence on every side of the trend of events. A Japanese financier, Megata, had assumed virtual control over the finance ministry. The entire Korean telegraph and postal systems were placed under Japanese control. Under the pretext of military necessity, the Japanese Army (which was in Korea ostensibly only to fight Russia) took over large areas surrounding Seoul, dispossessing 15,000 families in the process. Under the same excuse, all Korean "waste lands" (more than half of the entire national territory, comprising all the undeveloped mineral resources) were granted to a Japanese corporation headed by Mr. Nagamori. To this the foreign representatives in Seoul objected and the grant was rescinded, only to be renewed later when the Japanese domination was absolute. Japanese agents, posing as representatives of the military, went through the country seizing choice properties, with the simple explanation that they were needed for maintenance of the Japanese military forces. Japanese money-lenders were established in every city, lending money freely at a monthly interest rate of twelve per cent—and taking the property of the borrowers when repayment was impossible. Koreans were roughly treated by the Japanese soldiery, were forbidden access to any areas the Japanese chose to designate as "off limits" and were subject to summary judgment by Japanese military tribunals. The handwriting on the wall was plain.

Plain as the evidence was, Rhee was disheartened to find that there existed little semblance of any effective Korean nationalist movement at the time of his release from prison. A few months before his pardon, he received a letter from Philip Jaisohn, the founder of the Independence Club, who was then in America. Dated April 6, 1904, the letter read:

So far Japan is on the right side and waging war for the principle which every civilized being must uphold and support. I sincerely hope God will be with the nation which fights for righteousness and civilization . . . Japan or any other nation cannot help Korea unless Korea helps herself and is willing to be helped by another. If Korea continues to act like a child she will surely become a part of some other nation.

In his first talks after his release from prison with some of his earlier friends, Rhee found them enthusiastic over

Japan's successes in the war against Russia. In part this was because it was the first time an Oriental nation had succeeded in a war against a Western power. Partly, too, their rejoicing was because of the highly publicized feudal backwardness of Russian society. Another cause was the outstanding success of the industrialization program in Japan, following the Meiji Restoration, which made Japan look like the rising star of progress for all Asian peoples. Finally, the widespread acquiescence of the old Korean reformist group in the strutting assertiveness of the Japanese military resulted in part from their recognition of its superiority over the obvious incompetence of the decaying Korean monarchy. It was clear to Rhee that to his former associates Japan's imperialistic ambitions were hidden beneath a cloak of progressiveness.

It was not until he began to talk to Prince Min Young Whan and General Hahn Kiu-sul—the two most influential reformers in the court circle—that he found kindred souls who were as disturbed as he was himself by the course of events. These men understood that little if anything could be done inside Korea to check the trend of Japanization. They and Rhee agreed that an appeal should be made to the President of the United States, based upon the Amity Treaty of 1882.

Later Rhee learned of another effort made by the emperor of Korea to save his toppling nation. In October, 1905, he was induced to send to the United States Homer B. Hulbert, the friendly and courageous American who was the editor of the Tri-Lingual Press, with a letter from the emperor to President Roosevelt. Hulbert informed the American minister in Seoul of the nature of his errand and set out promptly. When he arrived in Washington, however, he found to his amazement that he could not see either the President or Secretary of State Elihu Root, to deliver the letter, and he received a cold response to all his inquiries in the State

Department as to the proper means of fulfilling his mission. As Hulbert wrote in a statement later presented to the Senate Committee on Foreign Affairs:

I supposed that the President would not only be willing but eager to see the letter; but instead of that I received the astounding answer that the President would not receive it. I cast about in my own mind for a possible reason, but could imagine none. I went to the State Department with it, but was told that they were too busy to see me. Remember that at that very moment Korea was in her death throes; that she was in full treaty relations with us; that there was a Korean legation in Washington and an American legation in Seoul. I determined that there was something here that was more than mere carelessness. There was premeditation in the refusal. There was no other answer. They said I might come the following day. I did so and was told that they were still too busy, but I might come the next day. I hurried over to the White House and asked to be admitted. A secretary came out and without any preliminary whatever told me in the lobby that they knew the contents of the letter, but that the State Department was the only place to go. I had to wait till the next day. But on that same day, the day before I was admitted, the administration, without a word to the emperor or government of Korea or to the Korean legation, and knowing well the contents of the undelivered letter, accepted Japan's unsupported statement that it was all satisfactory to the Korean government and people, cabled our legation to remove from Korea, cut off all communication with the Korean government, and then admitted me with the letter.

The event in Korea to which Hulbert refers was the signing by the emperor of a Japanese-drawn statement declaring a Japanese protectorate over Korea. In securing this signature, Marquis Ito, a special envoy from Japan, held conferences with the Korean emperor on two successive days, November 16 and 17, urgently pressing for his compliance, while Japanese troops surrounded the palace and paraded through the streets of Seoul. Memories of the murder of Queen Min by the Japanese in 1895 were vividly recalled. Prime Minister (General) Hahn Kiu-sul, who urged the cabinet to withstand this protectorate to the death, was arrested by Japanese soldiers in a corridor of the palace while on the way to confer with the emperor. After a night-long siege of the emperor and his cabinet, held incommunicado in separate chambers of the palace, the document was brought in to the emperor in the early hours of pre-dawn on November 18. Afterward the Japanese displayed the document with the emperor's seal upon it, but he always swore that he had never signed it. Meanwhile, over in the United States, Elihu Root wrote to Hulbert on November 25 that since "the emperor has made a new agreement with Japan disposing of the whole question to which the letter relates, it seems quite impracticable that any action should be based upon it."

The following day, November 26, Hulbert received from the emperor a cablegram which had been secreted out of Korea and dispatched from Chefoo, to circumvent Japanese censorship, reading as follows: "I declare that the so-called treaty of protectorate recently concluded between Korea and Japan was extorted at the point of the sword and under duress and therefore is null and void. I never consented to it and never will. Transmit to American government." However, it was too late. President Roosevelt had made his decision and the American legation in Korea was already ordered to be closed and its functions transferred to Tokyo.

Rhee urged Prince Min and General Hahn to go to the United States to plead for invocation of the mutual defense article of the Amity Treaty. The emperor, however, was so tightly in the toils of his Japanese captors that he could not give them an official appointment. Prince Min and the few others who were working together in a last desperate effort to save Korean independence decided that Rhee should be the one to go. He was provided with a student passport and with messages to the Korean legation in Washington, which he concealed in the false bottom of his trunk. Then accompanied by Lee Chung Hyuk (who took the anglicized name of Howard Leigh) he left Korea ostensibly to study in the United States. Their fare was supplied in part by Lee Chung Chin, who had been the deputy warden of Seoul Prison during their long imprisonment.

On November 4, 1904, at 1:00 P.M. they left Seoul, after a tearful farewell from Rhee's father, who was deeply stirred by mingled feelings of wanting him to stay and wanting him to go. Upon arrival at Chemulpo harbor (now Inchon) they secretly boarded the S.S. *Ohio*, which lifted anchor the following day at 3:00 P.M. Brief stops were made at Mokpo and Pusan, at each of which Rhee was fearful lest they be taken from the ship. Gradually, however, the coast of Korea receded from view, while he leaned moodily on the rail, staring at it with combined bitterness and dim hopefulness. He never doubted that his departure was well advised. It was all too evident that inside Korea nothing effective could then be done. But as a youth of twenty-nine, without official status, and without even money enough to proceed beyond Japan (let alone to live on after arrival in the United States) he wrestled with heavy doubts of his ability to counteract the heady ambitions of Japan or to overcome the indifference of the American government.

When the *Ohio* landed at Kobe, Rhee and Leigh were greeted by a number of Korean friends and by Mr. Logan, an American missionary to whom Rhee carried a letter of introduction. On Sunday, November 13, Rhee spoke in Logan's chapel to a large congregation, which made a contribution toward his passage fare. On the following Thursday he sailed for Honolulu on the S.S. *Siberia*, with a ticket purchased for 126 yen, which entitled him to a place down in the crowded hold amongst a mass of Korean laborers on their way to Hawaii. It was a strange setting indeed for a diplomatic mission entrusted with the salvation of a dying nation!

When the ship docked at Honolulu on the morning of November 29, Rhee was visited by Mr. Hong Jeung Sup, Korean interpreter to the American Immigration Bureau, who informed him that the Korean community expected his arrival and had arranged to hold a meeting for him. Alone among all the steerage passengers, Rhee was allowed to land. At dockside he was greeted by the Reverend Pyung Koo Yoon and by Dr. John W. Wadman, superintendent of the Methodist Mission, along with several others. They took Rhee to the Korean Church, near Nuanu Valley, where many Koreans were waiting to greet him. That evening they went to the Korean Plantation at Ewa, some twelve miles from Honolulu, where more than two hundred Koreans were gathered.

Dr. Wadman, in presenting Rhee to the meeting, said: "Our work here is growing so wonderfully and the wireless telegram of the Holy Spirit has transformed our brother Rhee so that he has come a long way from Korea to partake of this sacramental service. We would like to keep him with us, but as he is on his way to America we will wait until he comes back and then we will catch him." After Dr. Wadman conducted the sacrament of the Lord's Supper, Rhee made a long speech, which lasted until 11:00 P.M. The meeting was closed by mass singing of the Korean National Anthem —which at that time was sung to the tune of Auld Lang Syne.

After that long meeting was over, Rhee went home with the Reverend P. K. Yoon. They had received in Hawaii the information that Hulbert's mission had failed. The two men talked over the situation until dawn. They agreed that Japan, while professing to be a friend of Korean independence, really had already undertaken to undermine it. They also agreed it was essential to have Korea represented at the forthcoming Portsmouth Peace Conference. Since Japanese influence at the Korean court was sufficient to prevent any official representation, it was plain that Korea would not be represented at all unless steps to that end should be taken by Koreans outside the country. There in the early hours when dawn was graying the Hawaiian skies, Rhee and Yoon laid preliminary plans to do what they could to save the independence of their nation. Yoon was to remain for a time in Hawaii, raising funds and securing the full support of the entire Korean community, and Rhee was to proceed directly to Washington to do whatever he could.

At 6:30 in the morning, after virtually no sleep at all, they went back to Honolulu. There Rhee addressed another meeting, in which was taken up a collection of $30 to pay his steerage fare on the *Siberia* for the rest of his trip to San Francisco. The ship sailed at 11:30 A.M., while Rhee looked out over the rail at the waving hats and handkerchiefs of the people who had come to see him off.

Mr. Chung Soo Ahn was waiting at the San Francisco pier for Rhee and Howard Leigh, his companion who had been forced to remain aboard ship in Hawaii, when the ship docked at 10:00 A.M. on December 6. Three days later they went down to San Rafael, to call on Mr. and Mrs. Fish, whose son was a missionary in Korea. Their hosts took the two Korean students to the San Anselmo Seminary, where the president, Dr. McIntosh, offered each of them a three-year scholarship providing room, board and tuition. Following their graduation, he said, he would arrange to have them sent back to Korea as missionaries, with full support. As Rhee gazed around the beautiful stone building set atop a green hill and contrasted it with the misery of his surroundings during the preceding seven years—as well as with the uncertainties of his mission—he was strongly tempted to accept the offer and remain. Since he could not tell these new friends of his about the responsibility which was taking him to Washington, his refusal of their generosity was awkward and left both Mr. and Mrs. Fish and Dr. McIntosh feeling that these two Koreans were uncouth and ungrateful. Rhee finally broke away from them with an uncomfortable feeling he was fated to experience many and many a time during his long life, namely that understanding is a happy accident which sometimes occurs but that some degree of misunderstanding is the general rule.

Howard Leigh remained with Rhee and the two went on down to Los Angeles on December 17. There they were met by Hugh Cynn, one of their old prison mates and a boyhood companion of Rhee, who had first introduced him to the Pai Jai school (and who, half a century later, in 1952, was to be among his opponents in standing for election to the presidency of the Republic of Korea). Cynn was attending the University of Southern California and had a number of Korean friends in Los Angeles. He took the two homeless wanderers to the Korean Methodist Mission on Magnolia Avenue, where they spent several days. Then, the day after Christmas, Syngman Rhee left on the Santa Fe Railway for Washington, leaving Howard Leigh behind, since they were unable to raise money enough for two tickets.

Rhee's arrival in Washington was deceptively auspicious. His train pulled into the railway station—then located at the juncture of 12th Street N.W. with Pennsylvania Avenue—at 9:00 P.M. on New Year's Eve. With only a few dollars in his pocket, he found a room in the small Mt. Vernon Hotel, on Pennsylvania Avenue. Then he went at once to the Korean legation, on Iowa Circle, where he met the first secretary, Hong Chul Soo, and was delighted to learn he had received a letter from Prince Min asking him to give Rhee every possible assistance.

The legation counsellor, Kim Yun Jung, joined them and the three men talked the old year out and the new year in.

Rhee soon learned there was serious disagreement among the small legation staff. The minister, Shin Taimu, had been personally selected for the post by Lady Um, the king's consort. It was her driving ambition to have her own son, Prince Yi Eun, succeed to the throne. However, the emperor's second son, Prince Eui Wha, next in line to the childless crown prince, was then studying in the United States. Shin Taimu's chief function (or so it appeared to Counsellor Kim Yun Jung) was to send back adverse reports on the behavior of Prince Eui Wha, in order that he might be discredited. In the months ahead Rhee was to meet Prince Eui Wha several times, for the prince, who was attending Roanoke College in Salem, Virginia, came to Washington frequently. So far as Rhee could see, the worst report to be rendered on him was that he was idle and had little interest in education. Rhee rather regretted the harmless amiability of the prince, for, remembering Lady Um's kindness to him during his prison days, he would have liked to have pleased her by passing on tales of princely wildness. In any event, as matters turned out, he was to be far too busy to give thought to the personal ambitions of Lady Um.

Kim Yun Jung had an interesting story of his own to tell during that long New Year's night. He (along with a number of other *Yangban* youths) had been selected by the Korean Students Society in Japan as a recipient of one of its five annual scholarships for study in the United States. When Kim arrived in Washington he had contacted Dr. Hamlin, pastor of the Presbyterian Church of the Covenant, on Connecticut Avenue at N Street, who arranged for him to enroll at Howard University, a school for Negroes. Kim made a favorable impression upon Dr. Gordon, president of Howard, and upon Dr. Charles Needham, president of George Washington University, who was serving as an adviser to the Korean legation. With their assistance, Dr. Horace Allen, the American minister in Seoul, was persuaded to use his good offices with the emperor to have Kim appointed as first secretary, then counsellor, to the legation. After this was accomplished, Kim had his wife and children, Frank and Cora, sent over to join him.

During the next several weeks Rhee saw Kim frequently and neither he nor Hong ever had a good word to say for Minister Shin. In Rhee's own talks with the minister, Shin insisted that he had no authority to make any representations whatsoever to the United States government without explicit instructions from Seoul. Both Rhee and Shin knew very well that no such instructions could possibly be sent, in view of the tight Japanese control over the court.

Rhee came gradually to talk fully and confidentially with Kim Yun Jung about his own secret mission. Kim assured Rhee earnestly that Minister Shin would never do anything to assist with the mission and must on no account be informed of it. Kim then indicated that if he were made minister he would co-operate fully and do all in his power to make the mission a success. Rhee asked if he would make an official request of the State Department to invoke the Treaty of 1882 and Kim replied that he assuredly would do so.

In the meantime, Rhee presented letters from Prince Min and General Hahn to Senator Hugh A. Dinsmore from Arkansas, who had served a term as American minister in Seoul, and who was very sympathetic to the Koreans. Dinsmore was delighted to hear from his two old friends and promised to arrange an interview for Rhee with Secretary of State John Hay, the famous author of the Open Door policy for China. Dinsmore felt sure that Hay would favor full justice for Korea, and so did Rhee—for Hay was known throughout the Orient as the man who prevented the partition of China following the 1899 Boxer uprising.

While these arrangements were being made, Rhee called at the office of the Washington *Post* and talked with a reporter, who wrote a story published in the January 15, 1905 issue, telling of Rhee's protest against what he pointed out was a Japanese plot to seize Korea. This was the very first presentation of Rhee's views in the American press—and it received as little attention as did many of the great number of interviews that were to follow during the next forty years.

As the weeks passed, Rhee was learning something else which he also had many later occasions to relearn, namely, that even the most friendly officials often have other business which intervenes to prevent or delay their efforts on behalf of a voteless foreigner. On February 16 he received a letter, handwritten by Senator Dinsmore, which read: "Dear Mr. Lee: Your note came yesterday morning. I have been sick in bed with grippe ever since I saw you, and, therefore, have been unable to attend to my promise to you. I am sitting up in my room now, however, and am writing a note this morning to Secretary Hay asking him if he will kindly mention a time when it will be convenient for him to see you. When I hear from him, I will let you know."

A few days later Rhee was excited to receive a pencil-scrawled note from Senator Dinsmore, dated Friday, which simply said: "I send you Mr. Hay's note. If you will come at nine o'clock sharp, we will go to the Department." The next morning Senator Dinsmore drove in his carriage to the house at 12th and Eye Streets, N.W., where Rhee had a room, and together they rode to the Department of State. They were ushered into the Secretary's office for an interview that lasted more than half an hour. Hay was a parishioner of the Church of the Covenant and was much interested in the missionary program in Korea. He told Dinsmore and Rhee of his enthusiasm at receiving letters from Horace Allen reporting that the American missionaries in northern Korea had refused to evacuate their stations even after the area was proclaimed a war zone. The Department had ordered a gunboat to Pyengyang to bring them out, but they insisted on remaining with their charges. Mr. Hay expressed his feeling that the Koreans must love the missionaries, and he added, "As long as the Koreans do not start any anti-Christian movement, there will be no trouble." Of course what he had in mind was the anti-Christian and anti-foreign Boxer movement in China. Rhee assured him that since the opening of Korea to intercourse with Western nations no single missionary in the country had ever suffered any harm or indignity of any kind. Then Rhee concluded, "We Koreans ask you, Mr. Secretary, to do for Korea what you have done for China." Hay seemed pleased at this reference to his Open Door policy, and then, in the presence of Senator Dinsmore, he said, "I will do everything I can to fulfill our treaty obligations, either personally or representing the United States government, whenever the opportunity presents itself."

As they left the Department, Senator Dinsmore said that he was fully satisfied with the conference, and so was Rhee. Rhee wrote out full reports on the meeting, addressed to Prince Min and General Hahn, and Senator Dinsmore had them sent to Seoul in the American legation diplomatic pouch. Rhee always felt that this assurance from Hay would have resulted in saving Korea's independence except for the tragic fact that Hay died that summer and was succeeded as secretary of state by Elihu Root. So close did events come to averting the tragic destiny that led from Japan's seizure of Korea to Manchuria and on to Pearl Harbor!

While working through Senator Dinsmore to reach the State Department, Rhee also was concerned to do what he could to secure effective working co-operation from the Korean legation. Following a long precautionary conversation with Kim Yun Jung (to be sure his loyalties were beyond question) Rhee sent to Prince Min a recommendation that Kim be named as minister to replace Shin Taimu. Shortly thereafter Shin was recalled and Kim took his place as chargé d'affaires. Rhee at that time trusted Kim implicitly, but later events showed that Kim even then was in secret communication with the Japanese minister in Washington, telling him in detail of Rhee's plans and activities and assuring him of acquiescence in Japan's plans for Korea in return for support in his expected appointment to the legation post. Unaware of all this, Rhee felt that Kim's new official status was at least a partial assurance of the success of his mission.

In June it was announced that within a month a peace conference would be held between the Russians and the Japanese, under Theodore Roosevelt's auspices, at Portsmouth, New Hampshire. The Korean government was not to be represented and few Koreans appeared to have any realization of the danger confronting their country. At that time Secretary of War William Howard Taft, accompanied by Alice Roosevelt and her husband, Congressman Longworth, was making a tour of the Orient. On their way through Hawaii the Korean community held an enormous mass meeting in their honor and, under the leadership of Pastor Pyung Koo Yoon, presented a resolution representing the 4,000 Koreans in the Islands, petitioning President Roosevelt to safeguard Korean independence by invoking the Treaty of 1882. This meeting elected Reverend Yoon and Syngman Rhee as envoys to President Roosevelt, to present the memorial. Dr. Wadman, the Methodist Mission superintendent, urged Taft to write a letter to Roosevelt introducing the two elected envoys. This Taft did, with results which later opened to them the doors of the Sagamore Hill Roosevelt home at Oyster Bay.

It was from this friendly Korean gathering that Taft went on to Tokyo, there to seal Korea's death warrant in the secret agreement of July 29 signed with Katsura. Of course, Rhee knew nothing of the Tokyo memorandum; he did read in the Washington newspapers a glowing account of the Honolulu meeting, reflecting the cordial friendliness of Taft and his party toward the Korean patriots. The surface ap-

pearances all augured success, and what lay beneath the
surface was too melodramatically hypocritical (both in
Washington and out beyond the Pacific) to be suspected by
any reasonable minds.

Mr. Yoon came to Washington with the copy of the
memorial and together he and Rhee carried it down to
Philadelphia to perfect its final wording with the assistance
of Philip Jaisohn. From there the two envoys went to
Oyster Bay, where President Roosevelt was spending his
summer vacation at Sagamore Hill. The newspapers (intent
on the forthcoming Portsmouth Conference, and short of
news about it) gave more than normal attention to these
young men and reported their every move. They reached
Oyster Bay on the morning of July 5 and registered at the
Octagon Hotel. Soon they were surrounded by a group of
reporters from metropolitan papers and the press associa-
tions, asking them all manner of questions. Rhee and Yoon
were tight-lipped in a desperate determination to do nothing
that could upset the diplomatic proprieties, and told the
reporters they could say nothing until after they had seen
the President. The reporters jeered at them good-naturedly
and assured them the President would never see them.
Russian and Japanese delegates were arriving and the air
was vibrant with big events. "The President has no time to
see you," the reporters said, "and you can stay here for
months with no results."

Rhee and Yoon called on Mr. Loeb, one of the presidential
secretaries, and gave him a copy of the memorial and also
the sealed letter of introduction penned by William Howard
Taft. Loeb promised to show them to the President when
he could, but warned that it might be some time before there
would be any reply. The two Koreans returned to their hotel
low in spirits. But that very evening they received a telephone call from Mr. Loeb asking them to come to the
summer White House at nine o'clock the following morn-

ing. Then the reporters flocked around them, asking what they expected to say and do, and congratulating them upon getting the interview. The two envoys brushed them off as quickly as they could and spent the evening in excited preparations.

The next morning, dressed in rented formal diplomatic frock coats and silk hats, they engaged a carriage and drove in high style but with pumping hearts and trembling limbs to the Sagamore Hill residence. Shortly after they were ushered into a waiting room, two or three more carriages drove up, bearing Count Witte, the head of the Russian delegation, together with several military and naval attachés, dressed in full regalia and dress uniforms. President Roosevelt, dressed in his "Rough Rider" outfit, walked out to the porch to greet the Russians. Then he led them into a conference room and quickly walked in to where Rhee and Yoon were nervously waiting. He came to them so quickly they had no time to make the bows they had planned, shook hands and said, "Gentlemen, I am very happy to receive you. What can I do for you and your country?"

The two Koreans presented their memorial, which was very brief, and through which Roosevelt quickly glanced. Then he said, "I am glad that you have come to me. I would be glad to do anything I can in behalf of your country, but unless this memorial comes through official channels I can't do anything with it. The Chinese government has presented a similar petition to me through their embassy, and if you will have this sent to me by your legation, I will present it, together with the Chinese petition, to the Peace Conference. You see, gentlemen, my position is simply to invite the two nations to come together to make peace. I have no power to interfere. However, if you send this to me through your legation, I will at once send the two memorials to the Conference. Have your minister take it to the Department of State, and if he doesn't find the secretary of state, let him

were struggling to keep their tempers in check and avoid making a public scene on the steps of the legation. But it was hard. After all the many hours of confidential talks and planning together, Rhee was finally aware that Kim had been duping him all along and had used his influence to help get himself in a position to play the Japanese game. This was indeed a maddening outcome to his years of patriotic endeavor and seven years of imprisonment.

Rhee went to Dr. Hamlin at his study in the Church of the Covenant to plead for his help, but Hamlin sternly urged him to drop the matter. Hamlin declared that the question was completely official and could only be handled properly through the regular diplomatic channels. He said the Treaty of 1882 was a mere formality and should not be taken seriously. He pointed out that the President and all the leading government officials were friendly to Japan. In this interview he seemed to exhibit all the firmness of Calvinistic Presbyterianism but little of the loving faith of Christianity. Rhee discovered, however, that Hamlin was not alone in considering the Koreans to be naive and foolish if they rested faith in treaties and international commitments.

Rhee then went to Philadelphia to talk the matter over with Philip Jaisohn, and he thought of an idea that might work. On August 7 Jaisohn wrote to Minister Kim suggesting that he give Rhee and Yoon a letter of introduction to the acting secretary of state (for John Hay had died), without any reference to the memorial. "The President desires to have the memorial come to him through the Department of State," Jaisohn wrote, "and it is your duty to your country and your courtesy to the President to help these men all you can without involving yourself officially in the matter of the memorial. The letter of introduction will answer the purpose and at the same time it will not involve yourself in any way as far as the memorial is concerned. I hope you will see the matter in the same light." This suggestion might very well have appealed to Minister Kim had he simply been trying to resolve his own dilemma as an official without instructions from his home government, but since he was in secret firmly committed to the Japanese, it meant nothing to him.

On August 10, back in Washington, Rhee received the following note from Jaisohn: "My dear Mr. Rhee—If Kim refuses to do it, I don't see what else you can do. The only thing you can do is to get the home government to take up the matter. However, I doubt very much that they will take it up. If you fail, you can have the whole matter published in the papers through the Associated Press and give the reasons why the memorial is not officially accepted by the President and why you cannot present it officially." Sound as these sentiments were, they brought no comfort to Rhee and Yoon.

Dr. Charles W. Needham, president of George Washington University, where Rhee was by that time enrolled as a student, replied to his plea for help with the following note: "I should think the only proper course for Mr. Kim would be for him to receive the memorial, if you desire him to do so, and inform the foreign office of Korea of its receipt and contents and ask for instructions. It would not be according to good usage, in such an important time and matter, for him to act upon his own motion. I am sure Mr. Kim desires to serve Korea to the best of his ability."

This note from the good Doctor Needham—who knew nothing of the fierce background struggle for the control of Korea, but was eager to impress upon his overage foreign student the niceties of good usage—marked almost the end: the end of the Rhee mission, the end of Mr. Kim, and the end of Korea. On September 10 Rhee received a note from Prince Min Young Whan commending him and Yoon for their efforts and enclosing $300 for their expenses. Soon thereafter Prince Min committed suicide as a last gesture of protest against Japanese seizure of his country. A bamboo shoot grew up through the floor of the room in which he died, and all during the generation of Japanese rule of Korea, a favorite subject of Korean art was a spray of bamboo leaves, or a simple sketch of bamboo shoots—a memorial which the Japanese never found an effective means to prevent.

Minister Kim was recalled from his post in Washington and appointed governor of a province in Korea. On his way home he traveled incognito, not daring to face the wrath of the Koreans on the west coast and in Hawaii. He left his son Frank at Mount Herman School, in Northfield, Massachusetts, from which he went on to graduate from the University of Pennsylvania. Frank then returned to Korea, fully expecting to find under the Japanese the same freedom and opportunities he had enjoyed in the United States. Within a few weeks he found he could not endure the atmosphere of oppression and sought a means of returning to America. In 1911, when Rhee was in Korea, Frank Kim came to him and told of an interview he had had with David Starr Jordan, the famed president of Stanford, who was stopping briefly at the Chosun Hotel in Seoul. When Frank was ushered into Dr. Jordan's room, he found a Japanese official sitting at one side. Frank indicated that he wished to talk with Dr. Jordan privately, but the Japanese politely replied he would keep confidential whatever was said. As Frank told this experience to Rhee, Rhee reminded him, "You remember, Frank, when I was asking your father to send that memorial to the State Department, as he had promised to do? Your mother was strongly against me then and I told you that someday you would find out what your father was doing for your enslavement." Frank replied, "Dr. Rhee, I was too young to know. If I had known, I never would have permitted my father to betray his country." This was the sorry outcome of Rhee's dependence upon Kim Yun Jung for help in the fight to save Korea from Japan.

History has recorded the outcome. The Portsmouth Treaty

accorded to Japan a protectorate over Korea, leaving only the form of ineffective internal autonomy. After the withdrawal of the American legation from Seoul, other nations promptly followed suit. In 1907 the emperor made yet another attempt that (for him) bordered on the heroic: he sent a secret mission to the Hague to ask the World Court to restore Korea's 4,400-year old independent sovereignty. Since the Portsmouth Treaty recognized Japan's jurisdiction over Korea's international relations, the Court refused to accept or even consider the emperor's plea. Japan responded by ending the protectorate in 1910, and instead assumed full control over Korea. The ancient nation then ceased to exist—except in the hearts of its people who would not let it die.

Chapter V

FROM POLITICS
TO PEDAGOGUE

W HILE S YNGMAN R HEE was still pursuing his elusive goal
of trying to save Korean independence through backstairs
diplomacy, he was also enrolled as a student in George
Washington University. To pick up this thread of his
development, which was to grow into a broad pattern of
educational leadership, it is necessary to return to his life
in Korea, even before the years of imprisonment, to find
there the roots of the scholar growing and intermingling
with those of the reformist-politician.

In a sense Rhee has never been out of the schoolroom.
His mother and father were determined that he should be a
scholar and were teaching him to read and memorize the
Chinese classics well before his sixth year. All his life since
then has been spent with books, paper, the calligrapher's
brush, or the small lap-weight portable typewriter which
for many years he has always kept within reach, and often
in use. In Seoul and Pusan since his election in his midseventies as President of the Republic of Korea, his days
have been filled with the everlasting study of reports, listening to explanations, discussing and evaluating policies, for
all the world like a practical-minded graduate student who
is putting academic theories to the test of work-a-day application.

Life for Syngman Rhee has been an unceasing quest to learn, and after learning to teach; and then to test and learn and teach some more. As has been indicated, his imprisonment had the effect of a long period of study to enlarge his horizons and of incubation to meditate upon and ripen his unusually rich accumulation of learning and experiences. By the age of thirty, when he entered college as a freshman, his education had already far surpassed that achieved by most professors. Yet there were also great gaps in his knowledge of the western and modern civilizations, and he was eager to learn.

Before he put his student's notebooks aside, Rhee was to spend six years in the classrooms and libraries of three of America's leading colleges, and after that he was an educator (off and on) for three full decades. This was a longer academic career than most professors expect to have and its accomplishments were notable in themselves. Yet the educational phase of his life was never disassociated from politics. For him, education and politics were always closely intertwined. In his view, democracy demanded education as a background for understanding, ethical religion as a stimulus to duty, and action as fulfilment. To omit any one of these three strands would, to him, constitute a betrayal of function; with his temperament, to dissever them would have been impossible.

An early view of the intermingling of these threads appears in a letter written to Dr. Rhee by Dr. O. R. Avison (his old mentor who had removed his topknot), under date of December 21, 1949, when Avison was living in retirement in Florida and Rhee was struggling with the problems of trying to erect a strong Korean nation on the shaky foundation of the southern half of its ancient peninsular site. "How well I remember," wrote Avison, "when you, Dr. Rhee, used to come to my home on the hill behind the Public Health Clinic [which later became Seoul's great Severance Hospital and Union Medical College] nearly every Sunday to practise your English on me and to talk over the future of Korea. Little did we think then of what would occur between then and now. You, Dr. Rhee, were even then a young rebel and I fear I did not discourage you as I should have done, but you really did not need any encouragement. You may remember how I warned you of the dangers of the course you were pursuing. I remember it very well and how, after sitting quietly for a time, you spoke up and said, 'Well, I am going to do it anyway.' And you did.

"How I smile," Dr. Avison's letter continues, "when I remember the anomalous position in which I was placed—visiting the king when he was either sick or thought he was and discussing with you the future of the kingdom when the kingship would be abolished. I fear we were two traitors. But all is now well with Korea, and 'poor' Korea is going to have its chance . . ."

Avison was only one of several missionaries with whom Rhee formed solid and lasting friendships. Another was the Presbyterian scholar-missionary, James A. Gale—to whom Rhee went to seek advice and baptism after his release from prison. The advice Gale gave freely, but he refused the baptism—on the grounds that since Rhee had been educated at Pai Jai, "the Methodists had a rightful claim to him." Gale joined enthusiastically in the advice Rhee was receiving to go to America, and wrote for him a lengthy letter of introduction to Dr. Lewis T. Hamlin, Minister of the Presbyterian Church of the Covenant, in Washington, D. C. With a complete misreading of Rhee's destiny, Gale wrote, "Mr. Lee was a political reformer only till the Lord called him to a higher service . . ." "He stands in the forefront of the honest, intelligent young men of the peninsula," Gale wrote, "and is respected by all except a few members of the conservative government, who desire no popular assembly or public gatherings . . . He has stood all sorts of fiery testings in his native land and through them all has proved himself an honest and faithful Christian."

Another American to whom Rhee turned for advice and help was Dr. Horace Allen, the medical missionary who became the United States Minister to Korea, and whose strange life of intrigue, service, and business opportunism has been well presented by Fred Harvey Harrington, in *God, Mammon and the Japanese*. Allen, at this stage in his career, was strutting with importance and at the same time struggling in the throes of rejection both by the Korean Court and by the United States Department of State. He had little time for the young man whom he regarded as an unsuccessful revolutionist and little taste for entangling himself in any deeper troubles than he already endured. Consequently, he brusquely advised Rhee to forget his grandiose plans of trying to create a democracy in Korea, to accept the fact of Japanese dominance, and to settle down to a life of acquiescence with things as they were destined to be. Instead of giving Rhee the letter of introduction he requested, he wrote to Senator Hugh A. Dinsmore, a former Minister to Korea, on May 13, 1905: "I refused to give Ye Sung Mahn a letter to a single person in America and tried my best to keep him from going." Among all of Allen's mistakes this one merits forgiveness only because of its failure to prove effective.

In one of his speeches while attending Princeton, Rhee said that on arriving in America he had felt like a country chicken in a city hall. His first impressions were of the tremendous contrasts between Korea and the United States. He was not so much overwhelmed by the material improvements, the modern inventions, the industrialism, or the towering skyscrapers (all of which he had anticipated through his reading) as he was inspired by the fact that human life and labor, which were held cheaply in Korea, were valued most highly in America. It was in New York City that this lesson was driven home to him most vividly on a day when he saw an immigrant junkman jump down from the cart he was driving and commence to beat his skinny old horse with a buggy whip. A crowd soon gathered to protest this action and Rhee recalled that one indignant lady called the immigrant a wicked man and threatened to have him sent to jail. Rhee mused for hours over this incident, which indicated to him that any man's business was every man's concern and that humaneness extended not only to people but even to beasts.

In Washington Rhee called on Dr. Lewis T. Hamlin, pastor of the Presbyterian Church of the Covenant, to whom he had been referred by missionary friends, whom he found more formidable and less friendly than he had expected. Hamlin nevertheless accepted Rhee into his church and baptized him on Easter Sunday, April 23, 1905. Reverend Hamlin also introduced Rhee to Dr. Charles Needham, the president of George Washington University, who awarded him a ministerial scholarship, which covered all his tuition expenses except for the library fee of one dollar a semester.

Syngman entered George Washington University at the start of the Spring semester, in February, 1905, and was listed by Dean W. Allen Wilbur as a "special" student, with one year of advanced standing in recognition of his Korean and Chinese studies. He took courses during the next two and a half years in logic, English, American history, French, philosophy, astronomy, economics, sociology, European history, and semitics (ancient languages). During all of the period of his enrollment at George Washington he had great difficulty earning enough to keep alive and often went to class weak from hunger. As a result, he earned only one grade of "A" during this college course (in the second semester of his class in European history). Most of his other grades were "B" and "C" but in French and mathematics he floundered and was graded "D." In those subjects he received some help from two friends and classmates, Merritt

Earl and Miss Winifred King (who later married and who remained his life-long friends).

One glimpse into the kind of seriousness which marked their relationships is preserved in a letter written by Earl on December 2, 1949. "One day," he recalled, "while tacking a G. W. U. pennant on the wall of my room, with one foot on the footboard of my bed and the other on the mantel, a rap sounded on the door. 'Come in,' I said, and Mr. Rhee entered. I excused my position and, as we talked, Mr. Rhee said: 'What are you going to be?' I answered that I was studying for the Christian ministry. Then he earnestly and pleadingly said: 'Oh, Mr. Earl, come over to my people.' I told him that I was sorry, but that I planned to enter the regular work when my preparation was completed." Several times during the next four decades Rhee paid brief visits to the Earls in their various pastorates, enjoying pleasant recollections of their old college days.

One of Rhee's means of earning money enough to live on while at George Washington was by making speeches about Korea. He liked this particularly since it not only enabled him to earn a few dollars but also to win new friends for his country. Besides, he enjoyed the exhilaration of the platform and warmed to the earnest attention and applause of the audiences. Rhee has an unusually resonant and mellow voice, with a richness of range and a delicacy of tonal variations. Quite contrary to the myth of Oriental impassivity, his face and his bodily movements are unusually expressive. He had had a great deal of experience as a public speaker in Korea, under the most adverse of circumstances, and early became a master of platform arts. As a speaker he was less notable for mastery of techniques than for possession of a body of vivid experiences and for a driving zeal which animated and indeed ennobled his talks.

Rhee's student speaking continued through his later years at Harvard and Princeton, as well as at George Washington.

He kept a notebook record of his lecture dates, and noted also the fees, which commonly ranged from two dollars to five dollars, but occasionally ran to as much as fifty dollars. Many of the talks were given under the auspices of the Y. M. C. A., though as time passed he began receiving increasing numbers of invitations from many different types of groups and in cities all through the East. Often he would show a series of 70 to 100 colored slides, and his theme usually dealt with the work of the missionaries in Korea and of the progressive improvement of conditions among the Korean people. He always took occasion, however, to plead for a better understanding of the interest the United States had in preserving (or, later, in restoring) Korea's independence and in helping to maintain it as a bulwark against the expanding ambitions of Japan. The normal reaction of his audiences was one of great interest and sympathy for the first portion of his talk, and of uneasy rejection of the latter part.

Rhee was greatly encouraged by the friendly reception he generally received and by the many letters of appreciation that were sent to him following his talks. President Patton, of Princeton, wrote in 1908: "He has special qualifications for addressing popular audiences in a way that is both interesting and profitable." Woodrow Wilson often recommended him to groups seeking a speaker. Dr. Charles Erdham, Dean of the Princeton Theological Seminary, wrote that Rhee "has spoken many times to great gatherings and is always heard with marked acceptance and interest." Dr. Horace Underwood, the founder of Chosen Christian College in Seoul, wrote from Korea to several groups in America describing Rhee's work as "a standing example of what the Gospel of Christ can do for the Korean people." Of course Rhee was proud of these commendations, and he carefully clipped and pasted into his notebook a story from the March 12, 1908, issue of the Pittsburgh *Telegraph,* in which the reporter described him as "a forceful talker."

On June 13, 1907, the Washington *Post* carried a story of an illustrated lecture which Rhee had given the preceding evening at the Y. M. C. A., on "Korea, Land of Morning Calm." According to the account, "Mr. Rhee illustrated his lecture with more than one hundred interesting views of Korea, its people and its customs. He occasioned much amusement by explaining that he could not show any slides of the 'real high class ladies' of Korea for the reason that they never leave their homes, but exhibited pictures of the middle class women, who are allowed to go about the streets 'wearing a long veil and always with one eye shut.' Several hundred people attended the lecture," the story concluded, "and the young Korean received an ovation at its close." All who have done any popular lecturing will understand how essential it is to intermingle some humorous comments with the serious message, and how mortifying it is to the speaker to have the humor remembered but his message disregarded!

During the spring of 1907, the senior class of seventeen members in the Columbian College of George Washington University was eagerly looking forward to graduation. Rhee was more than a little apprehensive of not graduating, for strain and lack of proper food combined to undermine his health and he was forced to miss a number of classes because of illness. Fortunately, Dean Allen Wilbur and the faculty were kind and understanding. When, on Wednesday, June 5, the commencement exercises were held, the Washington *Post,* with the breezy intimacy of a weekly country newspaper and with the sympathetic interest in Rhee which it at that period often demonstrated, noted in its account of the graduation exercises that ". . . none received heartier applause on presentation of his diploma than the young Korean. . . . Recent illness threatened to undermine his health, and the possibility of failing to get his degree filled him with dismay."

Each summer during his college days Rhee spent as the guest of a wealthy, elderly Methodist lady, Mrs. Boyd, who lived in Philadelphia and had a homey cottage on Emery Avenue in Ocean Grove, New Jersey. Rhee was first introduced to Mrs. Boyd by George Heber Jones, a missionary in Korea who was especially interested in him because of his prison trials. Mrs. Boyd used to call Rhee "Paul," and wrote him a weekly letter during the winter terms of school. As soon as the summer vacation approached, she would send a servant down to Ocean Grove to open the cottage and would ask Rhee to go there as soon as his examinations were over.

His first arrival in Ocean Grove was one evening in June, in 1905, just as night was falling. He inquired his way of the first person he met on the street, who happened to be a woman. She was frightened—partly because he was an Oriental and partly because in those halcyon days women were taught to be afraid of strange men on the streets after dark. She soon recovered her poise, however, and directed Rhee to the Boyd cottage. Beyond this cottage was another, occupied by a family named Boyer, with whom Rhee developed a rather formal summer-time friendship. He taught their small son, Erwin, to fly a Korean-style oblong kite, and with the three Boyer daughters he often engaged in the kind of sage discourse that in those days was considered fit conversation for young people. On one occasion, as Rhee was strolling along the beach with the eldest daughter, Ethel, and her brother, Erwin, a portly woman riding in a wheel chair and carrying a gold lorgnette stopped to ask Miss Boyer pointedly, "Young lady, is this man your husband and that boy your son?" "No, Madame," Miss Ethel replied, spiritedly, "the young man you inquire about is the grandson of the Emperor of Korea, and the little lad is my brother." Her exaggeration of Rhee's lineage was doubtless justified by the provocation of the challenge, but both of the sedate young people decided that their friendship might become a subject of summer colony gossip and henceforth Rhee spent far less time chatting on the Boyer porch.

Many years later, in 1950, Ethel Boyer (by that time Mrs. Kamp) wrote her recollections of the rather stiff formality of Rhee's personality as she noted it. She said he always wore a black alpaca suit, neatly pressed, carried his head high, and walked along the boardwalk with restrained dignity. "At twenty-nine years of age," she added, "he was a dynamic, forceful personality who had ONE GOAL in life—the independence of his people—which goal he combined with a deep concern for their individual material welfare. His innate dignity communicated itself to everyone, friend or stranger, so that he was always spoken of, as well as to, as Mr. Rhee. Never loquacious himself, he had a way of putting people at ease in his company, while his quiet reserve forbade undue impertinence from strangers."

Rhee's quiet reserve in those days was indeed partly "innate dignity" (or, more accurately, part of the cultural heritage of his Confucian upbringing); but it also stemmed from his feeling that he was alien to his surroundings in many ways: in race, in experience, and even more significantly in his views of what was important in world affairs. To the people with whom he talked the Treaty of 1882 was something of which they had never heard and could not possibly take seriously; the fancied danger of Japanese imperialism offering a threat to mammoth China and later even to the United States was so remote as to be ludicrous. The intense zealousness of this foreign youth for the restoration of the independence of his people was natural enough and even admirable, but it was so unrealistic and unimportant as to seem "quaint." There were very few people, not excepting the serious-minded Miss Boyer, with whom Syngman Rhee could really share his inmost thoughts. As a consequence, he had little choice except to live behind a veil.

The summer of his graduation from George Washington (1907), was a significant one for Korea. That was the time when the Emperor sent Lee Sang Sul on his mission to the Hague, to carry an appeal for Korean independence to the World Court. Mr. Lee traveled to Europe by way of the United States and sent Rhee a telegram to join him in New York City. There the two men somberly talked over the international situation and spent several days together perfecting the text of the appeal to the World Court. While Rhee was in New York City, he read of an address made in the 12,000-seat Ocean Grove Auditorium (a famous center of evangelistic and "cultural" speeches) by Dr. A. B. Leonard, editor of *The Christian Advocate,* whose influence in the Methodist Church was so great that he was known as "the maker of bishops." Leonard had just returned from a tour of the Orient, during which he had spent some days in Korea. In his speech he told of reforms instituted in that country by the Japanese, and he ended his talk with a prayer that Japan might rule Korea forever. Rhee wrote him a long and hot letter of protest. A reporter from the Asbury Park *Press* sought Rhee out for an interview, resulting in a story which appeared in that paper and also in the Newark *Morning Star,* for July 25, 1907, in which Rhee was quoted as declaring: "The Koreans as individuals will never submit to the Japs . . . The Powers are afraid to say a word for the cause of justice, in fear it may offend Japan, and thus may interfere with their commercial interests in the Far East. But do you not know that the whole of Asia is passing rapidly into the Japanese monopoly?

"Peace patched up with injustice to the weak ones," the interview concluded, "will never be permanent." The ideas set forth in this account summarized the view of the Far Eastern situation which Rhee was presenting at that time in his talks and which he never afterward has changed in any significant degree.

During the summer Rhee determined to enter Harvard for a Master's degree, though many of his church associates advised against it, warning him, "You may lose your faith." The Harvard of President Eliot's presidency was undergoing fundamental changes, part of which consisted of a thorough secularization of the curriculum. The Methodist Mission Board wanted Rhee to return to Korea immediately as a preacher under its auspices, and this, indeed, had been his announced objective when he was at George Washington. However, his own inclinations were strengthened by letters from his father urging him to remain for a while in America, for the reports of his political views were causing a stir among the Japanese officials.

Accordingly, Rhee enrolled that fall in Harvard. The nature of his interests, and the assiduity with which he was undertaking to build a solid foundation of understanding of the global situation, are revealed by the choice of the courses in which he enrolled. These included American history, up to the adoption of the Constitution; the history of Continental Europe from the Peace of Utrecht to contemporary times (two semesters); a special course in the expansionist and colonial policies of European nations; and a course in the Economics Department on the industry and commerce of nineteenth century Europe. In addition, he studied International Law and Arbitration, and the operations of American diplomacy. To a student with an Oriental background, most of this was wholly new and the mastery of the problems required long hours of midnight study. As a result, aside from his speeches, Rhee kept himself secluded during his year at Harvard, forming no lasting friendships while there and entering not at all into the social life of the college. He did well in his studies, proceeding to his Master's degree in the minimum time, but made no lasting impression on his associates, nor did they on him.

Rhee's Master of Arts degree was awarded in the Harvard spring commencement of 1908. He returned there for some further graduate studies in American history in the summer of 1909, but even so he never felt any close or friendly attachment to the oldest of American universities. His heart was not in the classroom during his sojourn in Cambridge. In Korea the Japanese were systematically taking over the government departments and were steadily gaining control of the farmlands and industrial properties. In Harbin, Siberia, a Korean nationalist youth, Ahn Chung Kun, shot and killed Count Hirobumi Ito, a Japanese statesman, much admired by the Western world, who was on his way to Moscow to discuss means of accommodating Japanese and Russian interests in Korea. (Reputedly his idea was to draw a line through Korea and China along the 38th parallel, with Russia to dominate the part north of that line, and Japan the area south of it.) In San Francisco two Korean youths (Chang In Myung and Chun Myung Woon) shot and killed Theodore Roosevelt's friend, D. W. Stevens, who had been appointed the fiscal adviser to the Japanese in Korea, and whose advice helped Roosevelt decide to ignore the "amity clause" of the 1882 Treaty. Stevens had come to the United States for a tour of lectures on the theme that Korea would be vastly benefited by Japanese rule. The Koreans in America sent a committee to interview Stevens in his rooms at the St. Francis Hotel in San Francisco to ask him to retract these statements. When he refused they attacked him and a brief scuffle ensued. Afterward, when Stevens left his hotel to enter his automobile, two Koreans stepped forward and shot him dead.

These two assassinations, one in Siberia and the other in San Francisco, plus all the unfavorable stories about Korea that were then being sent abroad from Japanese sources, strongly prejudiced the American public against Koreans. During the Christmas vacation recess of 1907, Rhee made a train trip out to California to talk over the situation with the Korean community there, and all along the route he found that people were afraid to talk to him. One of his history professors held him in such distaste that he refused to see him in his office and kept his thesis. When this professor left for his summer vacation, he turned Rhee's course paper over to his assistant, Arthur I. Andrews, a tall, scholarly young man who suspected there might be substance in Rhee's strictures against Japan. On June 16, 1908, Rhee wrote to Andrews:

"I am going away on the 25th inst. for the Summer and I hope to see you again before I leave here. . . I hope to come back here next year, but I cannot tell yet." In a postscript he noted that he had written papers on Cavour and on the French and English struggle in India (besides his unidentified thesis) which his professor had not returned. It was evident that the Harvard graduate work of that time, at least for Rhee, was far from being companionable.

Rhee spent the summer of 1908 in marked uneasiness and in strenuous activity. The time was even less propitious than during the preceding summer for his return to Korea. Yet with his country's sovereignty dying, he felt strongly impelled to do whatever he could in its behalf. For months he had seized every opportunity in the Boston area to speak on Korea (often to the detriment of his studies), but he was disheartened to find his audiences reflecting the pro-Japanese sentiments which were so prevalent in the press. At the end of June he returned to Ocean Grove and there was further saddened by the death of Mrs. Boyd, whose cottage had been his summer home since 1906.

He kept closely in touch with P. K. Yoon, who had been his comrade in the unsuccessful mission in 1905 to try to secure Theodore Roosevelt's help in maintaining Korea's independence. Together they had planned, during the spring months, for an international conference of Koreans to be held in Denver, Colorado, on July 11-15. Yoon went over to England to organize patriotic activities among the few Koreans who lived there. Upon his return, he and Rhee sent out a general call to Koreans to attend the conference, which they arranged to be held in the Grace Methodist Church in Denver. The call resulted in a widespread attendance, with delegates coming from Russia, China, England and Hawaii, as well as from various parts of the United States.

When their first meeting was called to order, on the evening of July 11, there were thirty-six delegates present, from as far away as Shanghai, London, and Vladivostok. Rhee served as chairman and made the opening address. His speech and all their business were in the Korean language. They prepared summary statements in English for the press, and the July 12 issue of the Denver *Republican* reported: "The purpose is the making of a nation, the throwing off of the yoke of subserviency ... They are going about it calmly, with quiet passion, and with no illusions." For the main session, President David Starr Jordan, of Stanford University, addressed them in an open meeting, attended by many of the people of Denver.

It could hardly be claimed that the assembly was a huge success. Their numbers were few and their financial resources were far too limited to cope with the tremendous propaganda machine of the Japanese Government, which spared no effort to deluge the United States and other Western nations with stories alleging Korean incompetence and picturing the presumed beneficence of Japan's colonial rule. Japan borrowed a leaf from Rudyard Kipling's theme of "The White Man's Burden" to govern the helpless and backward peoples of Asia. Only Japan sought to make this theme even more convincing by claiming that a strong Oriental nation was undertaking to play the "big brother" role to weaker and backward Korea. The desire of the Koreans at Denver to counter this heinous propaganda was intense and their devotion and energy were boundless, but the task was too great for their limited resources. The international organization they envisaged never developed and after their separation to return to their several homes they never found any effective way of again uniting their efforts.

The height of their ambition was reported in the July 14 issue of the Denver *Republican*, which cited resolutions adopted the preceding day to unite all the diverse Korean groups into one central body, and to establish a publishing house for the purpose of bringing out Korean language translations of Western books, to be circulated inside Korea, thus keeping the people in their homeland informed of events and developments around the world. The delegates saw clearly enough that the principal problem would be to counteract the effects of the bamboo curtain which Japan was erecting around Korea, with the aim of Japanizing the thoughts and the loyalties of the people kept inside. But vision alone, devoid of resources, was not enough.

In Syngman Rhee's closing address to the assembly, he ended with a hopeful prophecy which proved to be justified by subsequent events. "Politicians often say nowadays," he told the delegates, "that Japan is too strong a foe for Korea to fight successfully for its independence, and that Korea's hope is, therefore, gone forever. But this is only a cursory observation. Upon a careful study of our history, our geographical expression and racial distinction, Korea is too strong for Japan. We have maintained our peculiarities and integrity for over 4,000 years, and these no nation can sweep from the face of the earth."

This prophecy was Rhee's living faith. Despite all the solid evidence that Japan was in Korea to stay; despite the kindly warnings of his American friends that he must bow to the inevitable and reshape his convictions to accord with the realities; despite the substantial support given to Japan's position by American and British public opinion and by the diplomatic adjustments made by the Western Powers (which Rhee's studies in diplomatic history taught him were certain to have significant effects); despite the submission to the new order by many of his old associates of the Independence Club and the acquiescence in Japanese rule by Rhee's old friends, the missionaries; despite all the promptings of his senses and the urgings of reason, he could not and would not abandon his own solid and unshakable conviction that the independence of Korea was right and that, therefore, its re-establishment was inevitable.

Rhee went from Denver to New York, and secured a room in the Union Theological Seminary, where he lived for a brief time while attending classes in Columbia University. He planned to take a doctorate at Columbia, supplemented by courses at Union, but was too restless to settle down seriously to any specific plan.

Late in the summer, while stopping in the offices of the Presbyterian Foreign Missions Board, Rhee met Reverend Ernest F. Hall, a former missionary to Korea, who was then a member of the Board. Hall asked what he was doing in New York, and Rhee explained his plan, indicating at the same time his lack of enthusiasm for it. Mr. Hall said with brisk assurance, "You are not going to the Union Seminary. You are going to Princeton!" Rhee replied that this would suit him very well if there were any way of managing it. The next morning he received a special delivery letter from Mr. Hall, mailed from Princeton, enclosing a railway ticket, a railway timetable, and a note saying he would meet Rhee at the Princeton station. When Rhee arrived, Hall took him first to meet Dr. Charles Erdman, Dean of the Princeton Theological Seminary, then to meet Dr. Andrew F. West, Dean of the Princeton Graduate School. Arrangements were soon completed for Rhee to live in the Theological Seminary, taking occasional courses there, while at the same time enrolling for his doctorate program in the University's Political Science Department. This change of plans Rhee never regretted. Princeton is where he enjoyed the best of his college days and perhaps the least troubled months of his life.

In addition to the educational opportunities and the pleasant life in beautiful surroundings, Rhee was fortunate at Princeton in making friends who continued to mean much to him through the later years. Dr. Erdman was one such friend, whose many kindnesses Rhee never forgot. Dean West was another devoted friend who did much to make his graduate study possible, pleasant and successful. Above all, President Woodrow Wilson and his family became Rhee's intimate friends, and their interest in Korea and in Korean missionary work was so real that he found vast encouragement from them for the lifework he was planning for himself. Although President Wilson and Dean West were bitterly opposed to each other over the proper disposition of funds donated by Procter toward the construction of a new Graduate Building (a quarrel that finally drove Wilson out of Princeton and into the White House), Rhee enjoyed the cordial friendship of both men. Both of them were touched by his prison sufferings and interested in his plans. Both aided in finding speaking engagements for him and were impressed by his ardent advocacy of Korean independence.

On December 15, 1908, Woodrow Wilson wrote for Rhee a "to whom it may concern" recommendation, which read as follows:

Mr. Syngman RHEE is a graduate student in Princeton University and has commended himself to us by every evidence of ability and high character. He is singularly conversant not only with existing conditions in his own country, Korea, but also with the general standing of affairs in the East, and has been unusually successful in presenting those conditions to general audiences.

He is a man of strong patriotic feeling and of great enthusiasm for his people and should prove very useful to them. It gives me pleasure to recommend him strongly to those who wish to learn directly of the interests which should be studied and conserved in the great East.

Wilson, his wife, and his three daughters all took a great interest in the earnest and mature student from Korea, whose zealous intentness was so readily (if briefly) broken by flashes of warm humor. The Wilsons liked to gather around their piano for family songfests and Rhee was one of the Princeton students who was often favored with an invitation for these intimate occasions. Unlike the others, however, he never joined in the singing and the girls used to tease both him and their father as the restrained dignity of the student guest contrasted with the unleashed gaiety of the home-warmed college president. On campus Wilson often introduced Rhee to visitors, frequently with a half-joking, half-serious reference to him as "The future redeemer of Korean independence."

During his two years at Princeton Rhee lived in the Calvin Club, a living center for Seminary students. Even though he attended only occasional lectures in the Seminary, his religious convictions and activities kept him in close association with the Seminarians. Through the kindness of Reverend Hall, arrangements were made for Rhee to live in the Calvin Club without cost. Because of this residence, numerous references have been published of Rhee's graduation from the "Seminary of Princeton University." This, however, is only one of a great number of uninformed and false stories which have been circulated about him. As a matter of fact, Rhee's differences from his living companions were far greater than the similarities. He was ten or fifteen years older than his fellow club members and had experienced more responsibilities, hardships, and challenging adventures than all the rest of them combined were likely ever to encounter. When they gathered in the club lounge, as they did every Wednesday evening, for impromptu entertainments generally of a very hilarious character, he stood out among them as a solemn island in a sea of youthful exuberance. Each of the Calvinists was enjoined to offer something each Wednesday for the entertainment of the rest. While the others were inclined to give humorous readings, dance jigs, or sing rollicking songs, Rhee's own contributions usually were sedate and sometimes solemn readings. One of the Calvin Club members later wrote of him that he was "not a good *stunter*" and that his most popular contributions to their entertainment was his singing of Korean folk songs. Once in a while he was persuaded to tell some humorous or quaint anecdotes about old customs in Korea, but he always found this exploitation of the oddities of his countrymen distasteful and after a time or two his fellows failed to find much interest in them. Rhee was liked in a distant sort of way by his fellow club members, and he enjoyed the hominess of the Club life. From among the group of students he carried away few lasting friendships.

As in his previous work at George Washington and Harvard, Rhee studied hard while in Princeton and let nothing interfere with his studies except his work for Korean independence. Once again, as at Harvard, he succeeded in earning his graduate degree in the minimum allowable time. His majors were in International Law, with minors in American history and in Western philosophy. During the first semester, in the fall of 1908, he took seminars in International Law and Diplomacy, in American history up to the fall of the Federalist Party, and in the history of Philosophy. In the spring of 1909 he enrolled in seminars in the history of Philosophy, American history following the fall of the Federalist Party, and in further problems in International Law and Diplomacy. During the academic year of 1909-1910, he took his qualifying examinations and seminars in

American history from 1789 to 1850 and in International Law. The major portion of his time was spent in the Princeton Library, preparing his dissertation on American neutrality in Asia, centering around John Hay's "Open Door" policy toward China, of which Rhee heartily approved.

One of Dr. Rhee's comments on his class work at Princeton was a remark which, in later years, became a jest he used on several occasions, to the effect that he should have had his tuition refunded for the work he did under Professor Elliott, for he lived to learn there is no international law. There would have been more humor in the jest if he had not believed there was too much truth in it.

In June, 1910, he completed his dissertation on the topic, *Neutrality as Influenced by the United States.* Through the kindness of Dean West this study was published by the Princeton University Press, and in the next several years Rhee received a few small royalty checks. Two of them, for sums of $1.80 and $2.25, he put away to keep as souvenirs. During the course of World War I, while the question of neutrality on the high seas was of great importance, Rhee was pleased to be referred to on occasion as an "eminent authority" on neutrality. The book has all but disappeared and made no lasting contribution to scholarship; but it constitutes, nevertheless, an important part of his unusually fine education for statesmanship.

At the annual commencement of Princeton University, on June 14, 1910, the last of the Princeton graduation exercises attended by President Wilson, Rhee received the degree of Doctor of Philosophy from Wilson's hands. As Dean West slipped the traditional hood of the doctorate over Rhee's shoulders, and Wilson handed him his diploma with a hearty handclasp of congratulation, Syngman's predominant feeling was one of sadness. His preparatory days were ended. The time had come for him to return to his own country, but it was his nation no longer, nor was it even any longer

Korea. It had become Chosen, a tributary of Japan. The formal annexation occurred the same year in which Rhee earned his Ph.D.

One of Rhee's most vivid memories of Princeton was the extreme difficulty of the written and oral examinations for his doctorate—a memory not unlike that of others who have experienced similar ordeals. Yet he was rather proud that, alien as he was, and with an early education deeply embedded in Oriental history, philosophy, and literature, he came creditably through the severest kind of examination in American and European history, international law, and Western philosophy. He was always to remain grateful for the dual experiences and education which gave him the rare opportunity to bestride the East and the West, and in effect to combine in his own thinking a fusion of the two. This cultural integration was to become one of the great sources of his strength and leadership in the years that lay ahead. His countrymen also were impressed by the fact that he was the first Korean ever to secure a Ph.D. from an American university.

Rhee's psychological condition on completing his work at Princeton was not unlike his feelings upon being released from prison in 1904. Once more he was "free" to take up the destiny life was pressing upon him. And once again he felt terribly alone and desolate as he looked hopelessly around for any shreds of opportunity to accomplish the staggering task to which he felt himself called.

Chapter VI

PEDAGOGICAL POLITICS

Rhee's uncertainty upon completing his doctorate at Princeton was not, of course, accompanied by any doubt as to where his duty lay. The question was not whether he should return immediately to Korea, but what he should do and how he should conduct himself after his return. His problem became easier when Mr. G. G. Gregg, of the Seoul Y. M. C. A., called to see him and offered him a position (on behalf of Dr. John R. Mott, international director of the "Y") as an organizer, teacher and evangelist among the youth in Korea. Rhee instantly accepted this offer since it provided him the means of returning to Korea. Moreover, it assured him the means of working among the young and intellectually promising Koreans, and offered a type of work in which he would be relatively remote from contact and conflict with the Japanese, who were by then busily reorganizing his homeland. After farewells to President Wilson and his family, and to Dean West, Dr. Erdman and other friends, he started the long trip to his home in Korea which he had not seen for six years.

Not knowing when, if ever, he might leave Korea again, eager to complete and deepen his understanding of European countries, and grateful for the latitude of the Y. M. C. A. in permitting him to select his own route homeward, he sailed for Europe on the S. S. *Baltic*, leaving New York on September 3, 1910. From Liverpool he went on for brief stops in London, Paris, Berlin and Moscow. After four weeks of this sightseeing he took the long trip on the Trans-Siberian Railway across the bleak and endless plains of Siberia, with an interesting stop at Lake Baikal, and in late October passed through Manchuria. When crossing the Yalu River he endured for the first time the ignominy of presenting his credentials for the sharp and suspicious scrutiny of Japanese guards officiating in his own country.

On the way down the Korean peninsula, with a brief stopover in Pyengyang, Rhee brooded endlessly over the constant sight of Japanese officials and noted the covert and helpless resentment of the Korean people as they were ordered around. His father, at the Seoul railway station to greet him, was tearful and overwhelmed with joy at the return of his only son, whom he had almost given up the hope of seeing again. Syngman settled down with him in his small hillside home in Seoul and for many evenings they exchanged stories of experiences during the past six years, achieving a sense of comradeship and union greater than they had ever known.

Rhee remained in Korea for seventeen eventful and busy months, trying at first to find a helpful role for himself in the changed conditions that existed, and finally, when that proved impossible, meditating new plans for more successful activities. He called upon Yi Sang-Chai, a saintly old Christian scholar who was known as the Tolstoy of Korea, who had been one of Rhee's converts to Christianity during their imprisonment together, and between the old and the young man there soon developed an even closer and more affectionate friendship. Rhee also became well acquainted with Philip Gillett, the energetic and idealistic first American secretary of the Y. M. C. A. in Korea. From the first Rhee threw himself into the work of the Y. M. C. A. with complete concentration, hoping that in this Christian service he could help his countrymen without antagonizing the Japanese. He never for a moment contemplated coming to terms with the conquerors, but he thought it might be possible to live in their midst without either approving or actively opposing their rule. He toured the entire country, speaking at many schools and conducting meetings in the churches. The Japanese officials, however, were far too astute and thorough to leave Rhee alone. They sent him numerous invitations to governmental and social functions, all of which he ignored. His relations with them soon ceased to be merely formal and became dangerously antagonistic.

The Christian churches in Korea could not possibly remain utterly aloof from the political facts on the peninsula. The Japanese kept a careful eye on the religious services and publications, to note any tendencies of encouragement for Korean nationalism. On one occasion, a tract urging all Koreans to expel the devil that was within them was suppressed. A Japanese official called on the editor in high dudgeon, charging, "When you say devil, you are referring to the Japanese, and you are encouraging the Koreans to rise in rebellion against them!" Instructions were then issued to all religious publications forbidding them to use the term "devil" again. On another occasion, a missionary weekly called *The Christian Messenger* ran an editorial on spring. In accordance with the regulations, an advance proof of the issue was sent to the Japanese censor, and he suppressed the entire issue on the grounds that the praise of "the new life" that breaks forth in the spring was really an incitement to the Korean Christians to arise and set up a new government! Under these conditions, Rhee, who had freely spoken in the United States against Japanese seizure of his nation, was under close watch. In all his writings and speeches he had to use care to say nothing that even remotely could suggest any shade of dissatisfaction with the foreign regime.

In order to escape at least partially from the humiliation and ordeal of constantly guarding his tongue and even his mind from saying and thinking the things he most ardently felt needed to be thought and said, he gave up the Y. M. C. A. lecture work and, in March of 1912, accepted the principal-ship of the Chong-No Academy, the leading secondary school in Seoul. He found, however, that this was no av-enue to seclusion. Within a few days he was off on another speaking tour, this time on behalf of the national student movement. But his new career as an educational admin-istrator died aborning. A life-and-death challenge was hurled at the Christian movement in Korea, and Rhee barely escaped becoming embroiled.

For the last several months of 1911 rumors spread through Korea that all Korean Christian Churches were to have their charters repealed and that they would be placed under the administrative direction of churches in Japan. The Japanese correctly assumed that the individualism, the dignity, and the dedication which are inherent in the Christian teachings could not but encourage resistance to tyrannical rule. Since they did not dare risk foreign disapproval by simply sup-pressing the Christian religion in Korea, they invented what they termed the "Christian Conspiracy Case," and arrested 135 of the outstanding Korean Christian leaders. Rhee was saved from arrest only by the quick intervention of Philip Gillett and other Y. M. C. A. officials, including Dr. John R. Mott, who was making a timely visit to Korea. These men quietly advised the Japanese that Rhee was so well known in America that his arrest would stir up considerable trouble for them. Against the 135 who were arrested a charge was placed of conspiring to murder the Japanese Governor-Gen-eral. Three of these men died under torture in prison, nine were exiled, and 106 were given prison sentences ranging from five to ten years.

Bishop Harris, who represented the Methodist Church in North Asia, hastened from Japan to Korea. Dr. Arthur J. Brown, secretary of the Presbyterian Board of Foreign Missions, came to Korea and collected evidence which he at-

tested showed a Japanese plot to get rid of the most intelligent and progressive Korean leaders. Dr. Charles W. Eliot,
Harvard's great President, who chanced to be in Japan at
the time, made a personal investigation and then issued a
statement which concluded: "The standing of Japan among
Western nations would be improved by judicious modifica-
tions of her preliminary proceedings against alleged criminals." Dr. W. W. Pinson, secretary of the Board of Missions
of the Methodist Episcopal Church South, concluded his
investigation of the case with a report which read in part:
". . . it is clear that the gendarmes have thrust their sickles
in among the tallest wheat. These men do not belong to
the criminal or irresponsible class of society . . . These are
not the type of men to be guilty of such a plot as that with
which they are charged." Several of Rhee's old prison associates were among those arrested, and he had many uneasy
days and nights waiting for the fatal knock at his own door.
Finally, through the active intervention of Bishop Harris,
he was removed from the scene of danger.

An international conference of Methodist delegates was
to be held that spring in Minneapolis, and Rhee was elected
by the Korean Methodists as their lay delegate to attend the
conference, along with two missionaries and a Korean pastor. Bishop Harris was able to get permission from the Japanese authorities for Rhee to go, and finally, on March 26,
he had a last tearful parting from his father, who stood in
his doorway, waving, with his face turned away.* The delegates held a conference in Kamakura, Japan, and spoke at
a big meeting in the Tokyo Y. M. C. A. As Rhee boarded
the S.S. *Tamba Karu* in Yokohama harbor, on April 10, the
Japanese minister of a Methodist Church in Seoul came
down to bid farewell to him and Bishop Harris. He advised
Rhee most strongly to return within six months and, meanwhile, to say nothing in America that would be critical of

* Dr. Rhee's father died on December 5, 1913.

the Japanese, as the results would be harmful to the Koreans. It was not until the ship began moving out from the harbor that Rhee breathed easily, for he doubted to the last minute that the Japanese would really let him go.

During the voyage, Bishop Harris talked to Rhee again and again, urging him to accept the fact of Japanese rule over Korea, and to accustom his mind to it. Rhee always argued with him briefly, then kept still, realizing they would never agree. While at sea they heard news of the tragic sinking of the *Titanic*, several days after its occurrence. They landed at Victoria, British Columbia, and proceeded to Minneapolis, after a brief stop in Seattle.

The conference had its own atmosphere of politics, and even of intrigue. There was secret balloting for the election of bishops, following a great deal of informal, off-the-floor discussion. Rhee shared a room with Dr. W. A. Noble (his first English teacher at Pai Jai), who had been criticized for being pro-Japanese. This view, however, was unfounded and untrue. Noble showed Rhee a typed report of a secret plan to unite the Korean Methodist Church with the North Chinese Conference, as a way of preventing its being dominated by Japan. He explained that several missionaries sent into China ostensibly to introduce the simplified 25-letter Korean alphabet among the Chinese, as an aid to combating illiteracy, were secretly charged with this additional mission. This revelation was an eye-opener to Rhee and showed him how dangerously a man could be misjudged. Many years later, during the first years of Korea's liberation from Japan, Rhee was greatly helped on occasion by Dr. Noble's educator-son, Harold, who did what he could to arouse in America a feeling of concern for the plight of the Korean nation.

In another conversation, Dr. Noble warned Rhee against Bishop Harris, because he trusted the Japanese so much he could never really understand them. They had several talks about the political-religious situation in Korea. With Rhee's usual hot-headed zeal, he made a speech on the floor of the conference, pleading for the independence of the Korean Church, and was severely criticized for endangering the missionary work that must be carried on under the Japanese flag. The month-long conference ended with resolutions reaffirming the policy of working closely with the Japanese, thereby protecting the mission enterprises in Japan and in Korea. It was apparent to Rhee that he could neither return to Korea nor continue effectively to work officially on behalf of the Missionary Board. Dr. Horace Underwood, the American president of Chosen Christian College in Seoul, wrote offering Rhee a position on the faculty. Rhee replied that he would return if Underwood could guarantee his security from the Japanese, but this, of course, was impossible. For the next six months Rhee traveled to Chicago, Princeton, and Baltimore (where he attended the Democratic convention), and sat with Woodrow Wilson in his summer cottage at Sea Girt, N. J. during his nomination. After this he went on to Ocean Grove, New Jersey, and to Washington, D. C., visiting friends and trying to formulate new plans.

While Rhee was in Washington, in mid-November, the Washington *Post* sent a reporter to interview him at the Willard Hotel, where he was staying. The story, appearing in the November 18 issue, represented Rhee's best efforts to be conciliatory and to avoid any charge of trouble-making. Its tone is sufficiently well indicated by the following typical excerpt: "Within the space of three years Korea has been transformed from a slow-going country where tradition reigned into a live, bustling center of industrialism . . . Seoul can hardly be told nowadays from Cincinnati except for the complexion of its inhabitants." Obviously, he was trying as hard as he could to avoid trouble with the Japanese authorities—probably uncertain in his own mind of just what course he could or should pursue.

During the fall of 1912 he thought wistfully of securing a

professorship in an American college, but he knew that he could not abandon his work for Korea. Late that fall, Mr. Youngman Park, one of Rhee's old prison-mates, went to Hawaii to make arrangement with leaders there to raise funds with which to establish a Korean school, of which Rhee should be the principal. On the invitation of these leaders, Rhee went to Hawaii in January, 1913, and found they had raised the sum of $30,000. He also found an extremely troubled situation, in which he could not accept responsibility for the funds or associate himself with the plans that many were trying to advance.

Ill feeling between the Koreans and the Japanese in Hawaii was intense, and the Methodist Church was doing its best to conciliate these feelings. Dr. John Wadman, his old friend, still headed the Korean Methodist Compound School and Mission. The Korean community also supported a small, independent church, called *Cha Yu Kio,* and they wanted Rhee to accept its pastorate. At this time the Korean students in Honolulu's Mills School went on strike, in protest against what they considered preferential treatment for the Japanese and Chinese students. The atmosphere throughout the islands was one of sharp and bitter controversy. Rhee could not take sides without either embittering his old Methodist friends or betraying the independence-minded Korean leadership. Under the circumstances, he urged his supporters to go ahead with their plans, but declared he would have to return to the States.

However, the Methodists soon invited Rhee to take over the Korean Compound School in Honolulu, which enrolled Korean boys from the first through the sixth grades. Classes were conducted partly in English and partly in Korean. The mornings were devoted to "Western style" education—including classes in Korean history and geography—and the afternoons to teaching the Chinese classics. Dr. Rhee approved of this general curricular plan, believing it would help the students to develop into citizens of both the East and the West. After assuming this position, he made a tour of the Hawaiian Islands, inquiring into the conditions of the Korean plantation workers. He discovered that a number of Korean girls were living in labor camps and that their parents were planning to force their marriage against their will. He took them back to Honolulu, where he paid for their board in the Susanna Wesley Home. Miss Anderson, the superintendent said, "We can keep the girls here for a time, but they must go to the public schools to be amalgamated with the great racial mixture in Hawaii."

There, for the first time, Rhee encountered the great issue which dominated his work in Hawaii. He was against the principle of amalgamation. He felt strongly that the Koreans should continue to speak their own language, should be educated in the history and customs of their own country, and should dedicate themselves to the resurrection of their fallen nation. The Methodist Church officials were strongly opposed to the idea. Dr. Wadman, his old friend, retired from the district superintendency of the Methodist Mission in Hawaii, and was succeeded by Dr. William Fry, who was determined to end all racial segregation. Dr. Rhee secured a building as a dormitory for girls and instituted co-education—changing the name of the school to the Korean Institute. At first they had 27 girls enrolled, but the number soon increased to forty—with about three times that many boys. During all this time there were sharp differences of opinion within the Korean community as to whether they should be independent or amalgamated with other racial groups under the general program advocated by the Methodist Church. Just before World War I broke out, the Korean community in Honolulu founded its own church. After several moves to new locations, it was finally settled at 1832 Liliha Street, where, in 1939, the present building, a replica of the South Gate in Seoul, was erected.

In the fall of 1916, Rhee split completely with the Methodist Mission and opened a school of his own, which he dedicated frankly to the promulgation of Korean culture and the education of the second-generation immigrants as Korean patriots. The Korean community supported the school enthusiastically and the enrollment soon rose to about one hundred and forty. Then, in 1920, the Hawaiian Department of Public Instruction instituted a new requirement of a special examination for high school entrance, to be taken by graduates of all private grade schools. All private schools suffered from this special requirement and Rhee's Christian Institute was no exception. Parents who wanted to be certain their children could and would go to high school felt it safer to start them in public schools. At about this time also the Territorial Government opened a public high school in every county and instituted a poll tax to finance these new schools.

This series of blows might well have ended Rhee's Institute, as it did many other private schools in Hawaii, except for a tremendous series of events which dramatically changed his position in the Korean community. The revolution in Korea which led to the establishment of a government in exile with Syngman Rhee as its president will be reserved for discussion in the next chapter, in order to preserve here as a unity the story of his experiences in Hawaii. Inevitably, however, the new status conferred upon him affected very strongly the whole fabric of his relationships with the Hawaiian Korean community. Insofar as his educational work was concerned, his renewed political activities and his position of leadership saved his school from what otherwise would have been certain extinction.

The differences that developed during these years with the Methodist Church officials were painful to Rhee. Although he was baptized into the Presbyterian Church of the Covenant in Washington in 1905, he became a member of the Epworth Methodist Episcopal Church, in Cambridge during his attendance at Harvard, and he belonged to the Chong-No Methodist Church in Seoul during his sojourn back in his own country. In Hawaii it seemed to him more important to find a means of bringing all the Korean people together than it did to support any single denomination; accordingly he felt it a duty to organize a non-denominational Protestant Church, within which the essential unity of all the Korean people could best be stressed and developed. After leaving Hawaii in 1939 to take up residence in Washington, his wife and he for a time attended various churches of the capital city, then selected as their church home the Foundry Methodist Church, under the ministry of the Reverend Frederick Brown Harris, and they have remained on its membership roll ever since.

Despite the fond attachment Rhee has always felt to the Methodist Church, and despite the fact that his differences with its program and officials in Hawaii were completely impersonal and on a matter of principle, there developed an unfortunate bitterness which long persisted between them. Even thirty years later, when Rhee was inaugurated as president of the Republic of Korea, this feeling remained. As one of the Mission Board officials remarked with considerable acrimony, "If the Koreans had elected Kimm Kiusic as their president, we would support them, but since they chose Rhee, let them go their own way as best they can." As Rhee saw political problems develop within the church organization to such a degree that Christian charity and brotherhood could be forgotten, he became sorrowfully suspicious of professional churchmen and gradually drifted into habits of solitary worship, giving up regular church attendance.

Rhee's reluctant disputes with the Methodist Board were not his only differences of opinion in Hawaii. Indeed, his twenty-five years there were marked by disputation. Perhaps it is inevitable that any exiled independence movement must be characterized by a certain degree of disorder and bitter disagreement. The nature and degree of political differences that existed among the Koreans in America are doubtless of less interest to Americans than they are to the participants in the squabbles. The general outlines of the policy disagreements that developed should, however, be understood as a part of the background of later differences that emerged in Korea after the Liberation.

When Rhee arrived in Hawaii, the one significant political organization that existed was the Korean National Association (or KNA, as it was familiarly called). Ahn Chang Ho, a native of Pyengyang, was one of its principal leaders; Youngman Park was another. As has been indicated, Rhee was specifically invited by the Koreans in Hawaii to join them and to accept a position of leadership in their affairs. His work in the Independence Club, his prison sentence, his authorship of *The Spirit of Independence*, and the fact that he had earned the first Ph. D. degree ever to be awarded to any Korean all served to bring him into inevitable prominence in the guidance of Korean activities. Perhaps even more important than any of these factors, his stubborn insistence that Korean independence was not dead and must be ever pursued as the fundamental goal of all Koreans free to exercise their inherent political rights provided both a motive on his part for exercising leadership and a rallying point for the loyalties of a great majority of the Korean expatriates. However, Rhee had rivals of great ability.

Ahn Chang Ho, a man of brilliant intellect and strong will, though without much education, also had a large following. Rhee would gladly have worked with him, but it proved to be impossible to do so. Within the KNA, Ahn Chang Ho was the acknowledged leader of a subsidiary group, called the Heungsadan, a society led by the natives of Pyengyang, which still exists in Korea and which has a large following.

These men cling together with fierce loyalty and pursue their own special interests as a group. The historical background of their determination lies in the fact that when the Yi Dynasty ascended to the throne of Korea in 1392, the founder of this line achieved power only over the strong opposition of the people of Pyengyang. As a punishment for them, he decreed that never again in all Korean history should any high governmental positions be held by Pyengyang men. And actually, for over 500 years, until after the absorption of Korea into the Japanese Empire in 1910, this unjust injunction was infallibly observed. The result was the natural development of a spirit of resentment and a league of group-interest among the natives of Pyengyang.

Rhee sincerely believes that he has done everything he could to rectify the injustices of the past and to build anew a spirit of cordial co-operation between the Heungsadan and the people of all the rest of Korea. Both in Hawaii and back in Korea (after the Liberation) he consistently sought to elevate natives of Pyengyang to positions of trust and confidence and to show in every way his own determination to work with them. In those first years in Hawaii he went far out of his way to court their friendship and co-operation. When the Republic of Korea was inaugurated, his first nominee for the prime ministership was the Reverend Lee, a Pyengyang man. Pyengyang has had far more than its proportionate representation in Rhee's successive cabinets. However, it was true in Hawaii and it has later proved to be true in Korea that "rule or ruin" has been the first principle to which many of the Heungsadan members felt it expedient to adhere.

Ahn Chang Ho became Rhee's bitter opponent in Hawaii and among the Korean residents in California. Ahn could speak little English and could read nothing in the language. As a result, he had almost no contact with the great Anglo-American tradition of democracy or little understanding of its principles. He did not emphasize any detailed political program but, with an oratorical power that few could match in the Korean language, he appealed for personal loyalty to himself and to the Heungsadan. To complete his story, he went to China after the attack by Japan upon Manchuria and in 1932 was arrested by the Japanese, charged with complicity in a Shanghai bombing attack by Korean nationalists against the Japanese military leaders. He suffered three years of imprisonment, and was again arrested by the Japanese in Seoul soon after the attack on the Marco Polo Bridge, in July, 1937, which started the "China Incident." Released from prison in mid-December and suffering from the tortures he endured in jail, he died in the Seoul Medical College Hospital on March 10, 1938, at the age of sixty. He has been very highly and properly revered by the Korean people as a loyal and worthy patriot who gave his life for his nation. Nevertheless, he proved to be unsuited for any program of co-operative endeavor designed to develop a genuinely nationwide and democratic independence movement. With him and his American-Korean followers, Rhee never was able to develop a co-ordinate program, and with them he could never live in peace.

Youngman Park, who organized the movement that took Rhee to Hawaii in 1913, also became one of his principal political opponents. Their gradual drifting apart was on questions of divergent principles, and was marked by a great many discussions in which they both sought without success to reconcile the differences that pushed them farther and farther apart.

Fully as patriotic and nationalistic as Ahn Chang Ho and Rhee, Youngman Park believed staunchly that Korean independence could never be achieved except through a forcible revolution against Japan. Rhee's own conviction was that no such revolution could possibly succeed, and that the Koreans must strive above all to merit and to win the diplo-

matic support of the Western powers and the sympathy of
the American people. These differences of policy proved
irreconcilable. Mr. Park established a military academy for
Korean youths in Hawaii, and spent his energies and abilities
in the recruitment, training, and support of a small but high-
spirited "army." He wanted Rhee to support this program
publicly and to incorporate it in his Hawaiian school. Rhee,
for his part, felt convinced that such a warlike posture would
lose the Koreans the friends they would need if they were
ever to reverse the policies by which England and the United
States sought to enforce peace in the Pacific on a foundation
of Japanese domination of that area.

The climatic year in Rhee's relations with Youngman Park
was 1915. Park was then editing a journal called *The Korean
Herald*, through which he attacked Rhee regularly, in the
attempt to win Rhee's following over to his program. Efforts
to conciliate Park's opposition led to a story in the June 16,
1915, issue of the Honolulu *Star-Bulletin* which asserted that
the "old faction" wished to promote the welfare of Koreans
in Hawaii, whereas Rhee wished to use the funds collected
by the KNA "for military training of Korean youth, for leaflets to smuggle into Korea, and for stirring up a revolution
in Korea." This badly bungled story then went on to declare
that Rhee had by then changed his mind, and added, "Dr.
Rhee today . . . declares he is working only for the good of
the Korean people in Hawaii with no thought of Koreans
in Korea." This was not the first time Rhee's views had been
badly misinterpreted in the press, and has certainly not been
the last. Considerable excitement was caused within the
Korean community in Hawaii and California by this apparent change in Rhee's policies, and he received letters of
anxious inquiry from several American friends. He was
particularly concerned not to be misunderstood by President
Wilson, from whom he hoped that help for Korea might
somehow, some day, be forthcoming. Consequently, Rhee

wrote a letter which appeared in the June 17 issue of the
Honolulu *Advertiser,* pointing out that, "I have never
dreamed of starting a 'revolution' either in Korea or in
Hawaii." The letter went on to explain that, "It is a well-
known fact that I have been criticized by some of the national association leaders for not taking a direct interest in
the military school run by Y. M. Park."

The *Star-Bulletin* thereupon sent another reporter to interview Rhee, and in its June 21 issue carried a long dispatch
in which Rhee explained: (1) that he was in fact very much
concerned over the plight of the Koreans in Korea; and (2)
that his policy was to help them to attain the independence
of their nation and to accomplish this end without any resort
to armed revolution.

On July 7, 1915, Rhee wrote to Youngman Park in a
determined effort to end the misunderstanding between
them. "At the very bottom of my heart," Rhee wrote, "you
will find nothing but a friendly and brotherly feeling toward
you. And I want to assure you that there is no better friend
for you than your old prison mate. If you still want to throw
yourself into the hands of these men you will surely regret
[it] in the long run. I have to fight them and find out they
are working to ruin the Association for their own gain. . . .
Choose between the two and follow whichever you deem
as wisest." The letter concluded, "Your brother, as always.
Syngman." To this friendly overture, he received no reply.

In September, one Chin Kook, a violent Korean youth who
followed Ahn Chang Ho, entered the San Francisco Hotel
where Youngman Park was staying and shot him, intending
murder, but leaving him merely wounded. He then took ship
for Hawaii, where he intended to assassinate Rhee. During
the course of the trip, however, he committed suicide by
leaping overboard—probably motivated by fear of arrest
upon the docking of the ship at Honolulu. His trunk, including letters describing his plan, was forwarded to the Korean
National Association.

As a result of the irreconcilable differences which developed within the Korean National Association, Rhee founded the Dong-ji Hoi Society, which has flourished ever since, with a minimum of internal dissension, and with a loyalty to Rhee personally and to his program, which has never wavered. The principal chapter of this society is in Honolulu, with a second large chapter in Los Angeles, and with smaller ones in New York, Chicago, and San Francisco.

Under the auspices of Dong-ji Hoi, Dr. Rhee founded in 1920 a magazine called *The Pacific Weekly* (or *Tae-pyung Yang Jharp-Ji*), partly in Korean and partly in English, which still continues and which serves as one of the principal means of maintaining the communal unity of the Koreans in Hawaii and in the states. Rhee regularly wrote the editorials in it from 1920 to 1939.

On the whole, Rhee's quarter-century in Hawaii (from 1913 to 1941) was a turbulent period marked by a variety of struggles, hardships and discouragements. Far removed from what he felt he should be doing, limited in resources, powerless to affect the course of events in the Pacific, and beset by factionalism within the Korean community, he endured reverses and suffered limitations which would have utterly crushed a less determined man. As proved to be true of his seven years in prison, he utilized his experiences to broaden further his knowledge and to clarify his program. Many of the reforms and policies which were later instituted by the Republic of Korea owe their origin to the lonely and bedeviled months and years of the Hawaiian travail. Scars of lasting bitterness, too, remain. Many of the political vendettas in Korea (which have proved so puzzling to American diplomatic and press observers) have roots in those earlier Honolulu feuds. But also from the positive veneration which most of the Americanized Koreans developed for Syngman Rhee came the first real indication of what he was later to mean to the people of the reborn Korean nation.

Chapter VII

THE MANSEI
REVOLUTION

In the Spring of 1919 Syngman Rhee faced a major test of his philosophy of seeking Korean independence through peaceful appeals to the minds and the consciences of Americans and other Western peoples. Woodrow Wilson, Rhee's friend from Princeton days—who used to introduce the Korean as "the man who will redeem Korea's freedom"—was now leading the world in a crusade for the "right of self-determination of peoples." Rhee was positive that Korea was included on Wilson's list of submerged nations that were to be restored to self-government. But he also knew from his extensive studies of international affairs that no such restoration could be expected easily or automatically. Japan had won a claim to special consideration because she had done such fighting as had been required in the Far East to seize the German outposts in China. Assuredly Japan would never consent freely to the surrender of the Korean corridor to the continental riches of Asia. Not even Wilson himself would be able to accomplish the restoration of Korea unless the Korean people should do something dramatic in their own behalf.

As a matter of fact, Japan forehandedly faced the same problem and met it by circulating a petition all through Korea, in December, 1918, and getting numerous signatures attached to a declaration that the entire Korean populace

132

was grateful for the beneficent and generous rule by the Japanese and were rapidly and happily becoming assimilated into the Japanese nation! This maneuver was either a master stroke of humor or the naive act of a ruling clique which didn't know what humor was; in any event, it was like erecting a sign over a burning house asserting that all was calm and serene within; no fire engines were desired!

In Hawaii the dispute over methods that had raged between Rhee and Youngman Park was intensified. Park insisted that the occasion clearly called for an armed uprising inside Korea, to dramatize the determination of the people to win their freedom—and he pointed out that with the statesmen of the free world standing by ready to measure nationalistic aspirations on the yardstick of Wilson's Fourteen Points, such an uprising could succeed even against the overwhelming strength of Japan. Rhee replied that bloodshed was not the answer. The world was sick of killing, after four years of world war. Another armed outburst would be insufferable. Besides, the Japanese could win Allied sympathy by pointing out that the lawless Korean populace had to be restrained from murdering innocent civilians. If a test of arms should commence, the Western statesmen would be forced to stand by Japan, which had fought with them during the late war. Consequently, revolution would be the worst thing to undertake.

However, Rhee argued, there was a middle way—a way of protest without revolution. What was demanded was not a revolution for freedom, but a *demonstration* so sweeping that none could doubt it bespoke the will of the Korean nation. Thus was born a new concept—a nationwide demonstration of passive resistance, three years before Gandhi launched a similar program in India.

The Korean intellectuals in their homeland watched with considerable interest this debate between Syngman Rhee and Youngman Park. Despite the closeness of Japanese censorship, there was constant and reasonably secret correspondence between those who were keeping the spirit of independence alive outside Korea and their friends within the country. As events were soon to illustrate, this correspondence was so absolutely clandestine as to leave the Japanese officials completely in the dark.

Actually, the occasion for which Rhee and his friends were looking was provided by the old deposed Korean Emperor. When the Japanese circulated their petition asking the Korean people to renounce any wish for independence, the Emperor made a last gesture of courage and independence —almost the only one in his futile life. He refused to sign the petition, and thus won finally a place for himself in the respect and affection of his people. Very soon afterward, on January 20, 1919, he died: by apoplexy, according to the Japanese announcement, but since his blood pressure was low, this explanation was not widely believed. Two stories raced through Korea—one that he had been poisoned; the other that he had committed suicide in protest against the approaching marriage of his son to Princess Nashimoto.* The Japanese authorities did not announce the Emperor's death until two days after its occurrence, thus lending some color

* The marriage, incidentally, did take place and turned out very happily for the prince. Princess Nashimoto was a lovely and unusually intelligent girl, whom the Japanese crown prince (the present Emperor, Hirohito) had originally selected for his own bride. However, the royal household ruled against the marriage when it was found that her family was almost barren of sons. As the wife of Korea's Prince Lee, she has taken a leading part in many welfare programs, including the sponsorship of the Japanese Girl Scouts; while Prince Lee has devoted himself primarily to the growing and selective breeding of orchids, of which he has developed some twenty new varieties. When, after World War II, this royal couple lost the revenue from their Korean estates, they were reduced to renting their mansion in Tokyo and to living in the caretaker's cottage on the grounds. Prince Lee, however, did not surrender the green houses for his orchids! So far as postwar events in Korea are concerned, he has never shown the slightest interest in them. It is noteworthy that there is no vestige of a royalist party on the peninsula. The history of the Yi dynasty, which ruled Korea for five hundred and eighteen years, is distinctly a closed book.

to the suspicion he had been poisoned, and at first refused to permit any special period of mourning for him. However, in view of the universal demand by the Korean people, Tokyo finally agreed that on March 3 Koreans might assemble in their various communities to hold commemoration ceremonies.

Instantly plans to utilize the occasion for retrieving Korean independence began to be discussed. Kimm Kiusic (whose uncle had owned the printing press on which Syngman Rhee's early newspaper, the *Maiyil Sinmun*, had been published back in 1897) was dispatched from Shanghai to Paris to plead the Korean cause at the peace conference. Youngman Park, who had left Hawaii in 1915 to go first to Manchuria and then to Shanghai, was among a group of Korean revolutionaries who wanted to turn the occasion into a bloodbath of frenzied attack (however futile it must be) against the Japanese officials in Korea, in order to dramatize for the statesmen in Paris the strength of the Korean determination to be free. However, the policy of peaceful demonstration was finally adopted—apparently the first instance in all history of a nationwide deliberate policy of organized passive resistance.

The motivation of the *Mansei* Revolution was patriotism guided and directed by religion. Among the outstanding Christian leaders in Korea were Kil Sun Chu, pastor of Korea's largest Christian Church, and Yi Sang Jai, who had been a prison mate of Syngman Rhee's twenty years earlier. Associated with them was Son Byung-hi, leader of the *Chuntokyo*, a native religious sect teaching the existence of one Supreme Mind, *Hananim*, and seeking to combine Christian brotherhood with Confucian ethics and Buddhist philosophy. These three, with thirty others, constituted a "Committee of Thirty-three" inside Korea, which set out to organize not a revolution but a demonstration of independence. These men drew up a "Proclamation of Independence," which they had secretly printed in a dark cellar in Seoul from handcarved wooden blocks. This declaration, conceived by the union of religion and patriotism, read as follows:

We herewith proclaim the independence of Korea and the liberty of the Korean people. We tell it to the world in witness of the equality of all nations, and we pass it on to our posterity as their inherent right.

We make this proclamation, having back of us a history of forty-three centuries and 20,000,000 united, loyal people. We take this step to insure to our children for all time to come, life and liberty in accord with the awakening conscience of this new era. This is the clear leading of God, the moving principle of the present age, the just claim of the whole human race. It is something that cannot be stamped out, or stifled, or gagged, or suppressed by any means.

Victims of an older age, when brute force and the spirit of plunder ruled, we have come after these long thousands of years to experience the agony of ten years of foreign oppression, with every loss of the right to live, every restriction of the freedom of thought, every damage done to the dignity of life, every opportunity lost for a share in the intelligent advance of the age in which we live.

Assuredly, if the defects of the past are to be rectified, if the wrongs of the present are to be righted, if future oppression is to be avoided, if thought is to be set free, if right of action is to be given a place, if we are to attain to any way of progress, if we are to deliver our children from the painful heritage of shame, if we are to leave blessing and happiness intact for those who succeed us, the first of all necessary things is the complete independence of our people. What cannot our twenty millions do, with hearts consecrated to liberty, in this day when human nature and conscience are making a stand for truth and right? What barrier can we not break, what purpose can we not accomplish?

We have no desire to accuse Japan of breaking many solemn treaties since 1876, nor to single out specially the teachers in the schools or the Government officials who treat the heritage of our ancestors as a colony of their own, and our people and our civilization as a nation of savages, and who delight only in beating us down and bringing us under their heel.

We have no wish to find special fault with Japan's lack of fairness or her contempt for our civilization and the principles on which her state rests; we, who have greater cause to reprimand ourselves, need not spend time in finding fault with others; neither need we, who require so urgently to build for the future, spend useless hours over what is past and gone. Our urgent need today is the rebuilding of this house of ours and not the discussion of who has broken it down, or what has caused its ruin. Our work is to clear the future of defects in accord with the earnest dictates of conscience. Let us not be filled with bitterness or resentment over past agonies or past occasions for anger.

Our part is to influence the Japanese government, dominated as it is by the old idea of brute force which thinks to run counter to reason and universal law, so that it will change and act honestly and in accord with the principles of right and truth.

The result of annexation, brought about against the will of the Korean people, is that the Japanese are concerned only for their own gain, and by a false set of figures show a profit and loss account between us two peoples most untrue, digging a trench of everlasting resentment deeper and deeper the farther they go.

Ought not the way of enlightened courage to be to correct the evils of the past by ways that are sincere, and by true sympathy and friendly feelings make a new world in which the two peoples will be equally blessed?

To bind by force twenty millions of resentful Koreans will mean not only loss of peace forever for this part of the Far East, but also will increase the ever-growing suspicions of four hundred millions of Chinese—upon whom depends the safety of the Far East—besides strengthening the hatred of Japan. From this all the rest of the East will suffer. Today Korean independence will mean not only life and happiness for us, but also Japan's departure from an evil path and her exaltation to the place of true protector of the East, so that China too would put all fear of Japan aside. This thought comes from no minor resentment, but from a large hope for the future welfare and blessings of mankind.

A new era wakes before our eyes, the old world of force is gone, and the new world of righteousness and truth is here. Out of the experience and travail of the old world arises this light on the affairs of life. Insects stifled by their foe, the snows of winter, are also awakened at this time of the year by the breezes of spring and the warm light of the snow upon them.

It is the day of the restoration of all things, on the full tide of which we set forth without delay or fear. We desire a full measure of satisfaction in the way of life, liberty and the pursuit of happiness, and an opportunity to develop what is in us for the glory of our people. In this hope we go forward.

To this paean of praise for a new age of enlightened justice which the Korean leadership felt was being ushered in by Woodrow Wilson with his Charter of the Fourteen Points, the Committee of Thirty-three added a threefold injunction for the *Mansei* demonstrators:

1. This work of ours is in behalf of truth, justice, and life, undertaken at the request of our people, in order to make known their desire for liberty. Let no violence be done to anyone.

2. Let those who follow us show every hour with gladness this same spirit.

3. Let all things be done with singleness of purpose, so that our behavior to the very end may be honorable and upright.

Dated the 4252d Year of the Kingdom of Korea, 3d Month, 1st Day.

While this proclamation was being printed, the Committee of Thirty-three was developing inside Korea a closely-knit nationwide organization under the very noses of their Japanese masters and in the midst of a veritable network of spies and secret agents. They appointed a local committee for every *myun* (township) in Korea. They drew up instructions directing that the crowds assembling to commemorate the Emperor's death should carry concealed on their persons homemade Korean flags. When these crowds were assembled, the instructions directed, a leader appointed from among them, would read to them the copy of the Proclamation of Independence. Then the crowds were to parade down their village streets, waving their flags and shouting, "*Mansei! Mansei!* May Korea live ten thousand years!" The instructions concluded:

> "Whatever you do
> Do not insult the Japanese
> Do not throw stones
> Do not hit with your fists
> For these are the acts of barbarians."

Incredibly, this great national movement was organized without the knowledge of the Japanese. The instructions and copies of the declaration were carried from village to village concealed in the long, flowing sleeves of schoolgirls. The local arrangements were completed in secrecy, even though the number of Japanese police agents in Korea numbered one to each one hundred of the inhabitants and the spy system was presumed to be extremely effective. The Japanese officials did, however, sense that something unusual was in the air. They planned extensive police precautions for the March 3 date of mourning. In order to counter these plans, the Committee of Thirty-three suddenly moved up the date of the demonstrations, sending word for the assemblages to occur and the Proclamation to be read at 2:00 P.M. on Saturday, March 1. This date and this hour became the natal time for the modern democratic Republic of Korea.

At noon on March 1, 1919, the thirty-three signers of the Proclamation of Independence gathered for luncheon in the Bright Moon Café in Seoul. Promptly at 2:00 P.M. they solemnly read aloud their precious document. Then they called in the Japanese police and, without ostentation or struggle, gave themselves up. At the same hour, in every section of Korea, the independence demonstrations broke out.

The sudden and universal demonstration of the determined will of the Korean people broke like a stroke of lightning across the Korean sky. The publisher of the Sacramento *Bee*, who was in Korea during that first week in March, called it, "The Greatest Example in World History of an Organized Passive Resistance for an Ideal." An editorial entitled, "The Dignity of Life," in the Los Angeles *Times* (for April 6, 1919) commented: "In our opinion this Proclamation will stand on a plane of exaltation with our own Declaration of Independence . . . It is the voice of a prophet crying in the wilderness . . . May God grant a mad world the grace to stop and listen to that voice." To another observer, "The whole plan had a loftiness and sober dignity of thought and speech, in which some fine old strain of Confucianism mingled with rich and fervent Biblical phraseology. It was one of the most remarkable revolutions in history—and one which might well put any Christian nation to shame. The instructions issued should be immortal in the annals of revolt."

The first effect of these nationwide demonstrations was to dramatize the utter falsity of the fabricated petition which had been circulated by the Japanese the preceding December. The solidly determined character of the Korean nationalism was demonstrated. President Wilson's thesis that every free people must be recognized and supported in its birthright of freedom was given convincing support. All Korea was alive with a spirit of restrained but powerful national self-assertiveness.

The Japanese were astounded and reacted in the traditional manner of colonial rule—with brute force. Several thousands of the peaceful demonstrators were killed. Several hundred thousand were imprisoned, and many of them were subjected to beatings and tortures. At least fifteen villages

were fired and some thirty Christian churches were burned
by the Japanese gendarmes, some of them with their con-
gregations inside. The representative of the Board of
Foreign Missions of the Canadian Presbyterian Church in
Korea, sent back an official report, noting: "I read affidavits
... which made one's blood boil, so frightful were the means
used in trying to extort confessions from prisoners." Dr.
Horace Underwood, one of Korea's best known missionaries,
wrote of coming upon a village of forty houses, burned to
the ground, and of finding the church a mass of ashes, in
which were found the remains of several bodies. "The odor
of burned flesh in the vicinity of the church was sickening,"
he wrote. An American who held a position under the
Japanese in Korea, and therefore chose to remain anonymous, wrote: "A few hundred yards from where I am writing, the beating goes on, day after day. The victims are tied
down on a frame and beaten on the naked body with rods
till they become unconscious. Then cold water is poured on
them until they revive, when the process is repeated. It is
sometimes repeated many times. . . . Men, women and
children are shot down or bayoneted. The Christian Church
is especially chosen as an object of fury, and to the Christians
is meted out special severity." The nature of the determination of the Korean demonstrators, as well as the severity of
the Japanese reaction to it, was well illuminated in the
official report rendered to the Japanese government by Mr.
I. Yamagata, the Director-General of the Administration of
Korea: "The agitation has gradually spread to all parts of
the peninsula, while the nature of the disturbance has become malignant, and it was to cope with this situation that
the government was obliged to resort to force. In spite of
this, the trouble has not only continued, but has become so
uncontrollable and widespread that the police and military
force hitherto in use has been found insufficient, necessitat-

ing the despatch of more troops and gendarmes from the mother country . . ."

The peaceful demonstrations and the furious punishment of the demonstrators continued for several months, while foreign news correspondents and missionaries poured out reports and denunciations of the Japanese cruelties. The revolutionists published a daily newspaper, the *Independence News*, regularly through March, April and May, and at intervals thereafter, keeping the location of the press a secret by a veritable miracle of closely co-operative organization. In issue after issue, the paper pleaded with its readers, "Do not hit the Japanese, not even in retaliation." Many of the missionaries sent back word to their conferences that the Koreans followed these instructions, regardless of the wanton attacks upon them. The Japanese government sent an additional force of 6,000 soldiers to Korea, issued strict edicts against any public gathering, confiscated flags and posters, arrested every demonstrator they could lay hands upon, and gradually the great *Mansei* demonstration was suppressed. Once again the Korean independence movement was driven back underground at home, and was forced to exercise its open activities only abroad.

Before the demonstration was crushed, however, it achieved a notable triumph. In the week of April 16-23, representatives from every province in Korea met secretly in Seoul and organized a provisional government. A constitution was drawn up, providing for representative government, and embodying the guarantees of personal liberty which are contained in the first ten amendments to the United States Constitution. These representatives held an election and chose Syngman Rhee as president of the Republic of Korea. At about the same time, exiled Korean patriots in Siberia and in Shanghai held similar meetings and endorsed the action of the patriots in Seoul, reaffirming the adoption of the constitution and the election of Syngman

Rhee. Thus was born what proved to be the longest-lived government-in-exile in modern history. It continued to function until its voluntary dissolution, to open the way for new elections, following the liberation of Korea in 1945.

Rhee was extremely active during this stirring period. He went to Washington, D. C., there to plead the cause of the "self-determination" of the Koreans, in accord with Woodrow Wilson's peace aims. With Philip Jaisohn he discussed the establishment of a magazine through which their cause could be systematically presented to the American people. Rhee put aside this plan for a time while he sought desperately to get a passport from the State Department to permit him to go to Paris, where he hoped to lay the Korean case squarely before President Wilson and the peace conference. To Rhee's dismay, Wilson sent a message to the State Department indicating that issuance of a passport to Rhee would cause uneasiness among the Japanese and would consequently interfere with Wilson's plan to build a secure peace in the Orient upon the seemingly sound foundation of Japanese power and co-operation. Rhee was thunderstruck to discover that his friend and hero, the architect of peace based upon justice, was planning to sacrifice Korean independence for the sake of power politics. It was clear to Rhee that a peace based on such cold-blooded and shortsighted expediency could never last.

Rhee and his associates were beset with a mingling of determination and despair. Their nation, 4,252 years old, surely came within the province of "freedom for peoples" upon which Wilson's entire plan for lasting peace was professedly based. The Koreans had acted with great decorum and restraint. They had participated heroically in a well-organized, nationwide demonstration of their will to regain their independence. Under the severest of provocations they had adhered to the Christian injunction to turn the other cheek. Japanese atrocities committed against the peaceful

Korean demonstrators were widely reported by scores of trustworthy foreign observers. Rhee could scarcely imagine that in the face of all those facts their cause would be rejected. Again and again he called at the Department of State, trying to see Secretary Lane, who was friendly and sympathetic, or Acting Secretary Polk. But the doors remained closed. The decision against Korea had been sealed.

A Conference of Small and Subject Nations was held in New York City in the spring of 1919, with Czechoslovakia being the chief claimant to public attention and sympathy. With the support of the Koreans in Hawaii, Rhee attended that conference, to plead the Korean cause. It was at this time that he first called at the office of John W. Staggers, a prominent lawyer in Washington, D. C., who was an active promoter of the conference, to solicit his aid. Staggers refused to support the Koreans—on the grounds that President Wilson must be left with a free hand to try to win the co-operation of Japan—but, nevertheless, the talks Rhee had with him led to the formation of one of Rhee's deepest and most lasting friendships. In the long years ahead John Staggers was to prove a loyal friend to Korea and a warm comrade for Rhee through many lonely years of what appeared to be a hopeless struggle.

Leaving the Conference of Small and Subject Nations, Rhee went to Philadelphia, where, with Philip Jaisohn, he laid plans for a concerted drive to mobilize American public opinion in behalf of their cause. They secured the introduction into the *Congressional Record* for July 15, 17 and 18, 1919, of a detailed report from Presbyterian missionaries of atrocities perpetrated against the Korean people during the March-May demonstrations. On August 18 they had placed in the *Congressional Record* a statement on behalf of Korean independence by Homer B. Hulbert, the author of the best English-language histories of Korea. On September 19, a long brief supporting Korean independence (prepared by the

As Chairman of the National Assembly, Dr. Rhee is signing the newly adopted Constitution, July 17, 1948. (*U.S.A. Signal Corps*)

very able and devoted lawyer, Fred A. Dolph, who had become the counselor of the exiled Korean Republic) was entered in the *Congressional Record*. Another brief detailing the legal basis for Korean independence, outlining the cultural achievements of the Koreans, and showing the exploitative nature of Japanese rule in Korea, was inserted in the *Record* for October 24. The story was clearly and ably told, but there were few who read it and fewer still who seemed to care.

On September 19 the Korean patriots opened with fanfare and considerable ostentation a Korean Congress in Philadelphia. Mayor Thomas B. Smith joined in the parade through the main streets of the city to Independence Hall, where they rang the Liberty Bell, and where Syngman Rhee opened the first session in the same hall in which George Washington had presided over the Constitutional Convention. That opening session was addressed by Senator Selden P. Spencer, of Missouri, who did all he could to win public and official support for the Koreans. Nebraska's great Senator, George W. Norris, came to their aid and made a speech in support of Korean independence which appeared in the *Congressional Record* for November 14, 1919. As the president of the Republic of Korea, Rhee addressed formal letters to the heads of state of all the principal nations proposing the initiation of diplomatic relations. Everything that could be done was done. It is amazing that the small group of expatriates, without funds or powerful friends, achieved so much. But the visible results were nil. The Western world had won its war and was content to let the peace somehow take care of itself. The statesmen tied together a bundle of compromises and adopted it as a substitute for the war aims set forth so sublimely in Wilson's Fourteen Points. The public was heartily sick of war and world problems and resolutely turned its attention to personal and domestic affairs. Japan remained in firm possession of Korea and in one of the more cynical aphorisms of Anglo-Saxon law, "possession is nine-tenths of the law."

Unfortunately, the divisions in the ranks of the Koreans, which had proved a constant problem in Hawaii, still continued. Youngman Park, Rhee's erstwhile friend and rival in Honolulu, was named minister of Foreign Affairs in the cabinet of the new government—even though his views continued to differ widely from those of Rhee. Ahn Chang Ho was nominated as minister of Labor. Jealousies and struggles for preferred positions were numerous. One of the disputes which was hotly debated in the secret conclave held in Seoul was whether the executive of the new Republic should be titled "Chief Executive" or "President." The choice finally settled upon was *Dai Dong Yang*, or President, and this was the title conferred on Rhee.

The fact that Syngman Rhee was in the United States deprived him of any voice in the choice of cabinet members. The selection actually was a patchwork of compromises among contending factions, all of whom had to be represented in order to hold their support. The impossibility of holding an open election among all the Korean people made the personnel of the new government subject to decision by the delegates assembled in Seoul. The natural result was a lack of harmony and mutual trust within the cabinet. When these new officials fled secretly from Seoul and reassembled in Shanghai, Rhee began to receive a flow of radiograms and letters chiefly notable for their recriminations and contentiousness. These disagreements emanating from Shanghai were reflected in the Korean Congress which convened in Philadelphia. Many of the delegates were more intent upon sparring for personal advantage than in working together to achieve their common goal. Even while their hope of national independence was slipping inexorably from their grasp, they fought among themselves for the shadowy appearances of priority in a government that had little more than a paper existence. Despite the notable and noble achievement of the organization and conduct of the *Mansei* demonstrations, it was evident that the Koreans were still suffering from the factionalism which had contributed to the failures of the old monarchy. As a result Rhee adjourned the Philadelphia meeting and left it in disgust. Its only tangible accomplishment was to vote for the establishment of the magazine Rhee and Philip Jaisohn had contemplated, *The Korean Review*, of which Philip Jaisohn became the editor, and which continued publication for a period of three years.

Rhee gave his own attention to organizing a League of the Friends of Korea, of which active chapters were soon operating in nineteen American cities. The number of local chapters might have been greatly extended, but a profusion of heavy duties pressed upon Rhee and time was fleeting. While engaged in this work, Rhee was living in the Portland Hotel in Washington, D. C., together with Kiusic Kimm, Henry Chung DeYoung, Ben Limb, and Myun Dong, all of whom were assisting him. Various news reporters called upon Rhee from time to time. Among them all he was most favorably impressed by a young reporter for the International News Service, Jay Jerome Williams, who became very sympathetic with the Korean cause and was possessed of a genuine crusading zeal. Williams came to report but remained to help. Along with John Staggers he has remained through all the succeeding years among Rhee's closest friends—a never-failing source of friendly counsel and sacrificial helpfulness.

One of the steps Rhee took at this time was to write a letter to the emperor of Japan, offering him "one more chance" to restore independence to the people of Korea, thus winning their gratitude and friendship, with the alternative that if this offer was refused the Koreans eventually would become free anyway and would distrust and despise the Japanese as would-be conquerors. This letter was

drafted with considerable care—in the thought that if it did
not impress the emperor of Japan it might at least win increased sympathy from American newspaper readers. Ben
Limb, who had been "drafted" as a secretary for Dr. Rhee
from his studies at Ohio State University, was dispatched
with the epistle to the Japanese Embassy. There he was
politely received by the first secretary of the Embassy, Koki
Hirota. The two men talked pleasantly for a time about the
revolution in Korea, the Korean independence movement
abroad, and the status of the Japanese residents in Korea.
Then Limb handed the letter to Hirota, who promised that
the ambassador would dispatch it to the emperor. The two
parted as amicably as though their relationship was one of
complete friendship. Hirota within a few years became the
premier of Japan, and Ben Limb, after the establishment of
the Republic of Korea in 1948 became, first, foreign minister,
and next, ambassador and chief of the Korean Mission to
the United Nations.

Rhee and Limb were soon to engage in a most exciting
mission. The political disagreements in Shanghai continued
and it became evident that the new government would break
apart unless a strong hand were introduced to settle some of
the quarrels. Rhee determined to go to Shanghai, and took
Limb with him as his aide. Since their capture would be a
considerable boon to the Japanese, the first necessity was to
drop from sight so that they could take a ship without their
identity being known. Accordingly, they announced to their
friends in Washington that they were returning to Hawaii
to raise funds. After they reached Honolulu, they went out
in the countryside and lived for a week in the sea-side
cottage of Mr. William Bothwick, operator of a funeral
parlor (who later became tax commissioner for the Territory
of Hawaii). Bothwick was preparing the bodies of some de-
ceased Chinese, which were to be sent to their homeland for
burial on the S.S. *West Hika,* which was to sail for Shanghai

on November 16. For Rhee and Limb this ship had two great advantages: the first, that it would not stop en route at any Japanese port, as did most ships sailing to North Asia; and the second, that Bothwick would be able to smuggle them aboard when he delivered the coffins. Thus it was that on the evening of November 15 Syngman Rhee and Ben Limb went aboard the *West Hika* without tickets and without the captain's knowledge, and hid themselves below deck among the coffins. All the next day they remained in the stifling hold, with their emotions supercharged by the danger of their mission and the nature of the cargo. Only late the next night, after the ship had cleared the harbor and was safely out to sea did they reveal themselves to the second mate, who took them to be a poor old Chinese and his son.

The captain treated them with great consideration. Rhee was assigned quarters in the hospital cabins, which were otherwise unoccupied. Young Limb was assigned to duty polishing the ship's brass and doing other light chores. The trip was uneventful and both Rhee and Limb enjoyed its tranquility after the hectic and wearing preceding weeks. The lumbering freighter required forty days for the crossing, and during this time the two men spent many evening hours in the ship's prow, watching the lifting of the waves and talking of the challenge of their cause. Upon arrival in Shanghai the captain considerately forebore to identify them to the port authorities, and shortly afterward they went ashore and made their way to the headquarters of the Korean Provisional Government, in the French district of the International Settlement.

Syngman Rhee remained in China for seventeen strenuous months. Because their finances were limited, and because Rhee wanted to send personal and urgent messages back to his followers in the United States, Ben Limb was soon dispatched homeward, traveling by way of Europe. While he was spending a few days in Paris, two police gendarmes stopped one day at his hotel and asked him to accompany them to the police station. There he was informed that Hirohito, then the crown prince of Japan, was to arrive in Europe shortly for a visit to the various capitals, and the Japanese had warned the French government that Limb was probably sent as an agent to assassinate him. Limb found the policemen very jovial in their examination, and after he assured them he had no intention of killing anyone, they exchanged pleasantries and soon parted. Actually Limb left Paris for New York before Hirohito arrived.

Rhee's problems in China were more serious. Every member of the cabinet and the National Assembly had his own special group of followers. The only financial resources consisted of free-will donations, and all those who gave or collected money felt privileged to help determine policies and choose personnel. The lack of international recognition of the government seemed to make it all the more imperative for every official to be especially solicitous about his own prestige and status amongst his fellows. With so much to worry them, and so little grounds for substantial hope, tempers flared easily and personal strife was almost their only effective means of securing an emotional catharsis.

Moreover, differences of policy were acute and could not easily be settled. Some of the Korean revolutionists favored close ties with the new Communist party which had recently come into power in Russia. Some wanted to work in close accord with one or the other of the several major factions in China. Some favored the development of an active program of sabotage, guerrilla activities, and assassinations of Japanese officials. Rhee insisted upon his long-established policy of peaceful appeals to public opinion and to the various governments upon whose support they must rely if they were to have any hope of success. Even those who were most loyal to Rhee personally or who were most in-clined intellectually to accept his philosophy were uncomfortably aware that his program thus far showed no tangible evidence of success.

Whenever Rhee could do so he devised means of leaving the International Settlement (usually in company with well-known foreigners, in order to circumvent arrest by the Japanese) and made trips to Nanking, Soochow, Peking, and other cities, both for a study of conditions and for conferences with Korean leaders. In this fashion the months passed. Rhee admonished his cabinet members to make studies of Korean needs in the various areas assigned to their responsibility. The one avenue of effective action that appeared to be open to them was the one Rhee had long opposed—namely, the organization of a volunteer army with which to make forays across the border from Manchuria into Korea and the secret build-up of disruptive forces inside Korea. Since Rhee remained convinced that lawless and violent measures could not achieve a victory and would only strengthen the Japanese case for ever-tighter controls and continuance of their police control over Korea, he argued endlessly against this course of action. But what he might propose as an alternative to it was not so readily apparent.

When U. S. Secretary of State Charles Evans Hughes, upon the suggestion of Senator William E. Borah, issued a call early in 1921 for powers interested in the Pacific area to meet in Washington to consider limitation upon armaments, Rhee seized the occasion as a rallying point for the exiled patriots and as possibly offering an opportunity to win an official international hearing for the Korean cause. Delegates from the United States, Great Britain, France, Italy, Belgium, Holland, Portugal, China and Japan were to meet in Washington on November 12, 1921. Rhee was convinced that lasting peace in the Orient could be assured only if Korea were restored to independence, so that it might play its historic role as the "buffer state" of North Asia. With his energetic optimism and unquenchable belief that reason could be made to prevail in human affairs, he had hopes of being able to sell this idea to the delegates of the great powers. Accordingly, on May 28, 1921, after a series of farewell sessions with his cabinet and National Assembly (in which at least the surface appearance of a new harmony was achieved), he sailed from Shanghai on the S.S. *Columbia*. During eleven days in Manila, he studied political and social conditions on the Islands—concluding that a halfway stop to independence is like a halfway point on a railway trip: merely a position to be passed by as rapidly as possible, rather than a place at which to linger. Then he boarded the S.S. *Granite State* for the long Pacific crossing, a passage which he always has loved and regards as one of the idyllic ways in which to pass a couple of weeks. Arriving at Honolulu on June 29, he was given a gala welcome. July and the first part of August were passed very pleasantly among friends in Hawaii; but by the end of August Rhee was back in Washington working to get ready for the opening of the Disarmament Conference.

This process of getting ready involved a complex pattern of activities. The first step was to create the strongest possible impression that his mission was official. Since no Korean government was recognized, and since Korea was not invited to play any role whatsoever at the conference, this stage of the preparation required special care. Newspapermen, with the able assistance of Rhee's friend Jay Jerome Williams, were courted, entertained, and given "story angles" on the heroic struggles of the oppressed people of Korea. Interviews were held in which, as it turned out, the story of Rhee's being smuggled aboard the S.S. *West Hika*, for the trip to Shanghai, "in a coffin" (which was not strictly true), proved to be especially popular. Critical items also appeared in the press alleging that Rhee was only one of several Korean claimants for leadership and that he did not really represent the masses of the people. These stories always hurt Rhee's feelings more than any other type of criticism, for they pictured him as being personally ambitious and struggling to elevate himself above other legitimate aspirants and, indeed, above the welfare of the Korean people themselves.

The second step in his preparations, then, was to request from the provisional government in Shanghai a set of official credentials. These were sent to him promptly, by radiogram, under date of September 21, 1921, and were forwarded to Secretary Hughes, but failed to elicit any reply from him. After the conference was convened, the credentials were dispatched to the conference secretariat, again without receiving any acknowledgment. Rhee and his associates were not surprised, for they had no expectation that their representation would result directly in a repudiation by the conference of Japanese rule over Korea. They did hope, however, to be accepted as "observers" at the conference, and they did expect to secure an amount of newspaper publicity which would make it difficult for the conference to ignore them completely.

This attempt to secure newspaper coverage for their cause was the third and, indeed, the major step in their preparations for the opening of the conference. Rhee's lawyer, Mr. Dolph, prepared a brief setting forth the case for recognition of the Republic of Korea, and this brief was introduced into the *Congressional Record* for December 1, 1921. The brief reviewed the recent history of Korea, commencing with the United States-Korea Treaty of 1882, in which the United States pledged itself to "use its friendly offices" in case Korea should require aid to maintain its independence. The brief also quoted an interesting article written by a Japanese publicist, Adache Kimosuke, which had appeared in the *Review of Reviews* for October, 1907. "We shall be frank about it," the passage read. "We shall say that we are carrying things with a high hand in Korea. We have gone into the back yard of our neighbor and are telling him to kindly move on simply because we need his home. We are doing just as the Americans have done with the Indians, the rightful owners of America; just as the British have done with the Hindus; just as the Russians have done with the Tartars; as Germany did in South Africa, and France in Cochin China. Nippon has joined the house of the great powers. She has become civilized."

The Korean delegation never was permitted to present its case before the conference. In personal talks with some of the delegates and with many newspaper reporters, Rhee was disheartened to find that they cynically accepted the continuance of the age-old pattern of power politics—the rule of the weak by the strong—in utter disregard of the high ideals proclaimed by the Allies in fighting the World War. The "New Era of Justice," which had been hailed so confidently in the Korean Proclamation of Independence of 1919, was sacrificed to seeming expediency: and thereby were planted the seeds that developed inevitably into World War II. Humanity, it turned out, had not yet become ready to cast off the old habits which had kept mankind in a continuing series of bitter conflicts for over 5,000 years. The old pattern persisted; and the old price, it was apparent to Rhee, would have to be paid in blood and destruction, over and over again.

It was also disheartening to him to find that everyone with whom he talked was deeply impressed by the crying need of Japan for greater resources with which to feed its teeming population. To his argument that the Koreans also had need of at least their own resources, with which to maintain a decent standard of living for themselves, the answer was often a shrug of the shoulders. Let those take who could; let those lose who must. This view of 1921-22 might be dismissed as simply a historical period view except that thirty years later the same kind of logic has been repeated

again and again—and this even after Japan conclusively
demonstrated that it was using its possession of Korea not
for self-sustenance but to build armaments and to open further roads of aggression against both its Asian neighbors
and the Western Powers. Rhee has always been both angered and bewildered by the strange logic of the West which
regards the claims of strong nations as having a sort of innate and natural priority over those of weaker states. He
has argued again and again against the view that when a
nation has developed sufficient strength to be classified as a
great power, different rules apply to it than those that apply
to smaller and weaker countries. In his view history shows
that this kind of reasoning leads only to war. He would substitute for it not an abstract principle of perfect justice,
which is perhaps impossible of attainment in a world of con-
flicting national sovereignties, but the Jeffersonian theory
(applied to nations and not merely to individuals) of the
greatest good to the greatest number. This line of reasoning
led him to the conclusion that the Western powers, for their
own sakes, should sanction and support the independence of
Korea as a sure means of keeping Japan off the continent.

Chapter VIII

DIPLOMACY
WITHOUT RECOGNITION

DURING THE TWENTY YEARS from the end of the Disarmament Conference to the attack by Germany upon Poland in 1939, Syngman Rhee persisted in his painful and lonely endeavor to accomplish what seemingly could not be done. He was a David without a slingshot, assailing an army of Goliaths. His goal was the resurrection of a nation that was dead in every respect except for the cardinal one that it still lived on in the hearts of its people. The Koreans were enslaved. If this term seems harsh, it may be recalled as the one used by Franklin Roosevelt, Winston Churchill and Chiang Kai-shek in their Declaration on Korea at Cairo, in 1943. The Korean people were abandoned diplomatically by the powers that (as history was soon to demonstrate) should have been their staunchest allies. They were so deeply submerged that when a book was finally written about Korea in 1944, the most appropriate title seemed to be *Forgotten Nation.*

Syngman Rhee was the president of a republic-in-exile that lacked everything except unalterable determination. It was even without debts! Its officials were unpaid, undisciplined and recalcitrant. As chief executive, Rhee had responsibilities, but neither power nor resources. In these circumstances, with the aid of a few friends, and supported by the voiceless faith and muted pleas of his captive countrymen, his task was to try every available means to make the impossible come to pass: to make a dead nation rise again from its ashes, and regain for the Korean people the life-giving right of self-government.

Internally, no nation ever has existed or ever will exist except as it is imprinted into the hearts of its people as an undying ideal. Externally, no nation is more than a legal charter, recognized by other nations as their sovereign co-equal in the great global community. Without that recognized charter, a people may bleed and suffer but they have no recourse and no apparent remedy.

Korea's resurrection from this virtual extinction was forecast in the *Mansei* revolution of 1919. The founding of the provisional republic, however shaky its material form, provided an essential rallying point for Korean loyalties and efforts. So long as that republic could be kept alive, there was always a vital spark in existence which might someday be fanned into a flame of regeneration. Rhee's task was to prevent that spark from being stamped out by Japanese force or from being smothered by sheer indifference and neglect.

As soon as his election as president was announced, he founded in Washington, D. C. an office which he called *The Korean Commission*. He would have preferred to call it the Korean Embassy, but this he could not do, for the exiled republic was without sanction or recognition. To have insisted upon calling its office an Embassy would have kept Rhee and his associates in a perpetually defensive position and would have handicapped them in doing any constructive work. By adopting the ambiguous term "Commission" they were able to claim what none could properly deny— namely, that they represented the true sentiments for freedom of a great majority of the Korean people. This commission was very active from its founding until after the dissolution of the Washington Disarmament Conference. Even then it continued in being, but was not reactivated significantly until after the Japanese attack upon Manchuria in 1931. Thereafter, despite the stubborn determination of the Western powers to ignore the patent dangers of burgeoning Japanese imperialism in the Pacific, with a consequent studied indifference to all claims for Korea, Rhee kept the Korean Commission active and insistent upon what he considered the just claims of his people for independence.

Syngman Rhee's philosophy as to how to wage the fight was set forth in a long report which he sent to the provisional government on July 5, 1919. In it he urged, "Our efforts must more or less for the time being be concentrated on the United States. Effectiveness will result from concentration." Then as always he placed his chief faith in the decency and fairmindedness of the American people. His own experiences in America gave him ample evidence of the native friendliness of the people and of the strong strain of idealism which impelled them toward justice as the one dependable yardstick by which to evaluate human problems. Rhee's years of detailed study of American history had taught him that the United States again and again has gone far out of its way to assist and encourage peoples striving for freedom. And beyond this faith in the character and temperament of Americans, he was convinced by his Oriental background and studies that vast forces were stirring in the Far East which would require American intervention, for its own self-interest, eventually to prevent the planned course of Japanese aggrandizement. For all these reasons Rhee was determined that efforts to free Korea should primarily take the form of appeals to American public opinion.

In the winter of 1921-22, however, during the course of the Disarmament Conference, Rhee's chief encouragement came not from an American but from a prominent Englishman. H. G. Wells came to Washington, D. C. to write a

series of newspaper articles on the Disarmament Conference. He received—and declined—literally hundreds of invitations but accepted one from Rhee and had dinner with
him. In the course of their evening's conversation, Wells
poured out his passionate conviction that only through world
government could the human race avoid self-destruction.
Rhee found Wells genuinely receptive to his views on the
Far East and to his explanation of the role that must be
played by an independent Korean nation in maintaining
the peace in that part of the world. As Wells departed at the
end of the evening, Rhee's chief thought was that if the
statesmen who governed the destiny of nations could only
be as well grounded in history as was H. G. Wells, the decisions by which international relations are shaped might be
far wiser.

In September, 1922, Rhee returned to Hawaii. But he
was far too restless to remain. In January and February,
1924, he sailed from Hawaii to New York, via the Panama
Canal, making many stops en route to visit friends and to
plant interviews in the newspapers along the way. After
several months in Washington, he returned to Honolulu in
the late fall of 1924, and settled down uneasily to five more
years of work with his school and with the Korean Church.
In October, 1929, he set off for San Francisco on another
trip across the United States, making stops in Butte, Chicago, New York and Washington, warning all who would
listen that the Japanese were engaging in activities inside
Korea which indicated plans for some warlike move beyond
the borders. There were few, indeed, who would listen and
in January of 1930 Rhee returned once more to Hawaii.

The attack launched by Japan against Chinese forces in
Manchuria in September, 1931, was a conclusive proof of
the soundness of the warnings Rhee had been issuing. He
felt hopeful that now, at last, peace-loving peoples would
listen to his pleas that Korean independence must be re-

stored as a barrier on the Japanese pathway of aggression against the continent of Asia. Furthermore, there were more than a million Korean immigrants in Manchuria, where they had fled to escape Japanese rule. These political expatriates were certain to fare harshly under this forcible extension of Japanese power, which again had engulfed them, and as their president (whether recognized or not) Rhee felt it was his clear duty to speak out in their behalf. So once again he set forth on the weary trail to Washington, arriving there in the spring of 1932. He found, of course, that Secretary Stimson had received little support for his policy of non-recognition of Japanese conquest in Manchuria; and Rhee got even less encouragement for his pleas on behalf of the Koreans.

After consultation with the provisional government in Shanghai and the loyal Korean community in Hawaii, Rhee decided to go to Geneva to make an appeal to the delegates attending the League of Nations, where Japan's conduct in Manchuria was under discussion. Therefore, just before Christmas, 1932, he sailed for Europe and went directly to Geneva. He engaged a room at the Hotel de Russie and at once commenced a series of interviews with delegates and newsmen. On January 26 the *Journal de Geneve* carried in French a long story Rhee had prepared on the pitiful situation of the expatriate Koreans in Manchuria, who were being subjected once again to the harsh treatment of vengeful Japanese masters. On February 16 he spoke over the broadcasting facilities of the League of Nations on "Korea and the Far Eastern Dispute." The February 22 issue of *La Tribune D'Orient* carried a long front-page article on Rhee's mission, together with his picture, based on an interview with Aly El Ghaïaty. The following day *Der Bund,* a German publication in Bern, carried a similar article written by Dr. Edwin Debries. In addition to these activities directed to winning a public airing of the Korean case, Rhee wrote a long letter to Sir Eric Drummond, secretary of the League of Nations, pointing out that through restoration of Korean independence, "Japan's positive policy of military conquest in Asia will be greatly handicapped."

Despite the sympathetic interest which Rhee found in many quarters, it very soon became apparent to him that the major powers were not going to take any significant action to check Japan's program of conquest. It was not difficult to discover that England and France felt that their own interests were being served in a degree by the establishment of a Japanese threat to the continental holdings of Russia in the Far East. If the Great Bear could be worried at his rear quarters, he would be less free to extend his activities in Europe. But it was not easy, of course, to establish such a thesis as this on the basis of public records. Rhee inquired politely but urgently at the League Secretariat for a copy of the Lytton Report on Japan's seizure of Manchuria and was just as politely but very firmly refused the privilege of seeing it. He received a hint that a copy of the report might be procured through discreet inquiries in Paris, so he spent four days, March 6-9, at the Hotel Trianon Palace in that city, without success. While there Rhee received a wire from his supporters in Hawaii assuring him of funds sufficient to permit him to spend as much as a year in Geneva, continuing his work with the League. The Easter week end, April 13-17, Rhee spent in Zurich, visiting with a former student of his from Seoul, Mr. Han-ho Rhie (a noted hockey star) and his family.

Back in Geneva the latter part of that month, Rhee had what appeared to be a significant luncheon on April 25 with Prentiss Gilbert, the American consul-general, who showed a broad and encouraging understanding of the role which a free Korean nation would play in maintaining the peace of the Orient. During their luncheon, several Japanese ostentatiously took seats at a table immediately beside them, and they consequently left the hotel and drove out into the country to continue their talk. At this same period the Chinese delegation to the League expressed an interest in presenting the case of Korea to the League. However, in the usual "behind the scenes" strategy conferences arranged by the reigning powers in the League, all Rhee's efforts were blocked.

At this point, he decided to go to Moscow. For one thing, Russia was much interested in stopping the expansion of Japanese power on the North Asian mainland. For another, Rhee wanted to explore the possibility of securing the co-operation of the Korean leaders who lived in Siberia and in Moscow. Rhee went to Paris to request a visa from the Russian Ambassador, but was told he should request it in Vienna. In Vienna the Chinese Ambassador, Dr. Taung, who was an old friend of Rhee's, invited him and the Russian Ambassador to dinner at the Imperial Hotel. At this dinner Taung urged the necessity for a united front on the Asian mainland against the rising menace of Japan, and pointed out that Rhee, as the leader of the Korean people, must be a vital element in the alliance. The Soviet Ambassador Peterwsky was convinced and wired Moscow for the visa, which was granted. Rhee entrained for Moscow (having to change trains at the Russian border), travelling third class and incognito. Upon his arrival in Moscow, he was visited by a Russian official who told him the issuance of the visa was a mistake, and he must leave Russia at once. Rhee asked the Chinese Embassy to intercede, but was informed that current difficulties between Russia and China over ownership of the East China Railroad had strained the relations between the two countries. Matsuyama, head of the Japanese Railway Commission, was in Moscow supporting the Russia position on the East China Railroad, and in order not to aggravate Japan and thus lose this support the Kremlin ordered Rhee out of Russia. On such shoals was wrecked the grand design of an North Asian alliance which might have prevented the Japanese conquest of Manchuria and thereby have diverted the whole later course of the history of our times. Rhee left Russia the next day and crossed Europe by train to Nice, from which port he embarked for New York.

While at the Hotel de Russie Geneva (before the trip to Moscow) Rhee first became acquainted with Miss Francesca Donner, who was to become both his devoted wife and a dedicated champion of Korean independence. Miss Donner was the eldest of three daughters of a well-to-do iron merchant in Vienna, who reared his family with a mixture of strict discipline and wise emphasis upon their development of a sense of individual responsibility. He granted them allowances, and insisted that they live within them. He let the girls help plan their own educational and social programs, and then required them to abide by the plans. Having no sons, he taught the girls the rudiments of practical business management and masculine self-reliance. Thus it was not surprising that eldest daughter Francesca was in Geneva, serving as a secretary to the Austrian delegation to the League.

The acquaintance of Dr. Rhee and Miss Donner commenced when the Maitre d'Hotel seated Rhee one evening at the table where she was dining with her mother. Rhee found her to be familiar with the Korean question, which surprised him, for he seldom met people who were informed about the situation. She confessed she had been following all the articles recently published by and about him, and that she had been eager to meet the man who was fighting for such a selfless cause. From that time began a friendly and cordial relationship. Francesca Donner was an eager auditor for Rhee's stories of the oppression of his people. From her own Central European background she could understand their plight with full sympathy. Their friendship grew from understanding to affection and inevitably to love. Upon Rhee's return to the United States after the Moscow fiasco, he opened the Korean Commission again in Washington, and Miss Donner arranged to enter the United States under the regular Austrian immigration quota. She ran into great difficulties when she gave as her reason her intention of marrying an Oriental. Finally the problems were solved, after Dr. Rhee went to the State Department to request its help in the issuance of her visa. On October 4, 1933, she arrived in New York on the *Europa*. Four days later the wedding was performed at the Hotel Montclair, with Dr. John Haynes Holmes and Rev. P. K. Yoon jointly officiating. The vows were said in both Korean and English.

Theirs was to prove a marriage complete and effective in every respect—as fine a working comradeship as ever a marriage can be. In all the years since, Mrs. Rhee has served as her husband's secretary, housekeeper, comrade, warmest supporter, adviser, and caretaker—as well as his wife. Korea owes her more than ever will be understood, for she flatly refuses interviews, publicity and all manner of public recognition of her services. When she is urged to see some of the newspaper correspondents who have wanted to write feature articles about her, she has always waved the suggestion aside with smiling insistence. She is truly a remarkable woman who has deliberately chosen to serve her husband and his cause from the shadowy background—and there, in accordance with her own strict preference, she deserves to be left.

In September the Rhees went to Honolulu, but the following spring Rhee returned once again to Washington, like a global Paul Revere warning of the dangers that were gathering against the free world. On June 12, the Washington *Daily News* reported, "A slight, smiling figure in gray, Dr. Rhee arrived here from New York, where he has been organizing Korean and Chinese sentiment. 'I am starting a maga-

zine to be called *Orient*,' he announced. 'It will deal with
affairs in the Far East—including Japan.'" All through the
remainder of that year Rhee worked zealously, attempting
to secure funds and support for such a venture.   He found
then, however, what he observed again and again in the
following years—namely, that money and support were more
easily to be found for publications on the Far East that represent views favorable to either the Japanese or the Communists than for publications opposing either.

With some hope that the newly elected President, Franklin D. Roosevelt, might reanimate the United States and
assert a more positive influence in world affairs than had the
preceding administrations, Rhee made another tour across
the country.   On September 16, 1934, in Butte, Montana,
with his secretary, Mr. Chang Kee Young, Rhee was quoted
in the Butte *Montana Standard* as saying, "It is the duty of
every American citizen to support the program of President
Roosevelt, especially his foreign relations policies—policies
that have indicated that the United States is ready and capable of caring for itself."

The Los Angeles *Times* for September 20, 1934, carried a
story of Rhee's mission under a headline that was anything
but encouraging: "Rhee Here in Korea's Lost Cause." The
story started off, "Leader of the lost cause of the Orient, Dr.
Syngman Rhee, president of the Provisional Republic of
Korea . . . is in Los Angeles meeting with Chinese merchants
and leaders in an effort to enlist their aid in his campaign
for Korean freedom."

How little Rhee himself accepted the conclusion that his
cause was "lost" is indicated in another story in the San
Francisco *Chronicle* for December 28 of that year, which
reported that "Breathing defiance of Japan," Rhee was on
his way to an undisclosed destination across the Pacific. This
"mission across the Pacific" will be discussed a little later
in this chapter. Meanwhile, together with his wife, Rhee

arrived in Honolulu on the S.S. *Malolo* on January 25, 1935, to receive a truly royal welcome tendered by the Korean community and by many other Hawaiian friends. With an inaccuracy not always confined in the press to small matters, the *Advertiser* reported Rhee's arrival with the statement that, "He was here last in 1922 and has since been traveling on the mainland and in Europe." The *Star-Bulletin* carried a longer story setting forth Rhee's plea that the Koreans in Manchuria be allowed to hold a plebiscite to determine their status, similar to that proposed for the inhabitants of the Saar. But, as Rhee well knew, the chances for success of his plan were slight because no pressure was being exerted upon Japan to accept it.

Rhee undertook extensive speaking tours of the Hawaiian Islands, reanimating the Dong-ji Hoi and raising funds for a new Korean Church. Once again he assumed direct supervision over the Korean Christian Institute. Refusing to believe that Korean independence could ever be a dead issue, he resumed and emphasized his pleas to his compatriots that revolutionary ideas must be subordinated to diplomatic appeals and education of public opinion. In April, 1939, he set off again for Washington to resume direct charge of the Korean Commission. It was obvious that the world struggle, in both Europe and the Orient, was rushing toward a climax, and Rhee was determined to omit nothing that could be done to serve his people's claim to renewal of their independence. Again, as on many other occasions, newsmen were far more receptive to his cause than were government officials. On May 17, the well-known reporter, Edwin C. Hill, sent out a feature story through Kings Features, Inc., which was widely printed. In it he reported, "An envoy from the Japanese Embassy arrived to make polite inquiries about Dr. Rhee's plans. He replied, also politely, that his plan was to give the boot to Japan with any and all opportunities, until his people were 'no longer enslaved.'

They both bowed and the smiling visitor departed." Mr. Hill's story concluded: Rhee "has been fighting for Korean freedom for forty-five years and says he is just getting a fast running start."

At this time the Washington office of the exiled republic was called the "Korean Nationalist Mission." During this year there was considerable newspaper publicity about the independence movement. On December 10 the Washington *Post* carried an interview with Rhee in which he reported an army of 30,000 Koreans fighting against the Japanese in China, under General Lee Chung Chun. This story carries us back to the San Francisco *Chronicle* account, which has been cited earlier, of Rhee's "secret mission across the Pacific."

Rhee's relationships with the provisional government assembly and cabinet in Shanghai, during all these years of separation (following his stay there in 1920-22) were fairly close through cable and correspondence, but were not always harmonious. As has been previously indicated, there were many cliques in the government and many divergent policies. As an "absentee president" Rhee could not control the situation nearly as well as he could have had he stayed with it. This was one of the prices that had to be paid for his conviction that his best work could be done in the diplomatic centers.

Just as Rhee, from his vantage points in Washington and Geneva, naturally was continually impressed by the necessity of seeking diplomatic support, so were his governmental colleagues in China continually impressed with the desirability of revolutionary activities. They were surrounded by Chinese nationalists who were actually at war with Japan and who, of course, sought their support in disrupting Japanese supply lines and bases in Manchuria and Korea. They received many evidences of friendship from the Chinese government, including asylum and the actual donation of sums of money and military supplies. All of these factors led them to follow a course which was not only not in accord with Rhee's but which actually imperiled his policies. Much as Rhee regretted this fact, he always understood the reasons for it and submitted to the necessities of the situation. However greatly their views differed, Rhee and his governmental associates always maintained a close basic accord. They discussed their divergencies as fully as circumstances permitted and operated, whether in agreement or disagreement, with mutual respect and recognition of the reasons for the differences.

The violence they had refused to sanction in the 1919 *Mansei* demonstrations began to appear more necessary following the Tokyo earthquake of 1923. At that time, when the sympathy of the world, and particularly of the United States, was aroused on behalf of Japan, the Japanese police utilized the disrupted conditions caused by the earthquake to destroy thousands of Korean residents in Japan. In Tokyo alone 800 Koreans were invited by the Japanese to military headquarters for "protection," and every one of them was slain. In Osaka and Nagoya mass slaughters also occurred. The government spread the rumor that Koreans were poisoning the wells, and for a time no Korean in Japan was safe. On September 5 the government ordered the attacks stopped, but by that time thousands were slain and 100,000 Koreans in Japan had been driven from their homes and deprived of their properties.

In 1929 the mistreatment of Korean girls by Japanese gendarmes in Korea led to nationwide demonstrations organized by students. For several months these disturbances continued, during which time thousands of students were imprisoned and beaten. In 1930 occurred the next significant outbreaks of violence, when mobs in northeastern Korea gathered around police headquarters and other government buildings to protest the savage treatment accorded the population by the Japanese. The police fired upon them and several were killed.

While Rhee was in Geneva the provisional government commenced its first significant direction of open revolutionary activities. In China, Siberia, and Manchuria, Korean military academies were established to train soldiers, saboteurs and guerrillas. In January, 1932, a patriot youth named Yi Bong Chan was dispatched to Tokyo with the mission of assassinating the Japanese mikado. He threw a bomb into a car that was supposed to be carrying the emperor on a procession through Tokyo, but through a change of plans the emperor was riding in another vehicle. Inside Korea, eight secret societies united, under the leadership of the *Eui Yul Tan,* and pledged themselves to the liquidation of high Japanese officials. Besides the attack upon the emperor, assaults against Baron Tanaka, author of Japan's blueprint for world conquest, and upon Korea's Governor-General Saito were the most notable "near misses."

The most successful of these attacks occurred in Shanghai, on April 29, 1932, when the Japanese staged a huge demonstration to celebrate their successes in Manchuria. The chief Japanese military and political leaders in China gathered on a platform to review the triumphant parade of their troops. A youthful zealot named Yun Bong Kil, carrying a bomb in a simulated bandage on his right hand, edged through the crowd close to the platform, and tossed the bomb upon it. General Shirakawa, who had commanded the troops which captured Manchuria, was killed. Admiral Shigemitsu, a noted militarist who later became Minister of Foreign Affairs, when the Japanese militarists seized control of their home government, lost a leg. And Admiral Nomura, who lived to represent Japan in Washington during the talks which screened the attack on Pearl Harbor, lost an eye.

In 1935 some 200 armed Koreans made a foray into Korea. It was at this time that Rhee planned what the *Chronicle* called a "secret mission" to Shanghai to persuade the cabinet and the assembly of the folly of this kind of activity, which could not win Korea's independence, and which, on the contrary, merely strengthened the Japanese propaganda that Koreans needed to be held in strict subjection. From Honolulu, however, Rhee sent confidential messages ordering a discontinuance of this type of warfare and received reluctant assurances that it would be stopped. For this reason—and because of the extreme danger, if not impossibility, of his venturing into China, where the Japanese were carrying affairs with a very high hand—Rhee remained in Hawaii.

The warfare, however, could not be entirely halted. Korean grievances were too pressing and Korean sentiments of independence were too deep-seated to be held completely in check. Year after year the sabotage and guerrilla activities continued. In 1936, for example, the Japanese governor-general in Korea reported 4,474 cases of guerrilla activities involving 169,961 persons. Kim Koo, who as a youth had slain Captain Tsuchida, one of the murderers of Queen Min, had become the premier of the exiled Korean Republic's cabinet. Kim Yak San, a guerrilla leader with few peers in the world, was another of the determined leaders of the revolutionary movement in China. General Lee Chung Chun, who led the Sino-Korean Northern Route Army which opposed the Japanese most bitterly in Manchuria in 1931, was another. Such men, backed by the tempestuous and indomitable spirit of the whole Korean nation, could not be readily held in check. All that Rhee could do was to seek to modify their methods while continuing his own work of seeking for a diplomatic solution of what even his friends came to describe as a "lost cause."

Chapter IX

PEARL HARBOR
TO CAIRO

THE LATE THIRTIES were dark days for Syngman Rhee. His policy of seeking to revive his lost nation through appeals to the self-interest and good sense of the West was seemingly bankrupt. His leadership never made any deep impress on the American officials to whom he tried to appeal, and as decade piled upon decade with his program barren of results, his own following began to disintegrate. Damaging divisions developed among the expatriate Koreans, and the Korean National Association in Hawaii came into the control of men who opposed Rhee with great bitterness. A Siberian-born Korean named Kilsoo Han, who had spent much of his life in China and Japan, came to Washington and (partly because he was a new face with a fresh appeal) won the sympathetic interest of some officers in the State Department. Those who had no intention of recognizing any Korean independence claims found a new reason for rejecting them in citing the lack of unity among the Korean claimants. Rhee was denounced as stubborn, uncompromising and ambitious, and was charged with clinging to the shreds of a discredited program in the vain hope of salvaging some kind of personal advantage. His most loyal friends and supporters were weary from years of fruitless struggle and sacrifice. In those days Rhee had little but his religious faith to sustain him. He was certain that the restoration of

171

Korean independence was inevitable—because it was demanded by the logic of the Asian situation. And he was equally certain that the course he was pursuing was the best means of achieving it. Yet aside from his wife and a small handful of Korean and American friends, he was left to nurture this faith almost in solitude.

When, after the outbreak of World War II, Rhee went from Hawaii to Washington, he and his wife moved into a small two-storied red brick house on Hobart Street, on a bluff above the National Zoological Park. At night he listened to the roaring of the lions in the zoo, and felt a kinship with their frustrations. One of his relaxations was to walk around the zoo, enjoying his life-long fondness for animals. For a year or so he drove a car, but his driving was so absent-minded that his wife and friends exercised all their ingenuity to keep him from behind the wheel. Since he often drove down the middle of the street, carrying on an animated political discussion—with vigorous gestures—while approaching cars swerved out of his path, it is probably a sheer accident that he never was involved in a wreck. When his friends would remonstrate with him, he would chuckle and assure them that he had no intention of getting killed before his life's task was accomplished.

His most fruitful recreation during this period, however, was in a return to the artistic interests of his youth. As a child he had acquired a very considerable skill in Chinese calligraphy, an art which is highly valued everywhere in the East. His parents used to boast of this and it was one of their greatest satisfactions. During Rhee's childhood his mother would never permit him to lift anything heavy, or even to throw stones for great distances, for fear the delicate nerve system of his hands might be affected. In his youth, friends had tried to interest Syngman in playing the ancient Korean harp or *Kumoonko*, but he refused to learn, lest the drawing of his fingers across the taut strings might interfere with his skill in calligraphy. Then, while he was in prison, the tortures to which he was subjected left his fingers sore and clumsy. For many years he had tried again and again to regain the delicacy of control over the brush which is necessary for artistic writing of the Chinese characters. He did not succeed until the year of 1939, in Washington, when to his great joy he found his old skill restored. In all the years since, the practice of calligraphy has been his chief relaxation and delight.

His thoughts turned to scholarship also—to the lessons he had learned in his early schooling in Korea and in the American universities. To Rhee there seemed to be a pattern of inevitability in the unfolding of the international situation in Asia. Time and again during the past years he had warned that Japan was directed fundamentally by a basic philosophy of military conquest and expansion, and that her innate aggressiveness could only be checked by a restoration of Korean independence, thus confining Japan to her islands. His warnings had been dismissed as special pleading. Now, with no apparent hope of persuading the diplomats to depart from the Wilsonian formula of a Pacific built around a strong Japan, Rhee decided to write a book in which his ideas might be set forth fully enough to be convincing.

Much of 1940 was devoted to this task, resulting in a volume entitled *Japan Inside Out*, which was published early in 1941. The comment on it which Rhee liked best was the one in which Pearl Buck wrote: "There is no personal hatred toward the Japanese, but there is a sure diagnosis of the danger that such a state of mind as theirs possesses for the human race."

"Postponement is not a settlement," Rhee wrote in this prescient book. "The forest fire will not extinguish itself. It is drawing nearer day by day. Years ago you heard faint whispers of impending trouble. It was so far away. It seemed as if it might be on Mars or some other planet. Later

on, you saw columns of smoke rising at a distance, or perhaps a glow of the flames reflected on the clouds, or, at
times, even heard the roaring or crackling of burning trees.
Yet it was still far enough away to cause you no worry or
alarm. Now that is all changed. You already begin to feel
the heat. It is coming too close for your comfort. You must
move from your own home or your own business because it
is dangerous for you to ignore it longer. You must give up
the international settlements in the Orient. You must lose
your business investments, mission stations, universities, hos-
pitals, and any and all other institutions that are yours . . .
Can you still say, 'Let the Koreans, the Manchurians, and
the Chinese fight their own fight; it is none of our business'?"

After pursuing through fifteen chapters the thesis that
Japan's aggression in Asia was a threat to the entire free
world, Rhee concluded with an appeal "that the United
States should employ all her power, economical, moral, and
military, now to check Japan in order to prevent an ultimate
conflict with her." In a final argument that sounds very
much like what he later said in regard to world communism,
Rhee concluded: "I cannot persuade myself to see how you
can escape clashing with a bully by making him stronger all
the time. Is it not clear that when he becomes powerful
enough to tackle you, he will surely attack you as he has
already attacked and robbed every one of his weaker neighbors? Is it not equally clear, then, that your true policy
should be to act quickly and keep him down by force before
he grows too big, so that he can never get out of hand?"
Speaking finally of Korea, he wrote: "Her destiny cannot be
separated from that of the free peoples of the world, not
from the lot of those peoples who once knew freedom and
have lost it for a while."

These words were soon proved by Pearl Harbor to have
a real pertinence for the time in which they were penned.
They gain added interest because, in the opinion of Syng-

man Rhee, they have as true relevance today in relation to the struggle that faces all free peoples confronting the menace of Soviet communist aggression. *Postponement is not a settlement*. Although written in 1940, these words express equally well Rhee's sentiments in 1954. History has come a strange circle, with Korea in the center again, as it was before. Once again Korean patriot voices are lifted, and once again they are not heard. International problems would be more readily solved if governments, as well as individuals, could learn from experience.

December 7, 1941, "a date that will live in infamy," as President Roosevelt told the Congress, was hailed by all Korean nationalists as a fateful incident that brought the United States into the war which, to the best of their abilities, they had been waging against Japan for a generation. Rhee arranged for the provisional government in Chungking (through Prime Minister Kim Koo and Foreign Minister Cho So-ang) to send him a cabled declaration of intent to do everything the exiled republic could to assist the United States in defeating the Japanese. The Koreans felt confident that now, at last, their provisional government would be recognized, for the old argument that Japan must not be affronted could no longer apply. However, when Rhee presented the statement from his government to Dr. Stanley Hornbeck, the chief of the Office of Far Eastern Affairs in the State Department, Hornbeck received it with careful circumspection and made it very clear that he was not accepting Rhee in any degree as the representative of either a nation or a people. Rhee was treated as though he were merely an individual who had walked into the State Department to present his own personal viewpoint.

Sorely disappointed and disturbed, Rhee wired Chungking asking the assembly and cabinet to adopt a formal declaration of war against Japan, so that the exiled Korean government might properly be included among the list of states entering into the democratic alliance. This declaration, too, was ignored by State Department officials.

Rhee's secretary, Chang Kee Young, wrote to Senator Guy Gillette, with whom they had had some friendly exchanges, asking for his intercession. On December 18, 1941, Senator Gillette replied: "I have discussed the recognition of Korea as an independent political entity with the State Department. I found them sympathetic but of course no action can be taken until the exchange of diplomatic representatives and attachés between the Japanese Empire and the United States Government has been effected. You can readily see that we could not and should not take any steps to arouse resentment which might find expression in abuse or misuse of Americans still resident in the Japanese Empire."

Since the United States was at that time in a state of war with Japan, Rhee found this determination not to "take any steps to arouse resentment" an attitude extremely difficult to understand. In company with John W. Staggers and Jay Jerome Williams, Rhee visited Senator Gillette in his office on December 22 to make sure there was no misunderstanding. The senator asked Rhee not to make any formal request that the Provisional Republic of Korea be recognized by the United States, for if such a request should be granted the Japanese would be offended and would find some means of retaliation. (On that very day three separate Japanese armies were sweeping almost unopposed through the Philippine Islands, converging upon Manila, where General MacArthur was without any effective means of defense.) Rhee said to Senator Gillette with great seriousness, "In that case, the war is lost. How can you fight the war without offending the Japanese?" Senator Gillette replied, "I have but told you what the State Department has said."

This interview with Senator Gillette was a staggering blow. Of course Rhee had been disappointed not to receive immediate recognition from the State Department after the

Following a strategy conference in 1951, President Rhee (with his faithful dog, Happy) is shown with Lt. General James A. Van Fleet, General Matthew B. Ridgway, U.S. Ambassador John J. Muccio and Lt. General John B. Coulter. *(ROK O.P.I.)*

attack on Pearl Harbor. However, Dr. Hornbeck had at least indicated that the Koreans' case was under consideration. Rhee had received a somewhat more cordial reception upon his call at the Department of War, where he left a statement indicating the desire to do all the Koreans could to help militarily. Following his talks with Army representatives, he wrote on December 17 to Dr. Hornbeck as follows:

"Yesterday afternoon I had a very interesting conversation with Major Wallace H. Moore of the Army Intelligence Service. He said it was at your suggestion that the Army wants to find out what they can do to help Korea. He said he would do all that he could to secure aid for the Koreans fighting in China." The letter went on to quote a cablegram from the Korean Republic Cabinet in Chungking stating that it had formally declared war against Japan, in order to qualify (as it hoped) for Lend-lease aid, and citing the fact that the Chinese government had formally recognized the role of the Korean army—which numbered 30,000 men, and which was equipped and supplied largely by Chiang Kai-shek.

This letter was not acknowledged and, after the talk with Senator Gillette, Rhee knew that it would not be. Actually, his efforts to win a recognition of the part Korea could play in the struggle against Japan had come to a head as early as June 6, 1941, at which date he addressed a long letter to President Roosevelt, together with a copy of credentials from the provisional government, setting forth in detail what Koreans could do to help undermine the vital Japanese position in Korea. A week later Rhee received a reply from Dr. Hornbeck, rejecting his offer of aid, and concluding, "We are still technically on friendly terms with Japan." Now it appeared that these same "friendly terms" were to be maintained—at least so far as Japanese claims upon Korea were concerned—after Japan and the United States were at war.

On January 2, 1942 Rhee had an appointment with Mr.

Alger Hiss, who served as a direct representative of Secretary Hull in discussing many Far Eastern policy questions. Soon after Rhee entered Hiss's office, Dr. Hornbeck called them both in to join him, and the three of them discussed the Korean situation for more than an hour. Rhee explained in detail what Koreans might do to assist in the defeat of Japan, and pointed out that they could develop their potentialities for sabotage and guerrilla activities only if their government were recognized, assisted with economic and military aid, and integrated into the general plans of the top command. The two men listened attentively, occasionally asking questions for clarification. Finally, Mr. Hiss declared that since Rhee's proposals involved a recognition of the Korean government, there was little or nothing the United States could do. To recognize an independent Korean government at that stage, he said, could offend the Soviet Union, which had a great interest in north Asia. To raise any political questions concerning that area, at that time, was premature, he declared, for the Soviet Union could not enter into such discussions—not being at war with Japan—yet its interests could not be ignored or circumvented. Rhee left this meeting believing sorrowfully that this young man with such great power was exercising very bad judgment. It did not occur to him to think that Hiss might be dedicated to serving Russian rather than American interests.

However discouraging the appearances, Rhee continued his efforts, writing on February 7, 1942, to Secretary of State Cordell Hull. To this letter he received on February 19 the following reply from Assistant Secretary of State Adolf Berle:

"Reference is made to your letter to the Secretary of State of February 7, 1942, with which there were enclosed a document addressed to the President of the United States dated June 6, 1941, a document addressed to the Secretary of State bearing the same date and a document entitled CREDEN-TIALS also dated June 6, 1941.

"As you are no doubt aware, the Department has stated in an announcement of its policy toward the activities of foreign political leaders in the United States that it is glad to be informed of the plans and proposed activities of organizations of aliens in this country who wish to assist in the struggle against Axis domination of the world. Accordingly, the Department is glad to be informed of the activities of Koreans who are assisting in the task of defeating Japan and her allies and, consequently, is making note of the information conveyed in the document under reference regarding the plans and objectives of the organization to which they relate.

"For your convenience there is enclosed herewith a copy of the Department's press release of December 10, 1941 in which there is set forth a statement of the Department's policy in matters of this kind."

To this communication Rhee replied on March 14, writing to Secretary Hull, and reviewing the preceding correspondence. His letter then continued:

"May I respectfully suggest that the matters accompanying my communication of February 7 do not seem to fall within the purview either of the reply of Mr. Berle or the press release referred to.

"The Provisional Government of the Republic of Korea is the sole representative of the Korean people, whether they are resident in Korea proper, Manchuria, Siberia, China or elsewhere, and regards itself, on the basis of the treaty of 1882, negotiated between the Government of Korea and the Government of the United States, not as a free movement in any sense whatever of that phrase, but as the only government agency of Korea that is in existence.

"It is the desire of my Government to be advised how the Government of the United States regards the aforementioned treaty between the two countries. It is the plea of my Government that the existence of this treaty be noted by the Government of the United States, for anything to the contrary would seem to further countenance the act of wanton aggression perpetrated by the Japanese Government upon the people of Korea."

To this letter Rhee received no reply. However, his appeals directed to Attorney General Francis Biddle, on behalf of the Korean nationals resident in Hawaii and in the continental United States, achieved a more favorable result. On February 9, 1942, Attorney General Biddle issued a statement specifically exempting from restrictions placed on enemy aliens all "Austrians, Austro-Hungarians and Koreans who registered *as such* under the Alien Registration Act of 1940 and who have not since that time voluntarily become citizens or subjects of Germany, Italy, or Japan.

"Such aliens," the statement continued, "are *not* required to surrender cameras, radios, or other articles prohibited to alien enemies; are *not* restricted as to travel or place of residence; are *not* required to secure certificates of identification; and are *not* required to observe other restrictions or regulations prescribed for aliens of German, Italian, or Japanese nationality. This exemption is designed to exempt the many thousand loyal aliens of Austrian, Austro-Hungarian, and Korean nationality who have never been sympathetic to the government imposed upon their homelands by military conquest."

Korean nationality! This was the phrase Rhee and his associates long had been struggling to have uttered by friendly governments! The attorney general's statement seemed to be a clear and unequivocal acceptance of the *de facto* existence of a Korea free from Japanese rule. With this encouragement he and his friends rallied and commenced a fresh campaign. On March 6, 1942, the Reverend Frederick Brown Harris, Minister of the Foundry Methodist

Church in Washington along with Mr. John Staggers and Mr. Jay Jerome Williams, in their capacity as trustees of the Korean-American Council, addressed a long communication to President Roosevelt. This communication set forth as persuasively as they could the major points in the case for immediate recognition of the Korean government, and for integration of Korean war efforts with those of the united allies.

They pointed out, in the letter, that the Koreans impressed into the Japanese army or conscripted as a labor force constituted fertile ground for psychological warfare appeals, and that the Korean expatriates in China, who already had organized an army of more than 30,000 men, would have the strongest motives to fight for the liberation of their homeland if they were given equipment and were integrated under the allied command. "Here is the moment for a tremendously effective political offensive," they concluded, "for who are better able to refute Japan's claims of establishing a new order in Asia than that new order's first victims, the Korean people?"

But however convincing this statement appeared to its sponsors, no answer was forthcoming. Rhee's diplomatic approaches were impeded by the efforts of Korean Communists and opportunists who were seeking to utilize the war that had broken out to establish a leadership of their own in relation to Korea. The most voluble and impressive of the new claimants was Kilsoo Han, as mentioned previously, who came to Washington declaring that he represented 300,000 Koreans in Japan, who were engaged as street-sweepers and in other menial positions which gave them entry into vital Japanese buildings and restricted areas. He claimed also to represent the Black Dragon Society in Tokyo, a secret brotherhood which was in a position to get strategic information on war plans. From time to time Kilsoo Han represented that he was in receipt of secret war data and offered to the State Department figures which it had no way of checking. By such means he won a degree of confidence in the lower echelons of the State and War Departments. He used this influence to undermine Rhee and the provisional government, stating that Rhee and his associates had been so long out of Korea (Kilsoo Han himself had not been in Korea since he was nine years old) that they no longer represented the people there and were, in fact, unknown to them.

In the latter part of 1942, Rhee was flatly informed by Dr. Hornbeck that in the opinion of the State Department he was wholly unknown inside Korea and the provisional government was no more than a self-constituted club with limited membership among a group of expatriates. Rhee and his friends gave very thoughtful consideration to this development and wondered if, in fact, the total failure of the State Department to take advantage of all the aid Korea could offer might be due to a reasonable skepticism of the validity of Rhee's position. Mr. Staggers offered a method of counteracting such doubt. It was obviously impossible to take a poll of Koreans inside Korea, and the opinions of the substantial majority of Koreans in the United States had already been ignored. Similarly, the *de facto* recognition accorded to the provisional government by China had not proved to be convincing to the State Department officials. Mr. Staggers suggested that one body of witnesses did exist whose testimony could scarcely be doubted. This was the group of American missionaries who had served in Korea and had been forced out by the Japanese during 1940 and 1941. They constituted the only group of Americans who had any way of knowing the real sentiments of the Korean people. Since they all had learned the Korean language and had lived on close terms with the people, and since their character and probity were above reproach, they seemed to be witnesses whose word would carry great weight.

Accordingly, Mr. Staggers undertook the arduous task of getting from the Methodist, Presbyterian and Catholic Churches and from the Y. M. C. A. the names and present addresses of as many of these missionaries as could then be located. With this information at hand, he addressed to them an objective questionnaire, requesting them to list the names of Korean leaders upon whom the Korean people depended to represent them politically. As the answers came back, the name of Syngman Rhee was almost the only one listed and it was supplied by almost every missionary who replied. With these data in hand, Mr. Staggers called upon Dr. Hornbeck and placed the papers on his desk. Dr. Hornbeck said that he would soon find an opportunity to read them. "No," Mr. Staggers declared, "I have gone to great trouble and expense to gather this information and I intend to sit right here while you take the necessary time to read through these documents." Dr. Hornbeck assented and for almost an hour went through the pile of responses, studying each one carefully. Finally he put them down and said uneasily that they appeared to be a substantial body of testimony and would merit the most earnest consideration by the Department. More than that he would not say, but Mr. Staggers left his office convinced that the fears of the State Department concerning Rhee's status, if indeed the officials actually had such fears, must now be allayed.

It was about this time that my own relations with Dr. Rhee began. My first meeting with him occurred in late August, 1942, at a luncheon to which Rhee and I were invited by our mutual friend, Reverend Edward Junkin, a Presbyterian minister who had been born in Korea. (The meeting place was the commonplace setting of a cafeteria on Connecticut Avenue, in Washington.) Rhee was dressed plainly, and his manner was agreeable and friendly; he seemed eager to please. But although there was nothing outwardly impressive about him, we had not talked long together before the magnetism of his personality was evident. He talked of Korea with earnestness and conviction, yet with the saving grace of humor and with a broad understanding of related world problems which removed him at once from the category of a zealot. Nevertheless, the facts he related of Korea's plight under Japan and of the determined fight of the provisional government to restore the nation's independence were arresting. I asked why he did not write up this story of Korea for the American public, and he replied, "I am not a writer; why don't you?" Thereupon commenced an acquaintance which brought me into increasingly intimate association with the further developments in Dr. Rhee's struggle for the re-establishment of his nation.

In February or March of 1943 I went to the Office of War Information and talked to Dr. Harold M. Vinacke, head of the Far Eastern Division (of which the field operational head was Owen Lattimore, operating out of San Francisco). Vinacke listened to the plea that Rhee be provided with facilities for making radio appeals to the Korean people to prepare for sabotage and other disruptive activities against the Japanese, and then asked coldly, "Do you honestly believe that anyone in Korea even knows who Syngman Rhee is?" I left his office wondering how American foreign policy possibly could be directed realistically by men who were so little informed of the essential facts. Yet from decisions such as that of the OWI there was no appeal.

At about this same time Rhee was advised by Major Wallace H. Moore of Army Intelligence to talk with Colonel M. Preston Goodfellow, who was on the staff of "Wild Bill" Donovan, chief of the Office of Strategic Services. Colonel Goodfellow was most cordial and receptive and fully agreed with Rhee that it would be a serious mistake for the United States to fail to take advantage of any aid the Koreans could offer. He said that even though the Korean government was not recognized by the United States, the War Department could "recognize" the leaders of the group sufficiently to develop some plan of co-operation. Together Rhee and Goodfellow worked out a plan by which Rhee should seek to gather a group of one hundred young Koreans who knew both the Korean and Japanese languages well enough to enable them to go about freely in Japan and Korea without being suspected of being outsiders. With such a group assembled, they could be secretly trained and at an opportune time could be parachuted into either Japan or Korea to develop a program of active sabotage and to establish contact with members of nationalist underground clubs within Korea which could assist them. Rhee agreed, on condition that he might be one of those parachuted into Korea.

Recruitment of such a group of Korean youths from among the second and third generations of Koreans in the United States proved to be exceedingly difficult, for few of them knew their own Korean language with sufficient exactness and fluency, and even fewer could pass muster in the Japanese language. Yet, since every Korean in Korea was forced to use the Japanese language, such bilingualism was a necessary qualification. Eventually Rhee got together a group of qualified Korean men and their training commenced. Through all the remainder of the war they awaited the time when this body of men could be utilized, together with another group of Koreans given similar training in China. However, as the plans for the defeat of Japan were developed, the campaign was directed up through the Pacific Islands, rather than calling for a landing on the northern Chinese coast. Consequently the Allied war plans never required the disruption of Japanese supply lines through Korea, and the Korean volunteers were not utilized.

Rhee's work with Colonel Goodfellow, however, was undertaken with great enthusiasm and hopefulness. On December 7, 1942, Rhee wrote to President Roosevelt, commenting on the anniversary of the "date of infamy," and informing him that "December 7 as of this year marks the beginning of the training of Korean nationals for warfare against the Japanese by the American War Department. The number is small, but the purpose, my dear Mr. President, is to make use eventually of the vast reservoir of Korean manpower in Asia to defeat the island savages."

At the end of November, 1942, Rhee received from Dr. Victor Hoo, Chinese Under-secretary of State for Foreign Affairs, a request for clarification of the aims and purposes of the Korean Provisional Government, and on December 5 Rhee wrote Hoo a letter which may be quoted as summarizing the policies and philosophy which governed his thinking:

My dear Dr. Hoo:

I am glad to respond to your request transmitted to me by Mr. John W. Staggers.

The immediate aim of the Provisional Government of the Republic of Korea is more actively to assist the United Nations in the war against Japan by:

(1) Adequately equipping the Korean National Army with weapons of warfare;

(2) Augmenting that army through accessions from the substantial reservoir of Korean manpower in the Far East;

(3) Establishing an espionage service both without and within Korea so that effective sabotage and revolutionary activities may be undertaken against the enemy.

I need not emphasize to you, my dear Dr. Hoo, the centuries' old and justifiable hatred of the Japanese by the Koreans, our ceaseless warfare against them during the past 37 years, the admitted skill of the Korean both as a regular and guerrilla soldier, and our earnest desire to play a major role in crushing Japanese militarism, routing the tyrant from our homeland and instituting a democracy for the 23,000,000 enslaved Koreans.

You have been advised by American military authorities of the first initial steps to implement our aim but much remains to be done and every moment is now precious. With vigorous Chinese-American collaboration, the military potential of the Korean nation can soon be realized to the immense benefit of our common cause where, as you know, nearly one year since Pearl Harbor has been permitted to elapse and this potential consequently has been virtually paralyzed.

The ultimate aim of the Korean Provisional Government is the complete demilitarization of Japan. Thereafter, the following:

(1) Banishment to Japan of all her nationals now resident in Korea.

(2) Return to Korea of all Korean national now held in serfdom in Japan proper.

(3) Search and recovery of all Korean books, records and works of art looted by the Japanese.

(4) Rigid restriction of Japanese fisheries, navigation (sea and aerial) and commerce.

(5) Return of Tsushima Island.

(6) An indemnity from Japan sufficient to cover her pillaging of Korean resources during the 37 years of occupation, as well as the damages which will result from the forthcoming military action in our country.

It is the purpose of the Korean Government, once the homeland is regained, to purge our nation of all Japanese influence, establish law and order, institute democratic processes, and to call for a general election wherein all adults—male and female—may exercise the rights of suffrage.

In the new world that will emerge from this war, a free, strong and democratic Korea can be one of the most powerful assurances of peace in the Far East.

Korea, even today, with more than one million Christians, is Christianity's greatest bastion in the Orient. And, as the future aerial gateway to Asia, it would fulfill a great role as the crucible for the tenets of Confucius and the teachings of Christ.

Korea, resuming her rightful place in the family of nations, will need the assistance of her age-old friend, China; material support and capital from America, and the understanding and friendship of her great neighbor, Russia.

Down through the 42 centuries of our existence as a nation, the Korean people have made priceless contributions to civilization—the magnetic compass, the first moveable type, the Orient's first alphabet, solar observatory, etc., etc.,—yet the industrial revolution caught us unaware but gave the imitative Japanese their chance. We are passing through Gethsemane but our will to fight for freedom and our belief that that great document, the Atlantic Charter, should apply to us now, can be our resurrection.

On December 7 Rhee sent a copy of this letter to Secretary of State Cordell Hull, so that the United States government would be equally informed of his program. A few weeks later he wrote to Hull, once again calling to his attention (as he had to Hornbeck and Hiss) Russian ambitions in Korea. He warned Hull again, as he had more than a year earlier, that failure to recognize the Provisional Republic of Korea would inevitably "result in the creation of a communist state" on the Korean peninsula. He concluded, "May I not beseech you again, my dear Mr. Hull, for the opportunity to come by and talk to you personally?" The letter went unanswered.

In view of such correspondence as this, besides Rhee's numerous personal appeals at the State Department for Korea to be allowed to take an active role in the war, he was both surprised and embittered when Secretary Hull made his widely publicized statement that no people which had failed to fight for its own liberties could expect American aid. Korea was obviously included in his category of "peoples who did not fight," and Rhee thought this reference was wholly unjust.

From Secretary of War Henry Stimson Rhee received somewhat greater satisfaction. Despite Attorney General Biddle's ruling exempting Koreans from restrictions applied to enemy aliens, the Army officers stationed in Hawaii persisted in many instances in lumping Koreans together with the Islands' Japanese. On March 30, 1943, Rhee wrote to Secretary Stimson, citing many such instances, and calling his attention both to Mr. Biddle's ruling and to the state of war existing between the exiled Korean government and

Japan. Rhee received from him the following reply, dated April 30:

I regret that necessary investigations have occasioned a delay in replying fully to your letter of March thirtieth, acknowledgement of which was made by the Adjutant General on April sixth.

The War Department has issued instructions to all field commanders to inform all concerned that Koreans who registered as such under the Alien Registration Act of 1940, and who have not, since that time, voluntarily become citizens or subjects of enemy nations, shall be exempt from restrictions imposed upon enemy aliens. Field commanders have been directed to examine into the handling of the matters brought out in your communication and to take immediate action to correct any injustice done to your countrymen and their descendants.

I am fully appreciative of the feelings of the many loyal Koreans now resident in this country who have never been in sympathy with the government imposed upon their homeland by military conquest. I am convinced that, by and large, these people are sincere believers in democracy and are loyal to the United States.

I thank you for bringing this matter to my attention and I would appreciate knowing of any subsequent difficulties experienced by Korean nationals or soldiers of Korean parentage.

Naturally Rhee appreciated the friendly and understanding tone of this communication. Actually, arrests of Koreans and enforcement of restrictions against them continued to occur under the jurisdiction of General Emmons, the military governor of Hawaii. When two of Rhee's countrymen were arrested in midsummer of 1943 for "violation" of the 8:00 P.M. curfew (which applied solely to enemy aliens) Rhee once again wrote to Secretary Stimson, and on July 7 received his renewed assurances that such restrictions would not be applied against Koreans. The fact that the Koreans in Hawaii nevertheless continued to be subjected to "alien enemy" regulations from time to time was ameliorated by their knowledge that Secretary Stimson was doing what he could in their behalf.

On July 12, 1943, Rhee received a letter from Assistant Secretary of State Adolf Berle, pointing out "that numerous and generous concessions have been made by various agencies of this Government to Koreans not only in continental United States but also in the Hawaiian Islands." Since Rhee felt that Koreans must of necessity be classified as either friends or enemies, he could not preceive the logic of "generous concessions" which fell short of recognizing that Koreans were independent of Japanese sovereignty. Rhee wanted Korean nationals in America to be treated as well as possible, but this treatment fell so far short of recognizing their nationalistic rights that he was far from satisfied.

It was not until the convening of the Cairo Conference, in November, 1943, that Korea's claim to independence received a hearing. Then, at the suggestion of Chiang Kai-shek (who had already extended *de facto* recognition to the Korean Provisional Government) Roosevelt and Churchill agreed to take formal cognizance of Korean claims. On December 1 the Big Three issued a statement which read in part, "Mindful of the enslavement of the Korean people, the aforementioned three Great Powers are determined that Korea shall, in due course, be free and independent."

Rhee was alarmed by the phrase, "in due course," which could mean the indefinite postponement of independence. He issued a series of statements condemning this restrictive phrase and addressed letters to President Roosevelt and to the United States' State Department asking for a clarification of its intent. No answers were received and the phrase was left suspended in the midst of the Cairo Declaration "charter of freedom," always threatening to blot out its essential meaning.

The year of 1943 ended on at least one note of hopefulness. Mr. Sumner Welles, who had been eased out of the

State Department because of his disagreements with Mr. Hull, but who presumably retained considerable influence with both President Roosevelt and the American people, wrote in his syndicated newspaper column: "With the restoration of Korean independence, one of the great crimes of the twentieth century will have been rectified, and another stabilizing factor will have been added to the new international system which must be constructed in the Pacific."

This statement by Mr. Welles neatly summarized much that Rhee had been saying for many years. As Rhee read it, meditated upon the source from which it came, and reflected on the number of newspapers in which it was published, he took renewed hope that the great spirit of justice and sympathetic understanding which he knew to be characteristic of the American people would assert itself effectively on behalf of Korea when eventually peace should be restored. At the very least, regardless of the dangerous qualification inserted in the Cairo pledge, Korean claims had finally been recognized by the major powers and the restoration of Korean independence had been pledged. In view of the many years of fruitless struggle the Korean patriots had had to endure, the Cairo statement loomed as a tremendously significant landmark on their road to national redemption.

Chapter X

A NEW ENEMY—
NEW INTRIGUES

SYNGMAN RHEE's struggles and difficulties during the many years he strove to counteract Japanese aggressive designs against Korea seem almost simple in retrospect as compared with his problems of dealing with the rising menace of Soviet ambitions in Korea. Russian designs upon the strategic Korean peninsula were not new in his experience. During his youthful leadership of the Independence Club, before the opening of the twentieth century, Russia had been one of the powers most persistently attempting to subvert the weakened and inept Korean monarchy. The last Korean emperor had spent an entire year in the shelter of the Russian Embassy in Seoul, protecting himself from Japan at the expense of yielding to the dominance of the Czar's ambassador, M. Waeber. The Russo-Japanese War, fought while Rhee was held in a Seoul prison, and the Portsmouth Treaty, which he had tried so hard to alter, marked a titanic (if unsuccessful) effort by the Russians to sweep Korea into their empire.

Rhee's studies in Far Eastern history had made him aware at an early age of the drive to the Pacific which had given Russia control of the Siberian Maritime Provinces in 1854, and which subsequently had led to the penetration of Russian influence into Manchuria. Rhee well understood Rus-

sia's need for adequate Pacific seaports (since Vladivostok
freezes up in the winter) and the consequent Russian hunger for control of Hamhung, Wonsan, and other Korean
warm water harbors. Similarly, Russia long had eyed greed-
ily north Korea's timber, coal, iron, and gold resources.
Moreover, Russian strategists have understood (as Western
statesmen until recently have not) that Korea lies at the
heart of the strategic triangle of North Asia and that a
strong power in control of Korea would be able to dominate
or at least threaten Japan, Manchuria and Siberia. For all
these reasons, before the end of the Russo-Japanese War
(1905), Clifton Breckinridge, the U. S. ambassador to Moscow, wrote to the State Department: "Korea and the country
around Peking, one or both," are the areas that "clearly meet
the requirements" of Russia in North Asia. And Czar Nicholas II made the Russian aim specific in a note he sent to
his Foreign Minister at about the same time: "Russia absolutely needs a port free and open throughout the whole year.
This port must be located on the mainland (southeast Korea)
and must certainly be connected with our possessions by a
strip of land."

The seizure of Korea by Japan—as a protectorate in 1905,
and through outright annexation in 1910—pushed the Russian threat into the background for a full generation. Indeed, the Bolshevik Revolution, occurring just before the
Mansei demonstrations in 1919, created a surface appearance of brotherhood between the Korean patriots and the
new communist Soviet state. After Japan's conquest of
Manchuria in 1931, the Soviets and the Korean expatriates
had a common enemy and fought battles together against
the Japanese in the borderlands of Manchuria and Siberia.
Several Korean patriots went to Moscow for their education, and a Korean branch of the communist party was organized in China. By 1942, Syngman Rhee was quarreling
openly with Kim Koo, the new premier of the Korean Pro-

visional Government in Chungking, because Kim Koo insisted on admitting communists into the cabinet. The Korean National Revolutionary Party (communist) in December, 1941, soothingly adopted a manifesto promising to support the Korean Provisional Government, "because the democratic countries of the world have now formed an anti-Fascist bloc and gone to war with the Fascist powers," and calling for a "representative assembly of all revolutionary organizations."

Although shortly after Pearl Harbor Senator Guy Gillette told Dr. Rhee that the State Department was withholding recognition from the Provisional Republic of Korea in order "not to offend the Japanese," Rhee realized within a few months that this reason could surely no longer apply. Yet the doors of the State Department remained closed to him and other Korean patriots as tightly as ever. It was not hard for him to deduce that the real reason was a determination not to affront Russia. When he talked to Alger Hiss and was assured that any solution of the Korean question would have to wait upon a postwar conference with the Soviet Union, he had no suspicion of how definitely communist influences had crept into the very confines of the State Department itself. But he did know that Secretary Cordell Hull had no intention of satisfying Korean claims for independence at the risk of disturbing the war strategists in the Kremlin.

Early in 1943 the London correspondent of the Chicago Sun reported that Anthony Eden had discussed with President Roosevelt the possibility that Korea might be absorbed into the Soviet Union. Cordell Hull, in his Memoirs, reports that on March 27, 1943, President Roosevelt suggested to him "that Korea might be placed under an international trusteeship, with China, the United States, and one or two other countries participating." Although Rhee had no way of knowing what was being said behind the closed doors of the world's chancelleries, he was deeply disturbed. An article published in the June, 1943, issue of *World Affairs* raised a question he was much concerned about at that time: "Why, one may ask, should the State Department treat Korea differently from the other governments-in-exile? The reason cannot be willful obtuseness—nor a love of Japan—nor any special anti-Korean bias. It cannot be the reasons which the State Department has officially given, for it has ample precedents for contrary action. Then why is Korea singled out for special rejection? The answer which any impartial examiner will find is—Russia." In the spring of 1945, Dr. Rhee circulated a pamphlet, "The Case for Korea," in which the following appeared as one reason why the Provisional Republic of Korea had not been recognized: "In view of the anxiety in some quarters to get Russia into the Asiatic War, recognition may have been withheld pending a clearer formulation of Russia's desires in regard to Korea. If this were a factor, it represented either a crass willingness to trade the independence of a small nation for the support of a large one, or a timid fear of developing any foreign policy until we were able to ascertain that it would please a powerful ally. Either motive would be one we should not expect to be avowed."

What is perfectly clear from the record is that long before the Western world was aware of the rising danger of Soviet imperialism, Rhee well understood that Russian ambitions were pointed toward Korea and that the United States Department of State was committed to a policy of at least partial (if reluctant) acquiescence in this aim. In the summer of 1943 the badly muddled and divided Chinese government got into the act. Rhee's Korean Commission office in Washington prepared a blueprint of the Korean underground organization and dispatched it to President Roosevelt. At a meeting of the Pacific War Council Roosevelt asked China's Foreign Minister, T. V. Soong (who was then in Washington) for his estimate of the worth of the Korean movement. Dr. Victor Hoo, Soong's assistant, asked Rhee and other members of the Korean Commission to form a coalition with Kilsoo Han (then a favorite of several State Department officials), thus uniting their divergent forces. Rhee replied that Han represented very few Koreans and that in his judgment to unite with Han would have no other effect than to encourage the Korean communists. In the subsequent meeting of the Pacific War Council, Soong reported to Roosevelt that the Koreans were too disunited to comprise any effective force. This is the same Soong who, in August, 1945, went to Moscow and signed a treaty handing over control of Dairen, Port Arthur and the South Manchuria Railway to the Soviet Union.

At the time of the organizational meeting of the United Nations in San Francisco, in April, 1945, Syngman Rhee wrote as follows in a memorandum addressed to his friends: "I knew that the shadow of Joseph Stalin loomed large at the Cairo meeting, even though he was not physically present—that Russian ambitions in the Pacific were receiving full consideration. I knew that England was fighting to maintain what holdings and status she could in the Orient, and I feared that the spirit of expediency and compromise which had led to the closing of the Burma Road in 1941 (leaving Chiang Kai-shek cut off from desperately needed supplies at a crucial period of his struggle for China's survival) might lead to similarly harsh decisions in respect to North Asia. I knew that the doors of the State Department were as tightly closed to me and to my pleas for recognition of the provisional government as before Cairo. I knew that my repeated attempts to have Korea numbered among the United Nations and to be considered as a worthy ally and recipient of lend-lease aid went unheeded. It was evident that the Cairo pledge was rendered deliberately ambiguous in order to keep the Korean question open for later decision. And it was also clear that the chief reason for this ambiguity was the undefined position Russia was preparing to assume in Asia. __

"My lifelong studies in international relations had dealt with Europe as well as with Asia. My travels in Europe also tended to sharpen my awareness of the significance of the trend of events in that part of the world. It was obvious that the nationalistic guerrillas operating in southeastern Europe were themselves divided into two groups—communist and noncommunist. When Roosevelt and Churchill agreed not to invade the European continent through the Balkans, it was also apparent that an agreement had been reached to leave this area primarily to Soviet influence. England's desperate efforts to aid the Greeks constituted a limitation of this policy and emphasized the need for Great Britain to protect its Mediterranean life line by keeping a friendly government in Greece. But the effective prohibition of any discussion of the communist problems presented by this and other areas (lest Russia be offended) prevented the development of policies adequate to safeguard southeastern Europe. In northern Europe Finland had prejudiced its position by fighting against Russia and by assisting Germany (though only in a desperate effort to maintain its own independence) and in Poland the Soviet occupation of eastern Poland gave communism a great advantage for exploitation of Russia's design of expansion.

"What was gradually unfolding in regard to Europe was much more open and apparent in China. There the Allies were insisting that the Nationalist government cease its opposition to the communists (who were openly in revolt against it, and who maintained a separate army and a separate government of their own) and accept a compromise coalition. It was evident that President Roosevelt's policy of 'unconditional surrender' by the Rome-Berlin-Japanese

Axis was being paralleled by another policy of Allied acquiescence in the essential pattern of Russian imperialism.

"My argument during the closing years of the war was that recognition of the Republic of Korea-in-exile was an effective means (and the only effective means) of blocking Soviet seizure of Korea. To the retort that the provisional government had been so long and so far removed from Korea that it no longer represented the people, and that it would be better to await the end of the war, at which time an election could be held in Korea to establish a new government, I replied that the Republic might be granted merely provisional recognition, with the understanding that an election under Allied supervision might be held as soon as Korea should be liberated. This point of view was presented over and over again by myself and my friends, in talks at the State Department, in news conferences, in radio talks, and in magazine articles written by some of our associates. However, I never received any indication that it was even considered by the higher levels of government. Reluctantly I came to the conclusion that President Roosevelt and Prime Minister Churchill had decided that Korea should have a government which would be independent only in form, but that actually it would be under the control of the Soviet Union."

As has happened many other times in his life, Rhee suffered by arriving at these views years before others in positions of power came to share them. Among the Koreans in the United States there were many (including the leadership of the Korean National Association) who came to believe the only "practical" solution for Korea would be a communist coalition government. These leaders represented themselves as "realists" and denounced Rhee as being "stubbornly unrealistic." They won some support from Dr. George McCune, head of the Korean desk in the State Department, who had been born and reared in Pyengyang and favored a north Korean leadership for the country.

When the San Francisco Conference was called, Rhee determined to do everything possible to utilize the occasion to secure a dependable guarantee of Korean independence. He called together all the leaders of the dissident Korean factions, established headquarters in the Maurice Hotel, and pleaded with them to stand together on a simple program of absolute independence for Korea, with the question of leadership to be decided later. A tenuous agreement to this effect was reached, and in the name of the United Korean Committee Dr. Rhee asked Alger Hiss for status as an observer representing Korea. This request was refused. At this point Dr. T. V. Soong of China again entered the picture. He invited the Koreans to a dinner on May 22 with the avowed purpose of drawing them together to support a program of coalition for Korea. In a memorandum dated June 11, 1945, Dr. Rhee declared that "McCune, together with Dickover and Ballentine in the State Department, joined with Dr. Soong in support of the coalitionists." Rhee refused to attend the dinner; the Korean National Association group withdrew from his delegation and set up separate headquarters in Los Angeles.

Early in May, Rhee was visited by a Russian who had left the communist party, and who convinced Rhee that he had authentic information of a secret agreement made at Yalta to turn Korea over to Russian control. On May 14 Rhee sent the following telegram to Senators Owen Brewster and Walter F. George and to Congressman Clare E. Hoffman:

"On advice of your friends here I am wiring you following information which calls for statesmen of courage to disclose to the American people. President Truman has been informed of secret agreement at Yalta which turns Korea over to Russian domination. We are positive of our source of information on this agreement, which we uncovered here. Secret agreement signed by United States, Great Britain and Russia, declaring Korea will remain in orbit of Soviet influence until after end of Japanese war and further declared United States and Great Britain shall make no commitments to Korea until after the Japanese war has ended. All this was signed at Stalin's request at Yalta. I respectfully call your attention to significance of this agreement compared with Cairo Declaration promising Korea her freedom. This secret agreement is now preventing Korea from becoming member of United Nations in San Francisco Conference . . . Facts we have uncovered plainly indicate Russia wants no democracy in Far East. This policy will end Korea unless America decides there is a limit to Russia's demands. Stettinius refused to discuss barring of Korea and is pleading for time to look up background. I am informed President Truman at first did not know of this agreement. He has been seen at White House about this matter and is being urged by freedom-loving Americans to intervene so that Korea may take her rightful place as member of the United Nations Conference. Every minute counts to save freedom of Korea now and I appeal to your sense of American justice to exert your influence to right this wrong."

When the legislators made no reply to this appeal, Rhee called a press conference and stated his charge of a "secret deal" publicly. News from U. N. organizational conference was scarce at the time, and newsmen gave these charges a wide coverage. The State Department in Washington released a formal repudiation. Rhee repeated his charge, and this time the White House issued a denial. By this time news coverage of Rhee's successive statements was considerable, and in the House of Commons in London Churchill was asked whether there was substance in the charge that the Big Three had entered into "secret agreements" at Yalta. Churchill replied that there were no secret agreements, but that many subjects had been discussed and some general understandings had been reached. It is almost a certainty that the 38th parallel division of Korea was among those "general understandings." Rhee's charge of a "deal" on Korea received no further official notice, nor was there any foreshadowing from Allied sources of the division of Korea until it was formally stated in mid-August, 1945, in Communique No. 1, issued by General Douglas MacArthur, as Supreme Commander of SCAP, in Tokyo. Whenever or however the decision was reached, this much at least is certain: despite the fact that it profoundly affected the present and future status of Korea, no Korean representative had any part in its consideration or formulation. To this day there never has been any official explanation from any source as to the genesis of the 38th parallel division—which has proved so costly in blood and so dangerous to world peace.

In review of all the available facts, it is almost certain that the fateful decision was reached through the following sequence of events:

In the first step, at Yalta, Joseph Stalin (who was determined to extend Soviet influence over the strategic Korean peninsula as a part of his master plan for conquering Asia) made it clear to President Roosevelt that, as part of the price for Russian participation in the war, Soviet troops would have to be admitted into Korea. It is probable that Prime Minister Churchill was not present at this conversation, for both he and Roosevelt have indicated that he had little to do with the Asian topics discussed by Roosevelt and Stalin at Yalta.

In the second step, at Potsdam, President Truman (newly installed in office, uninformed about many details of the Roosevelt-Stalin talks, and under the urgent necessity of reaching many important decisions quickly) accepted Stalin's declaration that agreement had already been reached for Soviet troops to enter and occupy a part of Korea.

In the third step, when Russia finally entered the war, just six days before the surrender of Japan, Soviet troops were rushed into northern Korea by land and sea, and immediately commenced pushing southward with all possible speed.

As the fourth step, agreement was formalized in the top military command in mid-August for a "temporary" dividing line to be established along the 38th parallel.

Finally, as the concluding step, American troops were assigned to occupy southern Korea. At first the plan was to have Lt. General Charles Wedemeyer, who was in northern China, and who was well acquainted with both Asian problems and communist tactics in that part of the world, take his command into Korea. On August 23, 1945, however, it was determined that difficulties of transport (plus the need to keep Wedemeyer where he was) invalidated this plan, and in a hasty reassessment of possibilities, the occupation duty was assigned to Lt. General John R. Hodge, who was in Okinawa, where he had brilliantly led the Sixth Army Corps in the conquest of that key island. General Hodge, unfortunately, knew nothing of Korea, or of occupation duties or of Asian history, psychology or problems.

On September 9, General Hodge landed at Inchon in the midst of a most unfortunate situation. General Abe, the Japanese governor-general of Korea, had radioed Hodge asking for full authority to maintain absolute police control, in order to prevent Korean reprisals against the 600,000 Japanese residents of the peninsula. Hodge had granted this request, and, to make it clear to the Koreans that he was not favoring them in any way, he issued a statement saying he regarded the Koreans as "breeds of the same cat as the Japanese" and would deal with them as conquered enemies.

This attitude came as a tremendous shock to the Korean people, who had greeted the surrender of Japan with deep rejoicing and were preparing peacefully and enthusiastically to resume their age-old nationality. During the period between August 15 and September 9, the Korean populace acted with commendable restraint and refrained from any

general acts of reprisal against their now-defeated overlords.
They did, very naturally, intend to welcome the American
troops of liberation with suitable manifestations of gratitude
and hospitality. When General Abe ordered all Koreans to
remain in their homes and make no display of any kind to
welcome the arriving Americans, the Korean people refused
to accede to his order. A crowd of 500 gathered on the
Inchon docks, waving Korean flags and bearing gifts of
flowers for General Hodge and his staff. As the Americans
landed and the Korean welcoming delegation moved forward to present the flowers and to extend their welcome,
the Japanese police opened fire upon them, killing five and
wounding nine more. Instead of being punished, the policemen were commended by General Hodge and the Korean
welcomers were pushed roughly out of the way while
Japanese officials took over the role of official hosts. General
Hodge compounded the follies of that unfortunate day by
announcing that for the time being all Japanese officials
would be retained in office, to continue their rule over the
Korean populace until a military government could be established. A nationwide storm of denunciation broke out
against this incredible order. Washington intervened and
ordered Hodge to relieve and replace all Japanese officials
within the shortest possible time. These were the foreboding
circumstances under which commenced the American occupation of south Korea.

Meanwhile, in northern Korea, the Russians had entered
the country a full month before the Americans and with
plans much better laid. They advanced systematically and
brought with them a group of expatriate Korean communists,
who had been trained in Siberia and at Yenan to take over
control of Korea and establish a puppet government. The
Soviet troops pushed south to the 38th parallel and across
it, to occupy and loot the city of Kaesong. After the landing
by the American troops, the Russians withdrew from Kae-

song, taking with them the city's large stock of ginseng (a root highly valued in Oriental medical practice) and all the money from the banks. Guards were quickly established on both sides of the 38th parallel, and on the northern side the building of fortifications was quickly commenced.

The problem General Hodge found in south Korea was not an easy one to solve—particularly since he had received no briefing, was accompanied by no experts, and had no officers who understood the Korean language or knew Korean history, customs or psychology. Politically, the situation confronting Hodge was peculiarly difficult for one who had no prior understanding of it. At the time of Japan's surrender, General Abe had called in a well-known Korean named Lyuh Woon Hyung, who headed an underground resistance movement comprising both genuine patriots and communists. Lyuh himself had been partly educated in Moscow and had been an active member of the communist party, though he declared he had severed those ties. Nevertheless, the People's Republic Party which he headed was largely under communist influence. Lyuh was well educated, spoke English (as well as Korean, Russian and Japanese) with complete mastery, was suave, affable, able and popular. He had been imprisoned twice by the Japanese for his nationalistic activities, thus identifying him (for those who did not then understand Moscow's pervasive influence) as a true patriot. Abe turned to him as the one Korean on the ground who could most probably achieve a smooth transition from Japanese to Korean rule. He gave Lyuh large sums of money and placed in his hands resources for communication and transportation to every part of south Korea. With such aid, Lyuh soon had People's Republic cells established in every province and in many of the *goons* (or townships) of the south. During the month before the arrival of the American troops sufficient progress was made to insure at least the surface appearance that Lyuh's party was genuinely a "people's movement."

After General Hodge had set up headquarters in the Banto Hotel in Seoul, Lyuh presented himself as the president of the People's Republic of Korea and requested that General Hodge recognize him as the civil ruler of southern Korea. This General Hodge brusquely refused to do, declaring that he would only confer with him as a private citizen. Even so, Lyuh was able to establish himself in the opinion of the occupation authorities as the foremost man in south Korea, with a claim to represent a significant organization of the people. The Korean Provisional Government officials in Chungking had their return to Korea blocked by T. V. Soong, Chinese foreign minister, and did not arrive to enter their own claim until mid-November. Meanwhile, Rhee was still in the United States, struggling with problems that seemed to multiply rather than diminish, despite the long-awaited liberation of Korea from Japan.

At just about the time Hodge was landing at Inchon, I talked with Dr. and Mrs. Rhee, to express my concern, as a friend, over the "extreme" course he was pursuing. I understood his nervousness about Soviet ambitions in Korea, but the newspapers were full of the glorious news that the United Nations had been launched successfully and that now at last the world was entering into the long-delayed era of international co-operation. The tragic failure of the League of Nations, contributing to the outbreak of World War II, had resulted (so it was an article of faith to believe) because the United States had remained out of it. Now the U. N. was organized with the membership of all the leading nations of the world. The problems posed by Russian obstreperousness were very evident, but surely the fact that the Soviet Union had joined this new partnership dedicated to the preservation of peace through the judicious settlement of problems around a conference table meant that the international difficulties would be safely and sanely overcome.

Filled with these sentiments, and disturbed by the general news accounts that Rhee was threatening to block an agreement on Korea by insisting upon bucking the policies of both the United States and the Soviet Union, I went to the Wardman Park to have dinner with Dr. Rhee and his wife. We dined on the back porch, where we had a small private room that looked out over the long rolling green lawn. During the dinner we confined ourselves to inconsequential social chitchat, but as the dessert was finished I spoke to Dr. Rhee with great earnestness, expounding at some length the sentiments summarized in the foregoing paragraph. To this lecture on the new internationalism I added the more particularized observation that Korea, located definitely within the Soviet sphere of influence in Asia, would certainly have to co-operate with the Russians. Under all the circumstances, it appeared inevitable that there would be a communist coalition government in the peninsula. I added that the course Dr. Rhee had adopted would lead to his exclusion from that government and that, as a result, after his lifelong struggle to achieve the independence of Korea he would fail personally just when the cause he had struggled for was succeeding.

After I had finished, there was a long silence, broken at last by Mrs. Rhee. She said, "Dr. Rhee and I have talked at length about the question you have raised. We believe that what you have said may probably be right. Korea may have a communist government. All that is happening makes it look that way. We know that we could not be a part of any such government because of the stand Dr. Rhee has taken. In any event, he would never join such a coalition."

Dr. Rhee spoke up at that point, at first slowly, then with a gathering rush of emotional tension. "What would you have me do?" he asked. "You know I have fought all my life to free Korea from Japan. Do you think that now I would conspire to turn Korea over to Russia, just for the sake of my own personal position? Mrs. Rhee and I have dreamed for many years of the time when we should return to Korea to rejoin my people. I know millions of them are waiting for me. Should I deceive them and tell them I am returning to lead them to independence when it would really be nothing but another slavery? You must know me better than that! This may be the end of my work for Korea. The big powers seem determined to follow their own course and they pay no attention to whatever I may say. But I will keep on warning them as long as I can of the mistake they are making.

"It is not only Korea that is being ruined. The United States will suffer more than any other nation, for you are the only people who stand in Russia's path of conquest. But what can I do more than I have to make the people see what is happening. As for us," and he turned to Mrs. Rhee with a wry smile, "we can always retire to a farm and raise chickens!" The incongruity of the suggestion made us all smile, and the dinner meeting ended on this somewhat awkward note. I left them, still thinking Dr. Rhee was wrong in his stand, but feeling more sure than ever that in his heart and in his motives he was undoubtedly a man of true nobility and selfless courage.

Chapter XI

RETURN TO KOREA

When a patriot who has crusaded and labored for the redemption of his country's independence is enabled to return to its shores for the first time after an absence of thirty-three years, it may be expected that his homeward journey would bear every mark of impatient haste. Yet Syngman Rhee did not arrive in Korea until two months after the defeat of Japan, and five weeks after General Hodge's landing at Inchon. Why? This question is one to be pondered by those who have repeated endlessly the story that Rhee was flown posthaste back to Korea to serve as the stooge of the State Department, which (so this story runs) wanted to establish a pro-American puppet regime in south Korea. Rhee, of course, was anything but a State Department favorite. How he got back into Korea is another revealing episode.

The nature of the problem confronting Rhee is well indicated in a letter written by his wife on March 9, 1945, in which she said:

I am enclosing an article by Mrs. Roosevelt. It is the first time that anyone (with real influence) mentioned our provisional government. We wrote her a letter and asked if we could call and express our gratitude personally. We received a note the other day that she would see us on Thursday at 4 o'clock . . .

We were prepared just to exchange friendly words but she

At home in *Kyung Mu Dai*, Seoul, on March 26, 1953—his 78th birthday—President Rhee examines a book of congratulatory messages sent by 103 78-year old scholars and officials on Formosa. (*ROK O.P.I.*)

asked immediately, "Are you trying to get lend-lease aid?" Then
Dr. Rhee told her how many times we approached the government for assistance to share in the fighting against Japan and
that up until now we have not received one dollar for lend
lease nor a stick of dynamite, etc.

He said that we believe the President has been misinformed
about us, otherwise it would be different. Mrs. Roosevelt promised that she would talk to the President. She said, "I will surely
tell him."

I wonder if you could write a letter to her commenting on her
article, particularly stressing the fact that it would be a grave
injustice to disappoint these peace-loving people who are looking up to the United States to extend a helping hand. A strong,
unified and independent Korean Provisional Government [has
been] established by the will of the Korean people in Korea and
maintained by all Koreans outside of Korea for 26 years. To
recognize that government is to carry out the will of the Korean
people whose declared intention is to hold the national election
within a year after the liberation of the country.

On the other hand, if the United Nations insist on unification
among all the groups outside of Korea as a prerequisite for the
recognition, the result will be encouragement for the communist
agitators, whose sole aim is to take hold of the nationalistic
democratic government now in exile and proportionate weakening of the position of the nationalistic leaders who are not co-
operating with the Chinese government. . . .

Eleanor Roosevelt's reaction to the meeting Mrs. Rhee
described was indicated in her syndicated column for March
12, 1945, in which she says: "I had never met Dr. Rhee before, but a beautiful spirit shines in his face, and the patience
which one feels his countrymen must have exercised for
many years is evident in the gentleness of his expression."
As for her proposed talk with President Roosevelt, nothing
came of it.

In a memorandum dated June 11 Dr. Rhee outlined other
phases of the developing problems. T. V. Soong was trying

to negotiate an agreement with the State Department to insure priority in Korea for the Koreans in Chungking with whom he had the closest ties—Kimm Kiusic, Kim Yaksan and Cho So-ang—who he felt would enter into a coalition with the communists and thus "solve" the Korean question. As early as December 7, 1942, Kim Koo had taken some communists into the cabinet of the exiled Korean Provisional Government in Chungking, and Dr. Rhee had been urging him ever since to rescind that policy. "I advised him against it at the time," the June 11 memorandum by Dr. Rhee said, "but perhaps he was unable to resist it . . . Meanwhile, Chiang Kai-shek was very much handicapped by the American support of the Chinese communist demands for complete unity and all those high Chinese officials playing power politics, including T. V. Soong himself, made the situation precarious for Chiang . . . As a result, both Chiang Kai-shek in the Chinese government and Kim Koo in the Korean government are isolated. . . ."

With this situation developing, Dr. Rhee made every effort to return to Korea immediately upon the defeat of Japan. He did not wish to travel by way of China for fear that T. V. Soong would keep him there until after Kimm Kiusic and his associates had time to establish themselves firmly in Korea. Accordingly, he planned to travel by way of Manila. He requested a passport from Mrs. Ruth Shipley, head of the Passport Division, and she secured authority to issue it from Secretary of State James Byrnes, just before his departure for London, on September 5. The next requirement was a military permit to enter the war theater. Colonel Sweeney in the Pentagon wired General MacArthur and the permit was approved by him. Colonel Sweeney thereupon prepared the permit, stating that Syngman Rhee, High Commissioner from Korea to the United States, was authorized to return to Korea by any suitable route. While Mr. Manning of the State Department was arranging transporta-

tion for Rhee, the Secretary of State's office called Mrs.
Shipley and informed her that the designation as "High
Commissioner" was objectionable and that the passport
should be canceled. On September 21 Mr. Manning called
Rhee, advising him to see Mrs. Shipley. This was late Friday
afternoon, and Rhee was unable to see her before Monday
morning. At that time he told her that he required no title
and wished to return to Korea with no publicity or fanfare.
Colonel Sweeney was thereupon advised to make out a new
military permit, omitting the title.

With this new permit in hand, Dr. Rhee again called on
Mr. Manning and was informed the State Department had
decided not to assist him with travel arrangements. Furthermore, Manning said Rhee would have to secure a new permit
from General MacArthur granting him specific permission
to land either on Okinawa or at Tokyo. Rhee would also
have to have assurance from MacArthur that he would be
flown into Korea by an Army plane. When Rhee asked
Colonel Sweeney to wire for this new request he said he
could not do so without specific authorization from the
State Department. And when Rhee asked Mrs. Shipley for
such authorization she replied that the State Department
could not intervene further in his behalf. It was almost an
additional month before these various difficulties were un-
raveled and Rhee's return to Korea was effected.

In view of the veil of secrecy behind which official decisions are made, it is impossible to be certain why the plans
for Rhee's return, which at first went so well, suddenly
encountered inexplicable delays. Some day the State Department files for this period will be opened to scholarly
inquiry and the story will be known. In the meantime,
speculation suggests that the original expectation of the
responsible American military and diplomatic officials was
that, following the disarming of the Japanese troops, the
Russians would co-operate in holding an all-Korea election

to provide a basis for a government of the whole peninsula
—with the proviso that it should be a government of limited
authority, subject to the combined military command. The
pattern established for Japan, Germany and Austria (of
operating through a controlled native regime) was probably
the one also intended for Korea. If this presumption is
correct, the return of Rhee to participate in the election
would not be objectionable.

However, within a very few days after the entry of
Hodge's Sixth Army Corps into Korea it became evident that
the Russians were not going to be co-operative. One of the
first definite indications of this was what happened when
Hodge sent a trainload of supplies into north Korea, there
to be exchanged for a load of coal; the Russians not only did
not send back any coal but they kept the train. Under these
circumstances it did not take long for the officials to learn
that the hope for a speedy reunification of the peninsula they
had so casually dismembered was not to be expected. The
next decision to be made was whether to establish a separate
government (with limited autonomy) in south Korea or to
hold the south Koreans under U. S. military authority, thus
keeping the situation fluid, while an attempt should be made
to negotiate with the Russians. The latter decision being
made, it must have been evident to the State Department
that the return to Korea of the most ardent and able advocate
of Korean independence could only prove embarrassing.

Whether or not this explanation eventually proves to be
correct, the fact is that Rhee's return was delayed until
October 16. The absurd charge that he was hand-picked by
the State Department to be its anointed agent in south
Korea, and that his rise in power there was due to the assistance of the American government is utterly ridiculous.
The simple fact is that Rhee was in effect *persona non grata*
with the Department of State because of his long fight to
try to induce it to recognize the provisional government, and

that he had to utilize every influence he and his friends could bring to bear to win the mere right to return to Korea in a private capacity.

After the difficulties were surmounted, however, Rhee's return was a triumphant procession which did much to repay him for all the long years of sacrifice and lonely struggle. MacArthur suggested to Hodge the wisdom of greeting Rhee as a home-coming national hero. The Korean people regarded him as an almost legendary leader, whose indomitable spirit had been an inspiration since 1897. To two generations the name Syngman Rhee had symbolized reform, democracy and independence. As soon as his arrival became known, a mass of cheering people filled the courtyard of the Chosun Hotel, where a three-room suite had been reserved for him by General Hodge on the third floor. With an understandable feeling of jubilation, Rhee wrote on October 21—sitting up in his bed at 5:30 A.M., for he had been awakened by the crowds gathered under his windows to shout "*Mansei!*":

It seems the whole nation is agog since my arrival was announced. Hundreds of people gather around the hotel entrance and ask for a chance to see me. General Hodge and I had agreed not to announce my arrival until we are ready but the next morning the general came and said the American news reporters were demanding an interview. So we rushed to the Palace and entered the press conference, with General Hodge and General Arnold escorting me. Then I spoke both in English and in Korean. Since that time to this, crowds gathered in front of the outside gate and many men and women managed to come inside and I could not find one minute for rest. Yesterday afternoon I had to call to them, saying that they must go away and do their work.

The letter ended on a note of haste: "They are coming already and I must stop so that I can mail this today." That was indeed a busy time. All the political leaders in south

Korea called and offered Dr. Rhee the chairmanship of their parties. Lyuh Woon Hyung and his brother Lyuh Woon Hong came and offered Dr. Rhee the leadership of the People's Republic Party. Pak Hun Yung, the chairman of the south Korean communist party, called to ask Rhee to assume the chairmanship of the communists! Rhee realized that in accepting these offers he would be committing himself to a coalition and that in effect he would be the prisoner of those he was presumed to be leading. Accordingly he declined them all and insisted that he would not affiliate himself with any political party. Instead he formed the Society for the Rapid Realization of Independence and asked all Koreans to join it. Soon local chapters were opening up in all the cities and villages below the 38th parallel line.

In a sense Rhee's return to Korea filled a political vacuum. Lyuh Woon Hyung had forfeited much of his popularity with the masses by his acceptance of the sponsorship of the hated Japanese governor, General Abe. His ties with communism were also soon to prove an even worse handicap. Kim Koo and Kimm Kiusic had not yet returned to Korea from China. After they arrived, Kim Koo proved to have considerable popular following, but as events demonstrated this was almost entirely because of his association through the provisional government with Dr. Rhee. As soon as Kim Koo tried to pursue an independent course (as happened in 1948) his following all but evaporated. Kimm Kiusic was to become the "fair-haired boy" of the American Military Government, but despite monumental efforts in his behalf by the AMG personnel he couldn't win the loyalty of more than a handful of Koreans. Chang Duk Soo, physically and intellectually vigorous and with the prestige of a Ph. D. from Columbia, had great promise, but was assassinated in the first months after the liberation. Kim Sung Soo, a wealthy textile manufacturer and sponsor of Posung College, was well and favorably known by the liberal intellectuals but unknown to the people at large. The only Korean whose appeal approached that of Syngman Rhee was Cho Man-sik, a Christian leader of the northern city of Pyengyang, whose exemplary character and patriotism had shone out from the sheltering protection of the Church. But in the first days of the occupation of north Korea, Mr. Cho was arrested by the Soviets and has never been heard from since. When Syngman Rhee appeared in Korea, the people—eager for patriotic leadership and for guidance out of the maze of international complications that beset them—turned to him as the one man they felt they could trust.

Rhee's rejection of the proffers of leadership of the various political parties in south Korea was denounced by many members of the Military Government and by the American newspaper correspondents who were on the ground. They were eager to see unity emerge from the tangled political scene, and were shocked when Rhee rejected what appeared to be the only chance to achieve it. At that date and in that place, coalition of unlike political elements (including communism) did not seem too high a price to pay for the unity they desired. Rhee's rejection, they decided, must be due to the ambitious determination to achieve power all by himself. What they did not seem to grasp was that Rhee's ascendancy could not possibly develop by any other means than his acceptance by the masses of the people. In most places that would be accounted a fair operation of the democratic process. But in south Korea in 1945-46, with the American personnel anxious only to get some kind of agreement with the Russians that would let them leave, the one test that was applied to any action was whether it would help to win the acquiescence of the Russians. To this end Rhee very definitely did not contribute.

Unfortunately, it was not alone the foreigners in south Korea who failed to recognize the danger of communism. Many Koreans, too, were favorably inclined toward Russia.

During the years of Japanese rule over Korea, Russia and Japan had been at loggerheads. The Soviet revolution of 1917-19 was an encouragement to the submerged Korean patriots. Communist guerrillas operated freely in Manchuria, harrying the Japanese after their 1931 conquest, and it was only natural that many Korean guerrillas joined forces with them. From time to time small quantities of arms and other supplies were smuggled into the Korean underground from Siberia. All these were reasons why the Korean people had come to entertain friendly feelings toward Russia and, therefore, an uncritical attitude toward communism. Strict Japanese police control had kept communist propaganda almost entirely out of Korea, but as soon as the war ended this bar was lifted. The American Military Government believed that democratic fairness required that communists be treated exactly like the other political parties. The communist party was assigned one of the best office buildings in Seoul for its headquarters (and was allowed to retain the building even after it was discovered that a counterfeiting press was being operated in the basement for the printing of paper *Won*—the Korean currency). Local communist cells were quickly spread throughout south Korea. They were well financed, partly with the counterfeit currency, partly with the money that had been taken from the Kaesong banks and with other paper currency from north Korea. The Russian army of occupation in north Korea quickly adopted a new paper currency for the northern area, calling in all the money in circulation, so that it had large quantities (forty percent, in fact, of all the paper Won in Korea in 1945) to be sent for the use of its agents in the south. With this money, the communists set to work systematically to buy newspapers and motion picture theaters. They also printed innumerable posters and leaflets, which were liberally distributed to give the impression that communism was widespread among the populace. In Korea, as in other parts of the world, it proved true that a small number of communists, by working hard and by being loudly articulate, could give the impression of constituting a mass movement.

Toward the end of December, 1945, the Moscow Conference (of Byrnes, Eden and Molotov) decided that the solution for Korea was a five-year trusteeship to be supervised by Russia, the United States, Great Britain and China. Rhee and Kim Koo issued a denunciation of it and called a protest strike of all government workers—which resulted in a shutdown of Military Government offices on January 1 and 2, 1946, and demonstrated the strength of the provisional government in the affections of the people. On January 1 a mass parade was held down the main streets of Seoul, aflutter with banners decrying trusteeship. Even the communists joined in this rejection—but in the very midst of the demonstration word arrived from Moscow that the communists were to support it. As a result, many of their signs were hastily changed, so that in "No Trusteeship" banners, the "No" was crossed out, and "Down with Trusteeship" was hastily converted into "Up with Trusteeship!" Within a very few hours the Korean attitude was so clearly manifested that Secretary of State James Byrnes quickly made a radio speech declaring that to the American government "trusteeship" meant only "aid and assistance."

Rhee, who was working closely with Kim Koo, knew very well that "aid and assistance" was not what the Soviet Union had in mind. He commenced a series of weekly addresses over the Korean radio, in which he pointed out that a trusteeship managed by four separate and, in some respects, inimical powers could not possibly work; that the five-year term could be lengthened and probably would be; that an immediate effect of the plan would be to extend Russian influence directly over the whole of the peninsula; that the plan violated the Cairo promise of independence for Korea;

and that since Korea had governed itself for over 4,000 years
a proposal of trusteeship was insulting and needless.

In January Rhee, Kim Koo and other like-minded leaders
held a series of consultations which led to the calling of an
Emergency National Assembly in February. This Assembly
recommended, and General Hodge accepted, a plan for the
establishment of a Representative Democratic Council of
South Korea, with Syngman Rhee as Permanent Chairman
and Kim Koo and Kimm Kiusic as Permanent Vice-Chair-
men. Lyuh Woon Hyung at first accepted membership on
the Council, but under the threats of the communist wing of
his following soon withdrew from it. In the months that
followed Lyuh was twice kidnaped by the communists.
Once he was taken north of the 38th parallel for an "educational" session, and once he was led up South Mountain
and held out over a cliff while his captors "reasoned" with
him. Actually, Lyuh was a very genial man (well acquainted
with American athletics) who was frightened by the radicals
whom he professed to lead. In July of 1947 while riding in
a car in Seoul, he was assassinated by a youth who was
identified by General Hodge as a north Korean communist
acting on orders from the northern occupation authorities.
Lyuh learned the harsh lesson that breaking away from
communism is far harder than joining it.

It was evident to Rhee that unless this burgeoning communist movement could be checked, Korea would be swept
by default into Soviet control. Accordingly, much as his
presence was needed in Seoul to cement his position with
the Military Government, to build an organization of his
own, and to mollify critical foreign newspaper correspondents, he set out in February, 1946, on a six weeks' tour of
south Korea, speaking in every city and in many of the towns
and villages about the evils of communism and the necessity
of combating it at all costs. Late in March, as a result of his

exertions, he came down with an attack of influenza and for two weeks was confined to bed.

The Representative Democratic Council, meanwhile, adopted a set of 27 principles Rhee had drawn up in America, which promised land reform for the peasants, votes for women, universal education, and other democratic changes that later were written into the constitution of the Republic of Korea. Colonel Preston Goodfellow was brought to Korea by the U. S. Army to serve as a liaison man between General Hodge and President Rhee and for a time Hodge believed that the Council might supply the "unity" which he sought. However, Rhee refused to try to achieve unity at the price of coalition with the communists and spared no effort to denounce them on any and every occasion. In the spring of 1946 General Hodge appointed a censor to read all of Rhee's speeches prepared for delivery over the Korean radio network, and had him delete all criticisms of Russia and of communism. When it appeared that Rhee was incorrigible on this subject, Hodge dropped the Democratic Representative Council from his calculations, and although it continued to meet for several more months, it never became an effective agency of the American Military Government. When I arrived in Korea on June 2, 1946, General Hodge told me that "Syngman Rhee is so much the greatest Korean statesman that he may be said to be the only one, but because of his persistent attacks upon Russia he never can have a part in any government which the United States may sponsor in Korea." Hodge urged me to do my best to make Rhee see that no solution for Korea was possible without Russian co-operation and that, therefore, he must cease his criticisms of Russian intentions. When I presented these views to Rhee, in his hillside home outside the East Gate of Seoul, he paced back and forth on the veranda and asked in some agitation, "Am I wrong in my views?" Then he went on to describe first the dominant position Russia had by then already assumed in the eastern European countries and, subsequently, the long history of Russian intrigue in Korea. His own conclusion was unshaken that to admit Russia in any guise into south Korea would merely be to surrender the independence of the nation.

While Rhee was active in Korea, the Korean Commission in Washington, D. C. was ably headed by Ben C. Limb (who later became foreign minister of the Republic of Korea and subsequently ambassador-at-large and permanent observer for the republic at the United Nations). On November 7, 1945, at Dr. Rhee's direction, Colonel Limb sent to John Carter Vincent, Director of the Office of Far Eastern Affairs in the State Department, a letter, in which he pleaded that the United States should adhere firmly to a policy of independence for Korea. To this letter, Mr. Vincent returned the following cryptic reply:

November 20, 1945

My dear Colonel Limb:

I have read your letter of November 7, 1945, with interest. The restoration and evolution of civilization, broken and all but destroyed by world war, is and must be the primary objective of all of us. No one man, no political party, no one nation can work out the right result alone. Full discussion and careful attention is essential to all procedural suggestion from all concerned. Consequently, right procedure to the attainment of our common object is bound to be slow, in the democratic processes which you and we prefer. We all need to be sure that we have the right procedural process upon which we may help you to build your own self-government and essential independence.

No responsible person is unaware today that Korea in all recorded history has been the crossroad and point of contact of the great movements of the peoples of eastern Asia, and, in later decades of the impact upon them of the western peoples. Nor is any responsible person unaware that Korea's ancient culture has influenced and been influenced by that historical fact. It is upon this awareness that we must all attempt to help you to

build up a synthesis of your very old culture with all that is best
in the modern for a solid and permanent future.

I can assure you that I welcome suggestions or comments by
you on matters concerning your country's future.

The friendly but noncommittal tone of Vincent's letter
typified the uncertainty of American policy toward Rhee at
this period. Mrs. Rhee was allowed to return to Korea to
join her husband, but only after several weeks of exasperat-
ing delay, sailing finally from Seattle on an Army transport
in January, 1946. Rhee's transcendent position of leadership
among the people of Korea could not be doubted, but
General Hodge adopted a determined policy of trying to
replace him with someone who would be more amenable to
suggestions of coalition.

The attempts to settle the problem of reunifying divided
Korea proceeded through the Joint Commission of representatives of the two military commands, north and south.
The first meetings were held in December, 1945, and soon
were broken off when it became apparent the Russians meant
to maintain an iron wall along the parallel. In May and June
of 1946 a second series of meetings was held. The Americans proposed that representatives of all Korean political
parties be consulted on plans for the future of the country—
with the result that more than 400 political parties were
registered, in a rush between the communists and the anti-
communists to assure for themselves majority representation.
The foreign newsmen, trying to make sense in their ab-
breviated dispatches of this hodgepodge of politics, soon
settled upon the simple (but misleading) terms of "leftists"
to designate communists; "rightists" to designate the anti-
communists; and "middle-of-the-roaders" to designate those
who were noncommunist but were willing to form a coalition
government. On the easy assumption that a middle position
is preferable to extremes, the newsmen—and their readers in

the United States and Europe—soon came to prefer the middle-of-the-road group, led by Kimm Kiusic and Lyuh Woon Hyung. Rhee, because of his strong and frequent denunciation of communism and his utter rejection of any suggestion of compromise with it, was soon labeled an "extreme rightist."

The communist negotiators from north Korea hit upon the expedient of insisting that no Korean could be admitted to consultation who refused to sign and abide by the Moscow Declaration setting up trusteeship for Korea. Their claim had some plausibility, on the ground that this was the agreed solution among the big powers and consequently must be imposed upon the Koreans. The American command replied that any and all Korean leaders who actually represented significant segments of the population must be "consulted" but this would prove no bar to imposing trusteeship, even if they opposed it. General Arnold, who headed the American delegation in the conference in its early stages, devised what became known as "Communique No. 5," a document attesting that all who signed it agreed to accept the validity of the Moscow Declaration but were not bound to abide by it. Arnold considered he had produced an "open-end" pledge which would satisfy the Russians and at the same time permit Korean leaders to sign it without being bound to accept trusteeship. Kimm Kiusic and Lyuh Woon Hyung signed. Rhee and Kim Koo explicitly declared that their followers should feel free to sign it if they wished, but they themselves would not do so. General Hodge issued some testy statements to the effect that Rhee was "blocking" an agreement with Russia for the reunification of Korea. Rhee replied that the general knew full well the big powers would do whatever they wished and that no Korean had any power to block their plans. Actually, the Russians never had the slightest intention of wiping out the 38th parallel division of Korea. If they could not get the whole country, they had no intention of surrendering the half which they already held. As General Arnold said in the summer of 1946, "Usually the Russian negotiators won't say anything at all. When they do say something, it is No. But if they ever say Yes, they break their agreement by the next day."

These Joint Commission meetings were held in Seoul, and the Russian negotiators brought large staffs, which worked busily with leaders of the south Korean communist party. To the Korean people the sight of the Russian officers riding through the streets was anathema. On one occasion (but only once) students and other demonstrators threw mud and stones at the Russians' cars. No one was hurt, but the Russians threatened to break off the talks and Hodge severely warned the Korean leaders that unless they held the people in check the failure to attain a free and reunified Korea would be their responsibility.

Rhee's position, often repeated, was that talks between the two military commands in Korea were fruitless: the real decisions would have to be made by the American and Russian governments, and the talks should be held between Washington and Moscow. For whatever the reasons may have been (and they presumably were largely the hope of keeping the Korean problem localized to the Korean peninsula itself) Washington long refrained from approaching Moscow on the matter. The attempt to settle the question inside Korea, and the hope to get both the Russians and the Koreans to agree on trusteeship as the solution, persisted until March, 1947. As late as April 10 of that year, Mr. Hugh Borton, chief of the Division of Northeastern Asian Affairs of the Department of State, was still explaining hopefully to a press conference:

"We are bound by the Moscow decision just as much today as we were when we made that agreement. I would also like to give you this statement—even under a four-power trusteeship it would be possible for the Koreans to extend their control over their own economic, political, social and cultural development and advancement. I will explain why I said that. Trusteeship can be an entirely different thing for one area, territory, country than it is for another. I say that because whatever form a trusteeship takes depends entirely on the trusteeship agreement itself. You are familiar with the trusteeship agreement for the former Japanese-mandated islands which was passed by my government to the Security Council of the UN. It was actually passed the day I left Washington. It provides for very strict control by the U. S. alone. Trusteeship for Korea, obviously, could be something entirely different. For example, its first article might say that on such and such a date Korea would be completely free and independent. It might further state in the second article an agreement to support Korea's entrance into the UN and then it would go on and convey a very limited power and authority that these four states would have. I have read in the Moscow agreement that Koreans would be consulted in the formation of the provisional government in reference to the drafting of a trusteeship agreement for Korea. I would not be excited about the idea of trusteeship. The thing that I would be excited about is what is in a trusteeship agreement when that time is reached."

Mr. Borton's fanciful portrayal of a hypothetical trusteeship agreement which would in reality be a velvet-covered pathway to independence was worse than a whistling in the dark. Since Secretary of State Marshall was already preparing to drop the trusteeship proposal and to suggest an entirely new approach to Molotov in Moscow, the Borton press conference can only be interpreted as an attempt to persuade the newsmen that the opposition led by Rhee to such a friendly and promising trusteeship as he described could only be shortsighted or worse. The eighteen-month attempt was about to fail. In the eyes of the public the onus of failure must be shifted from those who devised and had pushed the

scheme to someone who had blocked it. Russia was the
obvious villain but to blame the Soviets might impede
further plans for other solutions. The newsmen could readily
guess, of course, that Russia never would accede to the kind
of trusteeship Mr. Borton described. But blaming Rhee for
stubborn unco-operativeness was convenient and had, by
then, become a habit firmly fixed. In any event, whoever or
whatever was to blame, by the time Mr. Borton's statement
was made, trusteeship was already a dead issue. Rhee, who
knew it well, had other fish to fry.

Chapter XII

HALFWAY
TO INDEPENDENCE

In north Korea the Russians are riding a wild horse," the American newspaper correspondents jested sourly in the summer of 1946. "But in south Korea the Americans have a tiger by the tail and can't figure out how to get loose." Their figurative analogy had some point. North Korea was organized as a going concern under a communist regime that was first appointed, then, in the fall of 1946, "elected" on a single-slate ballot. A northern army was being developed. The seven and a half per cent of the population that owned farm rental properties was liquidated and the land was redistributed to farmers who met the requirements of the *Myun* (or county) communist committees. Factories, mines and hydroelectric power plants were being restored to operation. Prosperity was loudly claimed in the Pyengyang propaganda radio broadcasts and with some show of reason. Yet an average of 1600 north Korean refugees were fleeing from this workers' paradise every day to find refuge in south Korea. The horse was being ridden but it was indubitably wild.

Meanwhile, in south Korea, General Hodge operated under a Congressional enactment which provided him with funds and authority specifically limited to "combating disease and unrest." He could put down riots and alleviate severe hunger—little else. A State Department booklet issued in August, 1947, estimated that the industry and mines of south Korea (for two years under the control of the greatest technological power on earth) were producing only twenty per cent of their normal capacity. Unemployment was widespread, increased by the flood-tides of repatriates from China and Japan and the refugees from the north. In November, 1946, General MacArthur estimated that in Seoul alone at least 20,000 Korean families were sleeping in the streets, with no manner of shelter whatsoever—and November in Seoul is cold. The south Korean communists were crying for trusteeship and all the other political factions were clamoring for independence. The State Department could tell General Hodge little except to "maintain order" and to continue to work for an agreement with Russia. In the fall of 1945 Hodge had foolishly cut himself off from his best source of help when he had bluntly rejected a directive from Douglas MacArthur with the rejoinder that south Korea was a separate military theater from that in Japan, and was responsible directly to Washington. MacArthur gleefully accepted this "clarification" and left Hodge to stew in his Korean juice. Since all supplies for Korea came by way of Japan—where MacArthur's command took what it wanted —the Korean theater was in every respect the "end of the line." The Army PX's were bare, the Korean people received only such remnants of shipments from the United States as the Japanese didn't get, and the worst disciplinary threat offered to U. S. personnel in Japan was that "if you don't make good here, we'll send you to Korea." The Korean tiger may have been a mangy beast in many ways, but his growling was a constant threat.

In attempting to deal with the Koreans, Hodge had failed in his initial attempt to keep them under the control of the experienced Japanese officials. He was disappointed when Syngman Rhee refused, in October, 1945, to solve his problems by accepting the chairmanship of a coalition of all the existing political groups. He felt he could not support the Representative Democratic Council when the "leftists" walked out from it. The negotiations with the Russians failed utterly to provide any basis for reuniting the country.

In June, 1946, Hodge adopted another plan. He invited Rhee, Kim Koo, Kimm Kiusic and Lyuh Woon Hyung to unite in an advisory Coalition Committee. Rhee and Kim refused to join with the two leftists (on the grounds that they represented few south Koreans but did represent Russia), but Hodge stubbornly insisted upon keeping the Coalition Committee and named Kimm and Lyuh as its joint chairmen. With the advice of this committee he devised a plan for an "Interim Assembly."

This Interim Assembly was to have forty-five members, elected from all the provinces of south Korea, in November, 1946. The Assembly was to have merely advisory functions, and was strictly enjoined from passing any resolutions in the areas of foreign affairs or economic matters. Still further to insure that it could not get out of hand, Hodge declared that he would appoint an additional forty-five members.

The result was an overwhelming triumph for Syngman Rhee. When the elections were held, forty-three of the elected members were adherents of Rhee and Kim Koo. The American Military Government had conducted the election and its police had supervised it, but Hodge readily accepted the explanation of Kimm Kiusic and Lyuh Woon Hyung that "rightist terrorists" had frightened the people into voting as they did. Accordingly, he appointed forty-five members from a list presented to him by the Coalition Committee, "in order to assure the representative character of the Interim Assembly."

Following the announcement of these appointees, Rhee called on General Hodge for what proved to be a cold and bitter session. Rhee first tried to persuade Hodge to aban-

don his plan and was told brusquely that the general did
not intend to permit Rhee to "seize power." Rhee then said
that he had tried to defend Hodge to the Korean people,
despite all the mistakes that had been made, but that from
this point on he intended openly to oppose him. Hodge
replied that the United States could never be turned aside
from its chosen policies by threats, and assured Rhee that
he must co-operate in the program or be destroyed.

Rhee went from his meeting with Hodge to consult with
Kim Koo and their immediate lieutenants. Kim was in favor
of issuing an immediate announcement that the provisional
republic, based on the *Mansei* demonstrations of 1919, was
in fact the only lawful government of Korea, and calling
upon the Koreans to rally around it. Rhee never doubted
that the people would respond to such a call, but he knew
that the immediate result would be an outbreak in which
the unarmed and disorganized twenty million south Koreans
would be pitted against the 50,000 American troops in
Korea. He declared flatly that such a program as Kim proposed was utterly impossible, for if American soldiers were
killed the American people would forget the rights and
wrongs of the situation and rally immediately to the support
of their endangered sons. Once again, as he had for so many
years, Rhee argued that the only feasible road to independence lay through an appeal to the fair-mindedness of
the American public. He proposed that he should go to the
United States to present the case personally to the State
Department and to news-men who would not be, as were
those in Seoul, completely dependent upon the Military Government for livelihood, transportation, communication, and
interpretations of the situation.

Kim Koo and others argued strongly against Rhee's position, chiefly on the grounds that such appeals had not
succeeded in the past and that the time had come for action.
Rhee continued to urge that his proposal offered the only

hope, and finally a compromise was reached. Kim Koo agreed that Rhee might be granted the opportunity he requested, but only with the understanding that if Rhee could not promptly bring or send to Korea assurances of success, the revolutionary program would be put into effect. Suicidal though Rhee knew Kim Koo's program would be, he had no means of combating it. The temper of the Korean people did, indeed, call for decisive action. Yet he reminded Kim that the processes of government move slowly and asked that he be allowed several weeks for his attempts before Kim should proceed with his own plan.

With this much decided, Rhee returned to General Hodge and asked for co-operation in arranging his trip to Washington. Hodge declared himself "hurt" by Rhee's intention of going "over his head" to Washington. He reminded Rhee that he had several State Department political advisors and was in constant touch with the Department by cable. He insisted that no possible good could come from the trip and that much harm might result if the Korean people placed any confidence in it. Rhee could not explain to Hodge what the alternative to his trip would be, but simply insisted he was going to make it. The trip was announced in the Korean newspapers on November 25. The plan was unanimously approved in the press—even by the communist newspapers —"in spite of the fact," as the *Han Sung Ilbo* bitingly editorialized, "that it will cost the Koreans three hundred thousand dollars in gold." (Where such a sum could come from, the editorial did not reveal.) Actually, the Representative Democratic Council raised the sum of 500,000 Won (about $10,000) to finance the trip. On December 1, Dr. Rhee sailed from Inchon on the S.S. *Marine Jumper* for Tokyo, where General MacArthur provided passage on a military plane for him to the United States. In the stop at Hawaii Rhee was honored by a military guard, under command of General Hull, who (in 1953) became Commander of all U. N.

troops in Korea. He arrived in Washington, D. C., on December 7.

The issues that had to be decided in Korea were clear. Rhee's immediate complaint was against what he considered Hodge's undemocratic action in nullifying the results of the election by his appointment of forty-five middle-of-the-road members to the Interim Assembly. After Rhee's departure for America, Hodge appointed Kimm Kiusic as chairman of the Assembly. As an interesting commentary on the general tenor of Korean opinion, despite this stacking of the membership, the first resolution adopted by the Assembly was a denunciation of trusteeship—a vote from which almost half the appointed members abstained, but against which only one ballot was cast. The sole negative voter, Ahn Chai Hong, was promptly named by Hodge as civil administrator of the South Korean Interim Government (SKIG), which was organized to carry out specified administrative procedures under the direction of the Military Government. To Rhee the whole proceeding was as un-American as it was undemocratic and he did not believe Hodge's actions would be supported by the State Department.

In a larger sense, however, Rhee had little interest in this immediate question. Since the Interim Assembly and SKIG had no authority, he did not much care who controlled them. In his judgment it should by this time be abundantly clear to everyone that Russia would not agree to the establishment of a free government for all Korea and, consequently, he believed the time had come to establish a separate government, even if it had to be confined to south Korea. Immediately upon his arrival in Washington (where he took up residence at the Carlton Hotel) he asked me to leave my teaching position on the staff of Syracuse University to join him, and he established a "strategy council," of which the other members were John W. Staggers, Jay Jerome Williams,

Col. M. Preston Goodfellow, Col. Emory Woodall, Reverend Frederick Brown Harris, Col. Ben C. Limb and Miss Louise Yim. The following program, supported by a 4,000-word brief, was developed and presented to the State Department:

1. An interim government should be elected for southern Korea, to serve until the two halves of Korea can be reunited and a general election held immediately thereafter;

2. Without disturbing direct Russian-American consultations on Korea, this interim government should be admitted to the United Nations and allowed to negotiate directly with Russia and the United States concerning the occupation of Korea and on other outstanding questions;

3. Korean claims for reparations from Japan should be given early consideration, to aid in the rehabilitation of the Korean economy;

4. Full commercial rights should be granted to Korea, on a basis of equality with other nations, and with no favoritism extended to any nation;

5. Korean currency should be stabilized and established on the international exchange;

6. United States security troops should remain in southern Korea until the two foreign armies of occupation simultaneously withdraw.

There were marked differences between the hostility Rhee encountered in Korea from General Hodge and the relative friendliness accorded him in Washington. Hodge's failures as a military administrator were too obvious to be overlooked. Without any doubt he would have been transferred from Korea except for the fact that an active move was under way to shift occupation responsibilities in Korea, Germany and Austria from the Pentagon to the State Department. Rhee's argument that Hodge had acted unfairly and undemocratically in his appointments to the Interim Assembly was patently true. By this time, too, Washington was deeply concerned about Russia's world-wide expansionism and it was evident that new policies were demanded for Korea.

Rhee's overwhelming success in the November elections had impressed the State Department and it was ready, as never before, to deal with him as the presumptive leader of the Korean people. General John R. Hilldring, the Assistant Secretary of State for Occupied Countries, was close to Mac-Arthur, who admired and respected Rhee; Hilldring also was a fair-minded, blunt-spoken man who personally saw no reason why south Korea should not be allowed to organize a free government as a counter-balance to the controlled regime the Russians had established north of the 38th parallel. John Carter Vincent, chief of the Office of Far Eastern Affairs, appeared to oppose Hilldring's position behind the scenes but could not combat it openly. John Z. Williams, who occupied the Korean desk, and who "evaluated" Hodge's reports for the State Department, knew little of Korea but was not blind to the fact that the patent will of the Korean people was repeatedly violated by the Military Government.

Despite these favorable circumstances, governmental policies change but slowly and no State Department official of consequence felt himself in a position to talk with Rhee about positive steps to reform conditions. The weeks passed, and in late February Rhee received a coded message from Kim Koo saying that the time had come when he felt he must announce the sovereignty of the Provisional Republic. Rhee sent him a strongly worded radiogram to postpone any such action, and, under Rhee's directions, I had a series of talks with Assistant Secretary Hilldring about the urgency of the situation. Unless some genuine progress could be achieved through negotiation, the lid would soon be blown off in Korea. In the second week of March an understanding was reached with Hilldring that he would support a program very similar to that spelled out in the six points that had been submitted. In a final talk, Dr. Rhee and I met with Hilldring in his office and received assurances definite enough to be transmitted to Kim Koo.

Meanwhile, General Hodge was called to Washington for consultation and arrived on March 1. He electrified the public by announcing that the Russians were organizing an army of 500,000 men in north Korea, apparently for the purpose of launching an attack on the south. The Pentagon was alarmed lest American troops be trapped on the peninsula and be drawn into a war that might involve the Soviet Union. These factors were added reasons why Rhee's program began to look attractive to Washington officials. Secretary of State George Marshall went to Moscow for general discussions with Molotov and made one last effort for bilateral agreement on Korea by proposing that the Joint Commission discussions on reunification be resumed, with assurances that all Korean leaders, including those who rejected trusteeship, be consulted. Unexpectedly, Molotov agreed.

Rhee was greatly disheartened by this development, for he did not expect Russia to agree to a reunified and independent Korea and he did fear that the renewal of the talks would block any progress toward establishment of a government in south Korea. He desired to extend his stay in Washington, where the vital decisions would be made, but conditions in Korea (with Kim Koo becoming increasingly restive) made his return imperative. In order to determine State Department intentions, I called Hilldring's office and asked if there would be any objection to a release of a statement summarizing the informal agreement on the six points. The reply was a noncommittal statement that the State Department did not wish to exercise any influence over whatever kind of release Dr. Rhee might wish to make to the press. Consequently, the six-point program was published—followed by

a routine statement by the State Department press officer
that no new policy for Korea had been adopted.

What happened after that was a comedy of errors. The
State Department secured military clearance from Hodge
for Rhee's return to Korea, and plans were made by the Pentagon to fly him back in a military plane. Travel orders were
issued for Rhee, in conventional military style, dated March
27, by which he was "authorized and invited to proceed by
air on or about 1 April 1947 from Washington D. C. on the
Statesman to Fairfield-Suisun Army Airfield for further
movement by air on or about 2 April 1947 to Korea." In the
orders Rhee's trip was described as an "emergency mission"
and it was provided that "travel expenses will be borne by
the individual." On March 31 Rhee went to the Air Transport Command Terminal, as he was instructed to do, and
paid $900 for his fare to Tokyo. He prepared to report at
the ATC Terminal at 8:00 A.M. the following day.

Early in the evening of March 31, there came a telephone
call from Colonel Monson, in the office of Assistant Secretary
of War Howard Peterson, saying that Rhee's permission to
fly on the army plane had been canceled. As soon as offices
were opened the next morning, I called Major Simmons at
the War Department and was told that, "The State Department has informed the War Department that Dr. Rhee's
return to Korea was not considered of sufficient importance
to justify placing ATC transportation at his disposal." Thereupon I called at Secretary Hilldring's office, and he told me
with some consternation that he had just learned of the cancellation but had no idea what lay behind it. He put several
assistants to work tracing the message, and two hours later
informed me that the cancellation had been "suggested" by
a subordinate official of the Department (who may have
been John Carter Vincent) and that he was informing the
War Department this suggestion did not represent the views
of the Department of State. Nevertheless, the War Depart-

ment informed Rhee that the cancellation was "unalterable."

Hilldring expressed deep regret at this inexplicable development and before the day was over he telephoned to say that passage had been secured for Rhee and his aide, Chang Kee Young, on a Northwest Airlines plane which was making a "pilot run" to Tokyo (preparatory to establishing passenger service), scheduled to leave Minneapolis on April 5. The military permit issued by Hodge had been rescinded and Rhee did not know whether or not he might be allowed to re-enter Korea. Nevertheless, he took the flight. From Tokyo he flew to Shanghai and went on to Nanking for a conference with Chiang Kai-shek. With Chiang he had a long talk about the communist encroachments in their respective countries and about the need for securing more aid from the United States if these threats were to be held in check.

On April 19 Dr. Rhee wrote from Shanghai about still further delays:

I think we are leaving for Seoul on Monday the 21st. It is a long story to tell of all the red tape required for my passage. The Northwest Airlines plane finally left Minneapolis on April 8. As soon as I landed here from Tokyo (where I had a two-hour talk with General MacArthur) I was swamped with Chinese officials and banquets. Then Generalissimo and Madame came from Hangchow and we had a delightful and important conversation. They offered their own plane to take me back home, with the understanding that I would secure permission for landing in Seoul.

I wired my friends in Korea and it took two days to get the reply, which said that General Hodge demanded an official request from the Generalissimo through the Chinese Consul in Seoul. The Chinese Government wired the request at once. Then we were informed that we would have to have another permit from Seoul, identifying the plane by number.

I was so impatient that I was about to wire General MacArthur. But this afternoon the Foreign Office notified me officially that we are to leave Monday the 21st, at 9:00 A.M. So I feel that the way is at last open for me to return home.

An interesting incident: Soon after my arrival here the local Catholic paper published a letter from the new Foreign Minister, Wong, addressed to the chairman of the committee for my entertainment, asking him not to make a big thing of my visit. It was supposed to be confidential, but the Catholic paper got hold of it and published it together with a strong editorial comment to the effect that the Foreign Minister has nothing to do with arrangements made by the people of Shanghai. When I went to Nanking, Minister Wong was the first one to entertain me at his official residence, and the Catholic paper criticized him again for doing what he asked others not to do. Then it was revealed that the Chinese Ambassador in Washington, at the request of some of the "Far Eastern experts" there, had requested Wong to refrain from receiving me as a state guest. This story seems to have made the reception even bigger.

Upon Rhee's return to Korea, he faced a situation of explosive potentialities. Kim Koo, with whom he had worked for years in an atmosphere of difficult co-operation, was determined to go his own way. In Chungking, during the latter years of the war, against Rhee's strongest urgings Kim had reorganized the cabinet of the Provisional Republic to take in a number of communists and thus to effect a coalition. Rhee greatly respected Kim Koo's courage and patriotism but had serious misgivings about his wisdom. Kim neither spoke nor read English and was really ignorant of world affairs. He had little patience with Rhee's arguments that the United States faced grave international problems and would have to work out the Korean question slowly in accordance with its global program and responsibilities. Kim could see little further than the immediate situation and, as a Korean patriot, he saw little reason why he should be restrained by obligations the United States might have in Europe or elsewhere.

On March 2 Kim had convened a meeting of 1500 delegates from all over south Korea and proposed that the authority of the Provisional Republic be proclaimed at once. A vitriolic debate lasted that day and most of March 3, after which Kim Koo resigned as chairman of the Provisional Government and Syngman Rhee was elected to replace him. Thus Kim Koo's revolutionary plan was temporarily defeated. Meanwhile, in the Interim Assembly a bill was introduced proposing a constitution for an independent government in south Korea. The bill was referred to a committee, where it remained very much under active consideration.

Under these circumstances, it was necessary for Rhee to act quickly to prevent an open clash between the Korean patriots and the Military Government. As the best, if not the only, means of controlling the situation, he called a press conference upon his return to Seoul, and announced that he had a personal understanding with Assistant Secretary Hilldring that steps would soon be taken to establish an independent government in south Korea. General Hodge issued a counterstatement, pointing out that he himself was just back from Washington, and that positively there was no such agreement or policy as Rhee claimed. Hodge was aware of the restiveness of Kim Koo and many other Koreans, but apparently was convinced that Rhee was stimulating the revolutionary sentiments, rather than doing his best to curb them. Rhee called on Hodge to explain the problem and to ask for his co-operation, but was brusquely dismissed.

In May General Shtikov with a retinue of 38 Russian officers arrived in Seoul to reopen the Joint Commission sessions. From the first, he refused to honor the pledge Molotov had made in Moscow to admit all Korean leaders to consultation, and once again stalled the negotiations with a flat refusal to admit any Koreans who opposed trusteeship. Hodge made a valiant effort to convince the Koreans that trusteeship meant only "aid and assistance" and that the United States would not concur in the establishment of any Korean government that would not be genuinely democratic. On June 9 Rhee published an "open letter" to General Hodge, in which he requested an official definition of the words *trusteeship* and *democracy*. He insisted that "My true motive was and still is to find some basis for co-operation and common understanding between us." Pointing out that he was disturbed by Hodge's reiteration that "the Moscow decisions are 'immutable laws' which no one can change," Rhee concluded that "the fundamental question on which alone you and I can work together" was to devise effective means of establishing an independent Korean government.

For the remainder of that dismal summer of 1947 (while the Joint Commission meetings dragged on into utter and patent futility) Rhee was practically under house arrest. Letters from the United States could reach him only through a military censor. The telephone was removed from his house. Official and other prominent visitors passing through Korea were discouraged and circumvented if they wanted to see him. And his weekly radio talks and other means of reaching the Korean people were cut off. In sharp contrast (and in revealing illustration of how divided were the Departments of State and War at this time) in Washington Rhee's standing was never higher. Even those officials who liked him least were by now willing to accept the fact that Rhee was the chosen leader of the Korean people and would have to be dealt with on that basis. When General William Dean was called to the Pentagon from Fort Leavenworth to be briefed for his new assignment as Military Governor (under Hodge) for South Korea, Colonel Ben C. Limb, then chairman of the Korean Commission, was invited to explain to him the Korean political situation. At the State Department, Charles Saltzman, who replaced Hilldring as Assistant Secretary of State, was uniformly agreeable, if not always in accord with Rhee's views. Walton Butterworth, who replaced John Carter Vincent as chief of the Office of Far Eastern

Affairs, did not seem much of an improvement, but John Allison and Niles Bond, who worked on the Korean question, appeared willing to adjust their thinking to changes in the factual situation.

In August Secretary Marshall finally accepted the fact of the failure of the Joint Commission and issued an invitation for Russia, Great Britain and China to join the United States in seeking some alternative to trusteeship for Korea. The Soviet Union rejected this bid and on September 17 Marshall asked the General Assembly of the United Nations to place the Korean question on its agenda. When this proposal was made, the hallways and the lounges at Lake Success buzzed with worried comment. Delegates said to one another that Korea was a Russian-American problem, that it was a major power dispute which should not be unloaded upon the unsteady and toddling United Nations. The American delegates, ably seconded by Ben Limb and Louise Yim—as unofficial Korean representatives—assured the delegates from other nations that the United States was not trying to abandon or evade its primary responsibility in Korea. It would still provide financial and economic aid along with military and diplomatic support. What it did wish to accomplish was to get out of the bilateral deadlock with Russia; to avoid the charge that America wished to make South Korea a military base, which would be impossible if the U. N. rather than the U. S. was the sponsoring body for the area; and to lessen Asian fears that the United States was succeeding to England's role as a leading colonial nation in the Far East. On September 23, 1947, the General Assembly accepted the Korean question on its agenda, and on November 14 it voted 43 to 0 for the holding of a free election in Korea, to establish an independent government, under the observation of a United Nations commission.

To Syngman Rhee this vote came as a vindication of his lifelong program—a vindication both to his foreign critics

President Rhee is shown talking with north Korean refugees on Koje Island and Mrs. Rhee distributing a gift shipment of sewing machines, in midsummer, 1951. (*ROK O.P.I.*)

and to the doubtful among his Korean following. For months (since his return to Korea in May) Rhee's position had been exceedingly unenviable. He had sufficient political power to prevent Kim Koo from going ahead with his plans for revolution, but he had very little to offer to the patriots as an alternative. His claim of a special understanding with Hilldring came to appear increasingly dubious as the months passed. The program he had sketchily indicated was not put into effect. And his relations with the Military Government obviously were very bad. Rhee had no will to launch a new movement; and indeed, from his forced seclusion he had neither the means nor the freedom of consultation out of which new plans might have been developed. From his home, high on a bluff overlooking the Han River, he kept closely enough in touch with affairs to know that his rivals, Kimm Kiusic and Lyuh Woon Hyung were not enhancing their own popularity. Hodge and the whole personnel of the Military Government were depressed in a stagnant melancholy as black as Rhee's own. But it is scarcely true that misery finds any special consolation in having company. The plain fact was that Korea was drifting helplessly nearer to ruin, with no pilot at the helm. North Korea was becoming militarily stronger and Russia alone seemed to have a policy and the will to advance steadily toward its anticipated goals. Then out of this depressing blackness came the presentation of the Korean question to the United Nations. A stirring recital of Korean aspirations was laid before the General Assembly by Warren Austin, chief of the United States delegation. This was followed by a thrilling climactic vote of 43 to 0 for an election to establish in Korea a free government. After the darkness, there was beginning to dawn a glimmer of light.

Chapter XIII

HALF A REPUBLIC
—OR NONE

Back in August, 1947, before the Korean question was even presented to the United Nations, and while Rhee was still under virtual house confinement in Seoul, he was experiencing the very blackest period which traditionally comes just before the dawn. His fortunes well illustrated the old Korean proverb that "The darkest spot is just below the candle." Branded as an enemy of the United States by General John R. Hodge (whose own fumbling plans for Korea Rhee could not approve), Rhee wrote on August 12 to his friends in America: "I am fighting for the interest of the United States and Korea, as the interest of our two countries is the same and identical." So long as he had to oppose phase after phase of the State Department's Korean program (which closely paralleled the policies under which China was lost), this assertion did not appear to his critics to make sound sense. But after the vote of the General Assembly to hold elections in Korea a new situation began to unfold in which Dr. Rhee anticipated increasing understanding and co-operation. On October 7, 1947, in reply to assurances from his representatives in New York that the U. N. would favor an election, he wrote with sober satisfaction, "Most of the major obstacles have been brushed out of our path." When Secretary George Marshall stated that an election

242

would be held soon in Korea, Rhee wrote, "This refers to an election in the north and south" to which Russia would not consent, "but we can apply this principle to our election in the south for the present."

Amid all the grimness of those days, Ray Richards (a news correspondent for the International News Service, who became a close friend of the Rhees) tells a story that indicates Dr. Rhee could on occasion jest about even so crucial a question as Korean independence. The Rhees had a dog whose coat of fur they tried to thicken by keeping him out of doors on cold nights during that fall and winter. During the daytime, when it was warm, they freely let him in the house. When Richards called on them one day and found out about this plan, he chuckled and told Dr. Rhee, "There you have it! You Koreans put a dog out when it's cold and take him in when it's warm! How can such a people ever learn to govern themselves?" Every time the two men met during the next several months, Dr. Rhee would look at Richards with twinkling eyes and remark something about the dog and the inability of the Korean people to manage their affairs. As a jest the subject was in good standing, but no one in the Rhee circle ever cast doubt on the independence movement with any seriousness.

From Lake Success Colonel Ben Limb wrote to Dr. Rhee in mid-November, assuring him enthusiastically that he had found the delegates from Syria, France, China, India, El Salvador, Australia, Canada and the Philippines (who were to observe the projected Korean elections) all friendly and determined to get the elections completed not later than March 31. The Soviet Union had denounced the U. N. vote to hold elections as illegal, and the Ukrainian Republic had silently ignored appointment to the supervisory U. N. Commission. This attitude, however, was not preventing the U. N. from proceeding with its plans, and on January 8, 1948, the first group of the U. N. Commission delegates arrived in Seoul.

Dr. Rhee, along with General Hodge and Kimm Kiusic, joined the official welcoming party which greeted the delegates in the crowded Seoul Stadium. The speech which was made by Dr. Rhee so well portrays both his own feelings and the significance of the occasion that it merits presentation in full. It may be noted here that Dr. Rhee speaks easily, fluently and frequently. He is unrestrainedly articulate. On many occasions he speaks extemporaneously, generally with a simple theme developed with a prolific body of applications and specific illustrations. When he reads a prepared speech, as he did on this occasion, he presents it with a skillful utilization of emotional and intellectual emphasis on the main points to be unfolded. His voice is resonant, full-bodied and responsive to a wide variety of meaningful overtones. Even in his latest years he commands a dramatic expressiveness which might be envied by a professional actor. As a natural speaker, with his powers enhanced by long practice and thoughtful consideration of communicative requirements, he responds wholeheartedly to the stimulation of an audience and often shows a fine appreciation for the special requirements of particular situations. This address to the U. N. delegates—delivered in the presence of some 200,000 Koreans who had long waited for the fruition of his policies of peaceful appeals—represents a careful attempt on his part to set the right tone for their initiation into their labors:

Gentlemen of the United Nations Temporary Commission on Korea:

We welcome you with solemn gratitude and renewed hopefulness as you undertake one of the most significant missions in human history. It is not often that the united peace-loving nations of the world have undertaken such a task as the one to which you have been committed.

Forty years ago our nation was sacrificed to the ambition of one of the Great Powers, while the other nations of the world stood aside. During the past 28 months our long-suffering people have once again been the victims of circumstances wholly beyond our own control. We have seen justice delayed, pledges postponed, and the hopes of honest men frustrated. It has seemed through many dark months that a new blight had fallen across our land, even worse than that we were forced to endure while our country, however harshly ruled, was still united.

In those dark months we touched the depths of bitterness, but we refused to despair. We clung then—just as Koreans will always cling, so long as they may live—to the fierce determination that our country must once again be united and must once again be free.

We hail your arrival as a solemn event, not only in our own history, but in the history of the world. No longer do the Korean people stand alone. The free nations of the world have heard our voice and have answered it.

We take pride in the fact that the vote to establish the Temporary Commission on Korea was the largest affirmative vote ever cast on a disputed issue in the General Assembly of the United Nations. In this vote we see a world-wide recognition that our cause is a just one. We see in it a justification for the unfaltering demand we have made that Korea must be restored, indissolubly, to its own sovereignty.

The difficulties that lie ahead are not veiled from our eyes. We know that the task you have undertaken will not be easy. The obstacles that have prevented the reunification of our country during the past two years have not melted away as a result of the United Nations vote.

However, your mission to our country introduces a basically new element into our sadly troubled situation. The United Nations has voluntarily shouldered a responsibility for assuring that the promises which have been made to us will be kept. What has for too long been narrowly conceived in many quarters as a "Korean problem" has now at last properly been accepted as a general problem basically connected with the re-establishment of the stability of Asia and the continued peace of the world.

Troubled as our hearts still are by the magnitude of the issues yet unsolved, we nevertheless rejoice in the revolutionary change

in our situation that your mission portends. With the free nations
of the world standing by our side, we are confident that our long
struggle for freedom must at last succeed.

We need not review for you the events of the past two years.
Our people have been rent asunder, our hopes have been frustrated, our sovereignty has been submerged. Dire evils have
sprung up in our very midst, while we have been denied the opportunity to deal with them or to protect ourselves. These are the
conditions that led to the consideration of our situation by the
United Nations. It is precisely to remedy these evils that your
mission has been undertaken.

We greet you in a spirit of determined hope and of co-operation. Our goal is the same as yours—the re-establishment of a
united, democratic, and independent Korea that will be a corner-
stone of peace. It is vital to our welfare, as it is to the peace of
the world, that Korea should never again be subjected to international intrigue and the contending ambitions of major powers.

What we ask is very simply the inherent and inalienable right
to rule ourselves. In all our 4,000 years of history we have never
gone outside our own borders to attack a neighboring state. We
never expect to do so. But neither have we ever surrendered to
foreign aggression, and this we never shall do. There is not now
nor has there ever been any question of Korean infringement
upon the rights of any other nation. What we are determined to
achieve is the restoration of our own right to live as a free people
in our own way.

Located as we are in the strategic heart of North Asia, we can
and should be the keystone of peace in the East. This is the contribution we are prepared to make to the peoples of the world.
It is for the achievement of this high goal that we particularly
welcome your aid.

The thirty million people of Korea are asking for justice, not
for alms. Our case has been presented before the greatest forum
of free nations ever assembled in the history of the world. The
decision has been rendered that our sovereign rights must be
restored.

We pledge to you our active aid in your endeavor to enforce
that decision. We trust that an election may be held at the earliest

possible date. We trust that our long-sought freedom no longer will be needlessly delayed. It is our earnest hope that within a few weeks there will be established a free and sovereign government chosen by the Korean people themselves, ready to take its place among the nations of the world in the responsible partnership of free men everywhere who are dedicated to the cause of establishing and maintaining a just peace.

In this solemn hour we look to the future, not to the past. With the knowledge that our cause is just, and with the full support of the United Nations, we confidently expect that the obstacles will be overcome and that we shall succeed. The people of Korea will never rest until once again the control over our own destinies is restored to our own hands.

The first formal session of the U. N. Commission was held in Seoul on January 12, and in it the delegates drafted letters to General Hodge and to General Shtikov, requesting free access to all areas in Korea and the co-operation of the two commanding generals in holding the elections in their respective zones. Hodge replied immediately, affirming full support for their mission. The letter to Shtikov, and all their subsequent communications to him, went unacknowledged. Some of the U. N. delegates later expressed regret that, instead of writing letters, they had not simply formed a cavalcade of motor cars and traveled north to the 38th parallel and on across it—unless or until they should be stopped by communist guards. But, as one of them said wryly, "Who would have been willing to ride in the first car?"

Within two weeks it was evident that the Soviet Union would not permit the proposed election to be held in the north, and a very able report of the situation was drafted by the Indian delegate, Mr. K. P. S. Menon, who was selected to go back to Lake Success to ask the United Nations for further directions. At Lake Success a special "Little Assembly" was called in February to hear the report and decide what to do. The issue was clear: would the holding of a

separate election, to establish a separate government, in
south Korea advance or deter the hope for reunification of
the country. Canadian and Australian delegates argued that
such an election would solidify the division. United States
and English spokesmen (ardently seconded in off-the-floor
lobbying by Col. Limb and Miss Yim) declared that the
existence of a free and democratic government in South Korea would prove to be a rallying point for the loyalties of
all Koreans; that it was especially required in view of the
establishment of a communist regime in North Korea; and
that this was the only available way in which the United
Nations could carry forward its mandate to grant self-government to the Korean people. On February 19 the Little
Assembly authorized the Commission by a vote of 31 to 2,
with 11 abstentions, to observe elections "in all areas in Korea accessible to it."

A few days later, on February 26, there occurred a dramatic conflict in Dr. Rhee's home in Seoul which illustrates
some of the comic confusions which have marked many
phases of the handling of the Korean situation, and which
also indicates one of the ways in which Dr. Rhee has from
time to time suffered from inaccurate news reporting. At
about three o'clock in the afternoon Dr. Rhee was sitting in
his home talking with Mrs. Hughes of the International
News Service and with an unidentified reporter for the
French Press Agency when Dr. Harold Noble—son of Rhee's
first English teacher at the old Pai Jai School, half a century
earlier—came bursting breathlessly into the room. Without
any preamble, and paying no attention to the two reporters
who were present, Noble told Dr. Rhee the U. N. Secretariat
had approved a plan to hold a system of "staggered" elections, beginning at the southern tip of the Korean peninsula
and working northward, in successive stages. In this way,
he said, the elections would proceed until the 38th parallel
was reached, and would go on beyond it through the entire

President and Mrs. Rhee, with their dog, Happy, on the grounds of *Kyung Mu Dai*, shortly after their return to Seoul in the early Spring of 1953. (*ROK O.P.I.*)

country if the communists would approve. If not, the halting of the elections at the parallel would show the entire world the responsibility of the communists for preventing the reunification of Korea.

Dr. Rhee, describing the incident in a letter he wrote on March 2, said he told Noble, "Such a plan is not acceptable to us; no one ever heard of such a plan before. The main reason why our people would object to it is that it would create a dangerous situation. Let us suppose there are 10,000 communists in south Korea. If we hold an election all through the south, they will spread out in every section and we will be able to check them. If we hold an election in only one district or even in one province, they will all congregate and concentrate their weapons and forces to disturb that section of the country. Moreover, they would try to go from one district to another to vote in all the elections and that would be another problem to check."

Noble then asked Dr. Rhee, "Will you boycott the election?" Rhee replied he had been working for the election for over a year and surely was not planning to boycott it. But, he replied, the staggered election plan would be impossible, and he added, "We will go right ahead with our election program." Noble and Rhee engaged for several minutes in a heated exchange, in which Noble declared that if Rhee opposed the plan the U. N. Secretariat had devised the American troops would be withdrawn and the Russians would take over all Korea and Rhee replied that he was tired of hearing threats that if the Koreans did not accept fully all the plans presented by the Military Occupation authorities, the troops would be pulled out. "They should keep in mind that we are not working for the sake of Korea only. We are fighting their cause just as much as we are fighting our cause."

At this point the two reporters hurried out, and Noble warned Dr. Rhee that they would send out news cables and

"In two hours it will be all over the United States that you are boycotting the U. N. elections." Rhee remained adamant, and after another half hour Noble left, saying, "I have been your friend for fifteen years and this is our saddest moment." Rhee replied, "My friendship for you is always the same. Our political views have nothing to do with it." One hour later Noble returned, with a copy of the U. N. election plan in his hand and said, "I must apologize and I am terribly sorry. I made all the trouble for nothing. There is no plan for a staggered election, after all!" Rhee patted him on the shoulder and told him it was all right.

The sequel to this conversation was another flurry of press condemnation of Rhee in newspapers all around the world. Mrs. Hughes had gone from Rhee's home to the Duksoo Palace, where the U. N. Commission met, and found out that there was no such plan as Noble had described. Hence, she sent out no story. The French reporter, however, had rushed to the cable office and sent out news of the sensational rejection by Dr. Rhee of the U. N. plan for an election in Korea. The next day Richard Johnston of *The New York Times* called on Dr. Rhee and asked him for a statement of what had actually occurred. However, the story was so complicated that the news desk decided not to run it—especially in view of the fact that it was a tempest in a teapot, with no factual basis. The result was that foreign newspaper readers were left once again with the impression that Dr. Rhee was stubborn, unco-operative, and so confused that he opposed the U. N. election plan one day, and favored it again the next. By such events (multiplied many times in other circumstances) his reputation for being undependable and erratic spread. To a very large extent, that reputation is a factor of the difficulties of foreign news reporting.

The progress being made toward the holding of elections in Korea did not result in improving the relations between Dr. Rhee and General Hodge. On the contrary, their mutual suspicion and acrimony increased. On January 27, 1948, the usually sober and restrained *Christian Science Monitor* gave front-page display to a story by Gordon Walker, its chief Far Eastern correspondent, stating that "the official American viewpoint" in Seoul was "that Dr. Rhee would be unsuitable as a political leader, even of south Korea." The story continued, "As far as the local United States command is concerned, Dr. Rhee today seems to be classified in almost the same category as many Korean communist leaders, who either are hunted or else already in jail for activities deemed detrimental to the occupation operation." On February 2 General Hodge wrote to Senator Brien McMahon: "Regardless of Mr. [Jay Jerome] Williams' great regard for Dr. Syngman Rhee, Dr. Rhee has not been for over a year, and is not now, working in co-operation with the efforts of the United States to bring forth an independent and united Korea, but actually is making our task more difficult. He has done much in the past year to bring about distrust by Koreans of the occupation forces and of United States policies." According to another story by Gordon Walker (who was closely in Hodge's confidence) Kimm Kiusic was slated by Hodge for the presidency of the proposed republic.

There is no doubt that both Rhee and Hodge had come to a point where each readily thought the worst of the other, without much regard for evidence. Of course there were spite-mongers near both men who did their petty best to heighten the animosity. Since Hodge, for all his limitations and mistakes, came to entertain a high regard for the Korean people and did his best on their behalf, it is most regrettable that he and Rhee could not have maintained the cordiality of their earlier relations in the fall of 1945. When Hodge charged Rhee with "making our task more difficult," what he probably had in mind was the fact that his ostensible Military Government could not operate effectually unless supported by the real power which Rhee held by virtue of his popularity with the people. As the time came to work out plans for holding an election in Korea, the necessity became acute for a conference between Rhee and Hodge to insure a workable harmonizing of their ideas as to procedures. Hodge several times sent indirect hints to Dr. Rhee that it would be desirable for him to come to the staff headquarters in the Banto Hotel. Rhee ignored them, feeling that if Hodge did not care to call upon him, the least courtesy he could extend would be a direct invitation.

The impasse was broken in a strange manner. One evening in January General Hodge telephoned to Rhee, who was about to leave with Mrs. Rhee for an early evening meeting, asking if, on his way home, he would stop at Kyung Mu Dai, the official governmental residence which Hodge occupied, to give his reaction to an important notice which the Military Government intended to issue. Rhee agreed and a couple of hours later drove up to the door of Kyung Mu Dai. Leaving Mrs. Rhee in the car (since the call was not social and was presumably but to require a few moments) he went in. In the room which Hodge used as his study Rhee found many papers spread out, completely covering a large table in the middle of the room. Hodge greeted him grimly and told him "Now we can give some consideration to all these matters that have been piling up." Actually the conference lasted more than an hour and a half, during all of which time Mrs. Rhee sat outside in the car, in weather far below freezing, completely ignored by the guard standing by the door and with no invitation to enter. Both she and her husband resented the way they had been treated that night (though so far as Mrs. Rhee was concerned, this was doubtless simply an oversight on Hodge's part). What was true without any doubt whatsoever was that the two men who represented the only two sources of significant power in South Korea had drifted into ill-concealed enmity. Relations were not exactly cordial, moreover, between

Dr. Rhee and the other major political leaders among the Koreans. His differences with both Kim Koo and Kimm Kiusic came to a head as election time drew near and a choice among them was to be made. Two other personalities were introduced into the situation when General Hodge brought to Korea Philip Jaisohn, whose prestige for his founding of the Independence Club half a century earlier was high, and Younghill Kang, author of *The Grass Roof*, the most famous book by a Korean ever to be published abroad. Immediately upon his arrival Kang gave out an interview to newsmen, saying, "I don't like and don't trust Dr. Rhee. He's a politician, and I despise all politicians, Koreans or Americans. I'm a writer, an artist. Artists have no interest in the squabbles of materialistic politicians." Kang's sentiments clearly were such as to serve the purpose Hodge presumably had in mind, but his lack of tact rendered him unsuitable as a disruptive influence. Kang was shunted into a "back room" job and a few months later was quickly sent back to the United States. Jaisohn similarly lost for himself much of the goodwill he had upon his arrival, by saying in the hearing of a group of American and Korean newsmen that "The Koreans do not know how to make a bar of soap. How can they govern themselves?" This was in mid-April, when plans for the election were announced, but while the Canadian, Australian and Syrian delegates on the U. N. Commission were stating publicly that in their judgment it would be best to give the elected officials merely a consultative and not a governmental role. Suspicion, ill will, charges and countercharges flew in all directions.

A more sensational development was an invitation extended by Kim Il Sung, the premier of "The People's Democratic Republic" set up by the Russians in North Korea, for all "patriotic" South Korean leaders to attend a meeting in Pyengyang to plan for a coalition government under which the entire nation could be united. Kim Koo and Kimm

Kiusic, along with the representatives of the Nan No Dang, South Korean Labor Party (communist) agreed to attend the conference. Both denounced the projected United Nations election for a separate government in south Korea, asserting it would have the effect of perpetuating the 38th parallel division.

On February 12 General Hodge called Dr. Rhee, Kim Koo and Kimm Kiusic into conference at Kyung Mu Dai in an effort to persuade them to issue a joint statement favoring the U. N. election plan. Kimm Kiusic objected, saying he feared they were not in agreement. "Kim Koo and I have consulted one another," he said, "and we agree that any election for South Korea should be postponed until we can hold a joint conference with the leaders of the north." Rhee then tried to persuade the two other Korean leaders to change their minds. The discussion continued for two hours, without success. On Saturday morning, February 21, Kim Koo called a press conference and announced publicly that he was opposing the U. N. election. A newsman reminded him that he had said a few months earlier, "My loyalty to Dr. Rhee will never change. The pine trees on Namsan may change their color, but not I." Kim Koo remained silent for a time, then replied, "We may disagree on small details, but on the whole we stand together." When the reporter later told Dr. Rhee of this conference, Rhee commented that, "All the pine trees in Korea are dying." As a matter of fact, the disagreement on the election was one of the most vital issues in the entire postwar Korean situation. The simple question was whether plans should be carried forward to restore independence in South Korea, or whether all such plans should be held in suspension awaiting a possible development of a spirit of co-operation by Russia. In essence, this has remained the central issue during all the subsequent period of the war and the truce in the peninsula. Rhee had made up his own mind very early that expectations built upon the hope of reasonableness in the Kremlin were mere chimera.

On April 5 Dr. Rhee wrote: "The general belief is that the decision of the two Kims to go north will be much played up here. Already the communist press is praising them. They will make Kim Koo the vice-chairman and try to keep him there. Their propaganda is working hard to tell the northerners that Kim Koo is coming home to save the nation. It will go all right for a while, but they will insist either on carrying out the Moscow decision (on trusteeship for Korea) or pronouncing that the northern government is *the* government and must be moved down. All the military preparations (in the north) are pointing toward it. Kimm Kiusic will demand the withdrawal of the Americans—he has always clamored for it—the Russians will move across the border and watch how the American people react, and if America is pulling out you know the rest. Dr. Kimm is too smart and he still thinks he can outwit the Russians. The only thing is for us to go right ahead with our program in the south without any delay." A few days later the conference in Pyengyang was convened. On April 26 Dr. Rhee wrote, "If General Hodge was not in favor of it, the two Kims and their followers could not have gone. Kiusic was escorted up to the 38th parallel by a GI" and was "protected and entertained all the way." "We are informed," Rhee added, "that our opponents are hoping the conference will put up Dr. Kimm as head of the national government of united Korea, thus to postpone the election in the south."

At the end of April the two Kims returned to Seoul from Pyengyang, both announcing they could not support the plans of the communists, for they had become convinced the so-called national government that was projected was merely a plan to extend Soviet control throughout Korea. Kim Koo was unsparing in his denunciation of the communists, but Kimm Kiusic insisted they were reasonable men and it would be possible to work with them. He announced that he had received a personal promise from Kim Il Sung that under no consideration would the north cut off the flow of electricity to the south. (South Korea got almost all its electricity from the hydroelectric power plants on the Yalu River.) To anticipate a bit, the power from the north was abruptly cut off on May 14, and from that time Kimm Kiusic's loss of face in South Korea was so complete that he faded into background obscurity. To still further dip into the future, he remained in Seoul when the communist army captured it on June 29, 1950, and upon their retreat in September of that year the communists took him north with them. His death a few months later was reported through underground sources.

After the failure of their mission to Pyengyang, Kim Koo and Kimm Kiusic reiterated their objection to a U. N.-sponsored election in South Korea, and announced that they were asking their followers to boycott it. A flurry of news dispatches went out from Korea carrying this news, and intimating that such a boycott would nullify the significance of the election, which was scheduled to be held on May 10. The communists instantly took the cue, and the South Korean Labor Party announced that it, too, would boycott the election. Since the news reporters had been declaring in their dispatches for many months that Rhee was an extreme rightist who represented only a handful of wealthy landowners, this threat of a boycott by both the leftists and the middle-of-the-roaders seemed to augur a deathblow to the United Nations program for a South Korean government. The United Nations Commission hurriedly called a meeting to discuss whether the election should be canceled, but the plans were far too advanced to be dropped. No one in authority, however, ventured any forecast as to what would happen on election day.

From the comfortable distance of 8,000 miles away, and

especially several years after the event, it is difficult to picture the confusion, acrimony and disorder of that pre-election situation in Korea. The communists were officially treated as a genuine political party and were allowed full freedom of action. With ample funds from the north, they had secured control of large numbers of newspapers and other media of information (notably motion picture theaters) and were able to give the impression of being a large minority of the total population. The mountainous terrain of Korea, the severe shortage of transportation and communication facilities, the inadequacy of the Military Government (both in numbers and in knowledge of the language, customs and temper of the Korean people) to control the situation all united to make easy the communist program of sabotage, arson, murder and planned revolution. On Cheju Island the communists gained virtual control, spreading out from the central mountain mass to terrorize the villagers in nightly raids. Several hundred communist agitators and terrorists were arrested, but on the eve of the arrival of the U. N. Commission in January, General Hodge freed 669 of them in an amnesty to "restore full political liberty." At Taegu, in February, a communist coup was attempted and the police maintained command only after forty-eight persons were killed. More arrests occurred. When the U. N. Commission commenced its meetings, one of its first acts was to demand the release of all "political prisoners." General Hodge denied there were any political prisoners in South Korea, but under the urging of the Commission he almost emptied the jails of all the communists who had been arrested for their lawless activities. The communists openly announced, on billboards and in their newspapers, that they would attack any "traitors" who tried to vote in the "imperialist election planned by the United States through its puppet, the United Nations."

Dr. Rhee at first had no thought of standing for election

as a member of the Constituent Assembly which was to be elected on May 10. The function of this Assembly would be to draft a constitution and then elect a president, after which would be proclaimed the establishment of the independent Republic of Korea. His friends both in Korea and in the United States urged him to stand for election, since the prevailing view in the news sent out by the foreign correspondents was that he did not have any broad base of support among the masses of the people. If he should ignore the election and then should subsequently be chosen as president, not by the general electorate but merely by the elected assemblymen, the charge would be reiterated endlessly that the people themselves did not want him. Rhee yielded to these arguments, and permitted his name to be entered as a candidate from his home district in Seoul. Since there were no other means of determining candidacy, the regulation propounded by Hodge was that nomination should be by petition. Rhee's nominating petition soon was presented bearing 40,000 signatures—many times the 200 required under the regulation. Up to the end of the final day for submitting nominations, he was unopposed. But after the official deadline had passed, on April 16, an unknown man named Choi Neung Chin appeared at the headquarters of the Military Government alleging that he was a candidate desired by the great majority of the voters in Rhee's district, and that he was tacitly supported by Kimm Kiusic and Philip Jaisohn, but that Rhee's "hoodlums" had frightened people so that only 93 had dared to sign his petition. He requested an extension of the time limit. Although he had no evidence to submit, in view of Rhee's prominence the Military Government authorities decided it would be discreet to lean over backward and allow Choi an extension of a week, to safeguard themselves against charges of favoritism toward Rhee. At the end of the week, Choi again appeared—this time with a petition bearing the required 200 signatures. However, upon examination many of them were found to be fabrications. The military officials ruled that he would not be allowed on the ballot. Choi appealed his case to the United Nations Commission, which made an elaborate investigation, held extensive hearings, and finally issued a lengthy report stating that there was no evidence Choi had suffered any interference in his attempted candidature. The matter was ended officially, but the communist papers in Korea continued to drum away at charges of "coercion" by Rhee's "hoodlums" and many of these stories were dutifully reported to American newspapers as allegedly unbiased reporting of the news.

The morning of May 10, 1948, arrived and Korea was to have its first democratic election in its long 4,400 years of history. The vote extended to women (a notable fact in the Orient) as well as to men. Registration had been heavy, and when the polling places (guarded by American soldiers and Korean policemen under their orders) were opened at 8:00 A.M. long lines of voters had already formed. The balloting proceeded through the day, even though the communists conducted a campaign of violence in which over one hundred persons were killed. Voters were checked against the registration records, were handed ballots, and were then directed into the secret voting booths. In many instances election officials had to intervene to prevent husband and wife from entering a booth together—for this was their first experience with the secret ballot. Many voters upon emerging from their booths attempted to hand their open ballots to the officials, but were instructed to fold them and drop them into locked boxes. During the day the delegates and staff members of the U. N. Commission dashed around Korea (having previously divided the area into districts to be covered by the observers) visiting as many of the polling places as they could. Curious officers of the American Military Government, wondering what would eventuate from all the plans and all the mishaps of the preceding months, also went on private inspection tours of the polls. Probably there has never been another election in which parties and candidates participating had less control and were under such close observation. That night when the locked ballot boxes were delivered to the Military Government officials to be guarded and to have the ballots counted, there could be no reasonable doubt that what was recorded was a fair expression of the will of the voters. Syngman Rhee's election in Seoul was accomplished by a vote of over ninety-five per cent of all the registered voters in his district.

As for the widely heralded boycott, it simply failed to eventuate. Over 86% of all eligible voters had registered, and 92.5% of registered voters turned out to cast their ballots. In such periodicals as the *New Republic* and the *Far Eastern Survey* (published by the Institute of Pacific Relations) editorials promptly appeared declaring the election meaningless since all the leftists and all the moderates had boycotted it. Most American newspapers accepted the fact of a more than 90% turnout of voters as being anything but a boycott. The Koreans themselves were enormously pleased that their new experiment in democracy had been launched so auspiciously. The United Nations Commission withdrew to Shanghai, to insure an impartial atmosphere for its deliberations on the reports submitted by its observers, and on June 25 issued its own report that there had been "a reasonable degree of free atmosphere wherein [were exercised] the democratic rights of freedom of speech, press and assembly," and that the election constituted "a valid expression of the free will of the electorate in those parts of Korea which were accessible to the Commission and in which the inhabitants constituted approximately two-thirds of the people of all Korea."

When the election of 200 assemblymen was certified (from among more than 2,000 candidates) the elected members gathered in Seoul on May 22 and agreed to hold their first formal organizational meeting on May 27. At this point General Hodge again intervened (seemingly with a genius for making mistakes) and suggested that the Assembly not elect a chairman but simply accord the honor to its oldest member—who was a man named Sur, aged 78. At the session on May 27 many members spoke with great indignation against Hodge's proposal, both because they opposed it and because they feared it signaled an intention to try to dominate the Assembly. Rhee did his best to calm them down, assured them that General Hodge was probably simply trying to be helpful, and suggested they proceed with the election as planned. After some quiet was restored, Dr. Rhee led General Hodge into the Assembly Hall and introduced him to the members, saying, "If there is any one person who deserves more credit than any other one single individual, it is General Hodge, and I know he is rejoicing with us in what has been accomplished." Then, turning to General Hodge, General Dean, and members of their staffs who were with them, Rhee went on, "We are happy to see so many Americans here. You have been with us in a most difficult time. You were perhaps misunderstood and unjustly criticized but all these unpleasant experiences will soon be forgotten forever, but one great fact will remain and stand out prominently in history: you have come here to help us to restore our independence and you have accomplished it. Our people will remember this for generations to come with a high sense of profound gratitude and appreciation." General Hodge responded with a speech in which he promised to keep hands off of Korean affairs and offered to do whatever he could to assist the Assembly with its work of creating an independent government.

That same day General Hodge released publicly the text of a letter to Dr. Rhee in which he sought to lay down the basis for an orderly transition of authority, as well as expressing a variety of cautions, hopes and policies. The paragraph of most lasting significance is the one that read: "The policy of the United States has always been that Korea shall be a *united* independent nation under democratic government free of foreign domination. That same policy is reflected internationally in the 43 to 0 vote of the United Nations General Assembly when it voted to observe elections in Korea as a step toward establishing a Korean National Government and to advise Korean elected representatives in the formation of that government. This policy also reflects the wishes of the 30,000,000 Korean people, and we all regret exceedingly that the free election could not be held in Korea north of the 38° parallel at the same time as in South Korea. The United States and United Nations hope that this can be done and that representatives from North Korea can join those of South Korea in the establishment of a truly National Korean Government joining North and South Korea together in one nation. It is my hope . . . that the newly elected representatives will do everything in their power to form a truly democratic government and to unite Korea."

On May 31 the Assembly met again and proceeded to elect a chairman. Eighty-five of the members described themselves as independents, another forty-eight classed themselves as followers of Dr. Rhee, 30 listed membership in the Democratic Party (led by Kim Sung Soo), and the remaining 37 belonged to a variety of splinter groups. Dr. Rhee was elected chairman by a vote of 189 to 8. During the next several weeks the Assembly worked on the draft of a constitution, with considerable assistance from American lawyers attached to the Military Government. On the 19th of July, 1948, with the constitution adopted, Dr. Rhee was elected the first president of the Republic of Korea by a vote of 180, with 16 of the members voting for Kim Koo. On August 3 Dr. Rhee's nominee for prime minister, Mr. Lee Bum Suk, was confirmed by a vote of 110 to 84. Indications were that President Rhee would have a sound working majority in the Assembly, but that there would be a strong minority to serve a "watchdog" function. This expectation forecast the general tenor of executive-legislative relations in Korea during the years that lay ahead.

The process of turning over authority to the new government from the American Military Government proceeded in orderly fashion through a period of several weeks. The date for the formal inauguration ceremonies was set for August 15, notable as the anniversary of the defeat of Japan and the liberation of Korea. On that day General Douglas MacArthur came to Seoul for the ceremonies, the first time he had ever set foot on Korean soil. During the preliminary observances, he placed his arm around President Rhee's shoulders and remarked, "If Korea should ever be attacked by the communists, I will defend it as I would California." Attentive newsmen who heard and reported the remark wrote it down as an expression of rather inane sentimentality. That it was sincere was finally demonstrated in late June, 1950, when American troops under MacArthur's command poured back into Korea from their base in Japan to repel the communist attack. But all that lay far ahead. On the Inaugural Day, neither Rhee nor anyone else expected that the future would be free of heavy problems. This day, however, was not the time for qualms or fears. The sky was overcast with heavy clouds which promised, but did not deliver, rain. As Rhee stepped forward to deliver his inaugural speech, the clouds cleared away and beams of strong sunlight illuminated his white hair and crinkled face. Some of the observers saw an omen in the clouds, but to the Koreans the best symbolism was the breaking forth of the sunshine.

Rhee's inaugural address emphasized the importance of democracy and the need for protecting civil rights and individual liberties. He called for "the active support of every citizen, whatever his former beliefs may have been." In the light of subsequent events, perhaps the most notable portion of his speech is the paragraph which reads: "We await with hope and determination the missing third of our representatives from the north. The 38th parallel division is no part of our choice and is wholly foreign to our destiny. Nothing must be neglected to keep wide open the door to reunion of the whole nation. The Everwhite Mountains are as surely our boundary to the north as are the Straits of Korea to the south. No temporary international situation can obscure what has been established through the centuries as historic fact." The speech concluded: "We realize that without the goodwill and assistance of free nations, the many problems before us might be insuperable. But we know we have their goodwill and feel we can count on their assistance. Above all, we need and we count upon the loyalty, the devotion to duty, and the determination of all Korean citizens. With hopeful hearts and minds alert we take into our own hands today a sovereign republican government that will long endure."

Thus, at the age of 73—still looking toward the future, animated by hope and dedicated to the cause he had served for more than half a century—Syngman Rhee entered upon the heavy responsibilities of attempting to build the structure of a democratic government upon a foundation of 4,400 years of monarchy, Orientalism and Confucian codes of subordination. He was confronted with the task of restoring economic self-sufficiency in a country cut in half, with its mineral, coal and hydoelectric resources held by a foreign power and with its heavy population augmented in the south by some three and a half million refugees. He had to deal with an international situation that placed the world's most effective aggressor within the northern confines of his country and hungry to extend its conquest, while on the other hand he

Top: Dr. Rhee introduces Kim Koo to General Hodge, upon Mr. Kim's return to Korea from China in November of 1946. *Bottom:* President Rhee on one of his many visits to American wounded aboard the hospital ship *Jutlandia,* at the Pusan dock, in May, 1951. (*U.S.A. Signal Corps*)

had to deal with a sponsoring organization of sixty nations which comprised not only his worst enemies but many more countries which would willingly trade off Korean interests for such advantages as they might win for themselves. His people were not only inexperienced in self-government but were untrained for administrative and technological duties. Political parties in the Western sense did not exist, but the Korean electorate was beset by many factions which were bitterly contentious. Education had been in the Japanese language until 1945 and was designed to instil Japanese ideas, which meant that the knowledge of Korean history was incomplete and distorted. Because of the unhappy experience with the Military Government, many Koreans were confused as to where around the world were their friends, or if, indeed, their country had any real friends at all. The communists, who had enjoyed three years of opportunity to dig themselves into South Korea, were prepared to exercise every means at their disposal to disrupt and destroy the new government.

Under the searchlight of world scrutiny, liberals of many nations were determined to be critical of the procedures for dealing with communist subversion adopted by this new ward of the United Nations. Many so-called liberals were eager for the Republic of Korea to fail, to demonstrate that only through co-operation with the Soviet Union could suppressed peoples really find liberation. Miseries, inadequacies, shortages and troubles multiplied upon every side. And to compound the problems, many simple-minded Koreans believed (just as simple-minded people do elsewhere) that through the establishment of their own long-sought independent government, all their problems would be solved. "Today we rejoice in having our own government! Surely by tomorrow we shall have security, and education, and plenty to eat!" It was not alone the poorly educated and uninformed people of Korea who looked to their new president for miracles. Many well-intentioned but uninformed people outside of Korea took it for granted that if the independence Korea so long had sought did not answer all the people's needs, the fault must lie in the man at the helm.

Chapter XIV

THE PRESIDENCY—
BUILDING DEMOCRACY

FOR MORE THAN half a century Syngman Rhee labored with single-minded intensity to create an opportunity to help the Korean people achieve the decencies of democracy, a modernization of their ancient society and a redress for the ills of an outmoded system. When the chance came for him to lead them into the Promised Land, fate seems to have contrived every conceivable stratagem for turning his dream into a mirage. He himself was seventy-three years old—a decade or more beyond the usual age for retirement. The presidency which he was assuming was for only half a nation—with the division mischievously drawn between the living halves of an organic whole: industries to the north, agriculture to the south; hydroelectric power and coal to the north, light fabrication factories dependent upon such power to the south; fertilizer plants to the north, and in the south fields farmed for two thousand years and therefore unable to produce except as nitrates and phosphates were poured into them each spring.

Northward, across the artificial line of the 38th parallel, lived kindred millions—speaking the same language, treasuring the same traditions, thinking largely the same thoughts as their fellows in the south—but organized under a totalitarian regime and subject to a large army of repatriates

267

under Soviet control. South of the 38th parallel huddled
more than three million refugees from the north, homeless,
jobless, and restively competing for a livelihood in the midst
of the nineteen million overcrowded and undernourished
southerners. Mines, factories, farms and fisheries were all
in disorder and disrepair, lacking in equipment and technicians, short of raw materials, and uncertain in plans. Ownership of most of the heavy industries, transportation and
communication resources, and of many of the better homes
was vested in the new government (having been turned over
to it by the American Military Government after expropria-
tion from the former Japanese colonizers). Few indeed were
the Koreans who had resources with which to purchase these
means of production, and even fewer were those who were
willing to risk converting fluid capital into deteriorating
properties which would be subject to attack from the north,
sabotage from communist agents in the south, and to taxation
and regulations yet to be devised by a new and untried
legislature.

The further problems that confronted Syngman Rhee were
lack of experienced personnel, the unfamiliarity of the
people with democracy, shortage of everything needed for
economic recovery, a Japanized educational system that had
fallen apart when the Japanese were repatriated, a currency
not admitted to the international exchange and with little
gold reserve, a critical military defensive problem without
an army, undefined international inspection without international responsibility, and an American aid program pointed
toward relief instead of the industrial development that was
so desperately needed. Both the United States and the
United Nations were interested enough to insist upon precautionary controls, but were not interested enough to invest
the money and the attention required to help establish the
economy, the armed forces and the government structure of
Korea as an integrated going concern. Korean politicians

were confronted with the heady prospect of being able to advance their own interests for the first time in their lives, with no real organized political parties and with no rooted traditions to serve as guides for plans, procedures or conduct.

Syngman Rhee had asked for leadership—and he got it under conditions almost impossible to conceive. As an illustration of the minuteness as well as the pervasiveness of the difficulties, he could not even secure a secretary. Koreans with secretarial skills were practically nonexistent and foreign secretaries were not available. During the course of the Constitutional Convention, in the summer of 1948, he wrote to an American friend a long letter (pecked out on his own portable typewriter), which concluded: "I am not going to have this rough draft retyped, as we have not time to do it. Hope you will be satisfied with its mistakes and errors as I am typing it myself in the midst of all the confusion and noise. Do find for me a good stenographer!" In these circumstances Dr. Rhee entered into the last and greatest phase of his life's work—the building of a secure, democratic and free Korean nation.

"These people [the newly elected members of the National Assembly] don't know what democracy is," an associate of President Rhee wrote in early July, 1948, while the debate on the constitution was proceeding. "For most of their lives they had to take orders from Japan and resented it. For the past three years they took orders from the Military Government, and most of them liked it because that got them positions of influence. Now they don't intend to take orders from anyone, but they don't know how to make up their minds for themselves." The summary is as apt as it was disheartening.

As the new government began to take form, President Rhee was quickly immersed in problems that had no solutions. Hundreds of appointments had to be made, many of them to posts of crucial importance, but there were no

Koreans with democratic administrative political experience. No wonder many foreign observers doubted that the Koreans were as yet able to govern themselves. Not a few Koreans shared this doubt. Yet the problems piled higher every day and most of them demanded action without delay.

Without any doubt the one saving factor in the situation was the character and determination of Syngman Rhee. Despite his age, he was a paragon of tireless activity. Accumulation of years had not dimmed the sharpness of his mind. Weariness didn't keep him from giving detailed consideration to a multitude of problems. Three characteristics formed the fundamental basis of his leadership and they proved adequate to the harrowing responsibilities which he faced. The first of these qualities was an optimism that could never admit defeat and that always insisted problems could be solved. The second was an ability to see beneath and through the maze of complexities to the simple and clear issues which underlay them. And the third was the absolute conviction that the welfare of the Korean people and the interests of the great powers of the free world were so closely intertwined that his efforts to build a Korean democracy would inevitably gain the support of the Western nations. Without this clarity of vision and without this faith, there would be no bulwark of democracy in South Korea today. Out of this compound emerged a magnetic leadership which created at least a partial success against overwhelming odds. The rebirth of a free Korea is the direct and unquestionable result of the selfless devotion and transcendent abilities of Syngman Rhee. The great and indeed the crucial advantages of having democracy soundly implanted on the vast and teeming continent of Asia are owing directly to him. Those who have made him the whipping boy for the succession of disasters arising from the confusions of postwar policies in the Far East should ponder thoughtfully and humbly the question of where the free world would stand in the Far

East today had it not been for the devotion to democracy and the iron will of Syngman Rhee.

While the questions of the character of the new Korean government were still unanswered, President Rhee took time out on July 5, 1948, to write a long letter, of which a few excerpts will show the tenor of his thinking. Concerning the question of the interrelationships of Korean and American military security and responsibilities, he expressed the basic policy from which he never since has deviated:

. . . I was told the U. S. Army is making plans to withdraw during the next 60 or 90 days. Our position in that connection is that they ought to give us time in which to organize our national defense. When that is done they can do what they please. However, we will not ask or beg the United States to maintain forces here to protect us from foreign aggressors. Americans should decide to safeguard the United States interests in Korea, first from a sense of moral obligation, and second for the sake of American security. If the American people are sufficiently informed of these facts, I do know the Americans will not pull out and leave to the Soviets a free hand for occupying the south.

Turning to a consideration of the newspaper label of *extreme rightist* which was freely and frequently applied to him, President Rhee indicated that his own economic-political philosophy is liberal Jeffersonianism—neither radically socialist nor reactionary. "We are stigmatized," he wrote, "as reactionary. We do not have to answer this charge by words. Our actions will speak more loudly for us. I do not think they can find anything in our constitution when adopted that will show that we are reactionary. Everything that has been said in the U. S. Constitution to guarantee the freedom of citizens has been adopted in our constitution and we are going even further than the Americans have ever gone. Our laborers are demanding now an article permitting the laborers to participate in business co-operation with capital and also giving them a share of the profits. This motion was brought before the Assembly and they asked me to give my opinion. I think it is a little too much for the laborers to demand. I am sure that the resolution should be voted down . . ."

On still another subject which was to become a major issue in the second presidential election in 1952, President Rhee outlined the reasoning which he has continued to defend against those members of the National Assembly who wanted to change to the French system of legislative dominance over the executive:

There was another question which created a strong division of opinion. This was about the premier and the cabinet. Certain leaders of the Assembly who have high aspirations secretly advocated the idea of the premier being the head of the government. They were about to present a resolution to the Assembly to this effect when I learned of it and met with them. I explained that when England adopted its cabinet system, they had a king who could not be the executive head and whom they could not get rid of. But in Korea we have no king and there is no reason to create a president who would be outside of the government. The moment the Assembly voted against a premier the government would lose stability. Therefore, we should adopt the American system and insure stability at least for the duration of the presidential term of office. Overnight the committee changed its recommendation and decided to keep the premier in name, but to make him an assistant to the president, who will be the real executive head . . .

A few days later Dr. Rhee wrote, "While the Congress is in session downstairs, I am in my office trying to answer some letters which need my attention." He was deeply immersed in the problems of constitution-making, trying to foresee problems that would arise, and attempting to devise compromise solutions which would gain and hold majority support without weakening the structure of a government which would have to be strong if it were to have a chance

During an interlude between conferences in mid-July, 1953, President Rhee shows the Kyung-Hoi pavilion in the Capitol grounds to U.S. Secretary of State John Foster Dulles and Assistant Secretary Walter S. Robertson. *(Seoul Daily News)*

for survival against the many external pressures and internal problems. "So far," he wrote, "the draft [of the constitution] provides for a single-house Congress, which will elect the president and vice-president. My original suggestion was that a clause should be adopted for the establishment of an upper house after the government is formed." This suggestion of the need for an upper house, to insure balanced consideration of legislative questions, again came to the fore in 1952 and was finally adopted as a constitutional amendment, after a hard struggle. Another idea which President Rhee presented to the Assembly was also adopted in the summer of 1952: namely, that the president should, after the first election, be chosen by direct vote of the people.

Despite all the difficulties, the new government took office on August 15, 1948. Two months later President Rhee was writing, "Since the turning over of the government departments, a vacuum exists, due to the fact that the former AMG advisers sit around, wondering if their services are still wanted. We have asked twice for a list of available personnel, but have not yet received any answer. In the meantime, nobody does anything. . . . It will take a long time before we have an over-all survey and everything going easily."

On August 18 the Rhees moved into Kyung Mu Dai, the official residence which had been occupied by General Hodge. There was little furniture and they had the usual difficulties of new householders. Mrs. Rhee wrote that one of her problems was that the cook they engaged had worked for an American family in Seoul and the wife called to complain about her cook being hired away. She and Mrs. Rhee discussed the question amiably for an hour over a pot of tea, with the result that the cook stayed in Kyung Mu Dai. The big two-storied, green-tiled building sits on a hilltop above Seoul, surrounded by twenty acres of wooded grounds. It is handsome, but very hard to heat and requires a great deal of furniture and a large staff of servants. Under Korea's depressed circumstances the Rhees had no intention of living any more expansively than they had before. Consequently, they engaged only two housemaids, and closed up the entire house except for the reception rooms and two offices on the first floor, and a bedroom, small dining room, and sitting room for themselves on the upper floor. During all the years since, this same economy has been maintained. The first and only time the state dining room (almost as large as a basketball court) has been used during their occupancy of Kyung Mu Dai was when they entertained Secretary of State John Foster Dulles in August of 1953.

The grounds, on the other hand, were a sheer delight for Dr. Rhee. He has always loved physical exercise and the out of doors, yet the danger of communist assassination attempts (of which three were uncovered) had kept him confined to the small grounds around his former modest home in Seoul. At Kyung Mu Dai, with a police guard around the surrounding wall, he has been able to stroll at will through the grounds and along the wooded paths. He is especially interested in the goldfish in the pond beside the house, and goes every day to feed them. He also has arranged a small pool where the fish are bred and watches them as attentively as any farmer would watch a flock of new lambs. His favorite outdoor recreation is to putter about the grounds with pruning shears in hand, trimming bushes and directing the work of a gardener. During the first two years of his presidency (until the communist attack upset all schedules) he customarily spent half an hour every afternoon out in the back yard sawing wood. His friends learned that the gifts he most appreciates are sets of small tools, such as wrenches, screw drivers, pliers, etc. In the evenings, since he cannot read after working all day on papers, he enjoys spending a couple of hours writing Chinese calligraphy. Mrs. Rhee rubs up the inkstone for him, helps in the selection of the proper brushes, and criticizes the results—noting that one line is too heavy, another light or wavy, or judging the balance of a completed ideograph. Sometimes, she will read aloud to him for an hour from some current book—preferably a discussion of international affairs. Their life in their leisure hours is a simple one, comparable to that of middle-class educated Americans, even to the Saturday evening movie, which is shown in the reception room of Kyung Mu Dai.

Dr. and Mrs. Rhee are both very fond of animals, particularly dogs. They have two small dogs, which Dr. Rhee always feeds with scraps from the table, and which are devoted to him. They lie at his feet while he works, sit outside his office in the hall when he has high-level conferences, and walk with him around the grounds. In the summer of 1948 the Rhees had a three-legged deer, which hunters had found in the woods, and which they presented to him. This animal was a prime favorite for about six months, after which it developed such a temper that it had to be disposed of. During the winter of 1952 Dr. Rhee had another pet deer running about the grounds of Kyung Mu Dai, and coming up to him to receive the sugar and bread which he always had for it. In the spring of 1952 Korean soldiers found two small black bear cubs in the eastern mountains, where their mother had been killed by artillery fire, and they presented these to Dr. Rhee. The cubs wrestled, climbed and entertained visitors through the summer, and then were sent to Washington, D. C. as a present for President Eisenhower, where they are now entertaining a larger audience in the National Zoo.

For a time after his election to the presidency Dr. Rhee continued his tennis, which he had played intermittently for many years. Mrs. Rhee was his customary partner, and spectators were strictly barred. This game he gave up, too, when the communist attack was launched, and he has not returned to it since. Fishing was a sport he learned to love while in Hawaii, and he continued it in Korea when time permitted. When he could do so, he went out in Inchon Harbor in a small boat (or in Chinhae Harbor, during the period while the capital was in Pusan). When he could not take time for a fishing trip, he would try in the summer months to get in an hour of fishing, once or twice a week, in a large pond behind the Capitol building. Again, he discouraged spectators during these fishing periods, and used the time for meditation on government policies and problems.

Along with his light but regular exercise, the fact that he does not smoke or drink and that he eats simply doubtless contributes to his excellent health. Another factor is his ability usually to forget his problems when he leaves his desk. He and Mrs. Rhee prefer a few good friends to large numbers of casual acquaintances, but the confining duties of the presidency make friendship a luxury difficult to enjoy. Consequently, they have devised entertainments which they can manage singly or together. When bedtime comes, usually around 10:00 P.M., after evening prayers Dr. Rhee ordinarily falls quickly to sleep. By 7:00 A.M. he is up, and he and Mrs. Rhee have breakfast together, during which time he reads to her a chapter or more from the Bible. After this he works alone for an hour on the most pressing problems before him. By 9:00 A.M. he is out on the grounds for a few moments of observation of the goldfish and a brief walk, and 9:30 A.M. finds him commencing a round of conferences and the study of innumerable documents. He writes long and frequent memorandums, sometimes dictating them to a secretary, but often pecking them out with two-fingered typewriting on a small portable.

A large measure of his effectiveness in the presidency stems from the flexibility of mind which makes it easy for him to turn quickly from one problem to another, often wholly changing his mood in doing so. He may have a disagreeable discussion with one person concerning a policy which is not working well; and after that talk ends he may greet another visitor with such relaxed graciousness that it seems impossible he ever has to struggle with problems. During the course of a day he will talk with experts in half a dozen different fields and often he astonishes them by his grasp of not only the essentials but even of many of the details of the problem upon which they are working. Subordinates who report directly to him have found that he is not satisfied with generalities, but requires detailed statements of what is being done and of the reasons why some particular course of action is being recommended.

As an administrator, his greatest liability is his difficulty in delegating full responsibility. When this problem is discussed with him, he is prone to look at his inquirer quizzically and ask just how much responsibility can safely be intrusted to untrained and inexperienced aides. His secretary high-lighted another facet of the situation when he wrote, on December 3, 1948, "It is very difficult to make the Koreans understand he cannot attend to everything." Everyone who has a problem, whether he be a Korean, an American, or a representative of one of the several international organizations in Korea, tries if he can to get the direct attention of the president. When the government was first organized, with lines of authority not clearly defined, cabinet ministers developed the habit of bringing to President Rhee for final decision a great many of the problems with which they had to deal. This habit has persisted unduly—partly because of Dr. Rhee's own nature; partly because cabinet officers have been frequently changed, so that there are always new and inexperienced ones; and partly because Korea has been beset during the short life of the republic by a mass of problems too acute to permit of anything but top-level decision.

Because of his long lifetime of agitation, President Rhee has a high regard for the value of achieving favorable public opinion, and during his entire tenure in office he has given considerable attention to the press. He is fond of issuing statements for newsmen and perhaps does so too often for maximum effectiveness. During his first eighteen months in the presidency, he held weekly press conferences, for foreign and Korean newsmen. At these conferences, he would talk freely, normally with no prepared statement, and would answer every question that was asked. It is probably true that in all his life he has never turned aside a reporter with the noncommittal, "No comment," which is the customary safeguard of high officials. His custom is to talk with the press in English until all the foreign newsmen are satisfied, then to hold a continuing session in Korean with the local pressmen. However, after the attack by the communists, this regular weekly press conference was suspended and it has not been renewed. In place of it, President Rhee has adopted the practice of granting special interviews to selected newsmen—a method that frequently results in harsh criticism by those who are left out. In any period of crisis (and Korea is never long without one) newsmen will send questions to Kyung Mu Dai, accompanied by a request that they be allowed to come and see the president personally. Most of these questions are answered only in writing, with personal conferences perhaps once in two weeks. During this latter period he has granted general conferences only at infrequent intervals. Korean reporters practically never see him except at these general conferences, which is a subject of common complaint among them. Since President Rhee most often discusses international questions with newsmen, he is chiefly interested in addressing the foreign press. The Korean newsmen, of course, receive daily news reports from the Korean Office of Public Information.

President Rhee, however, far from neglects Korean public opinion. His favorite method of reaching the Korean people is through public speeches, which are naturally reported in full in the local newspapers. He is a prolific speaker and enjoys extempore addresses. If he says something indiscreet in one of these off-the-cuff addresses, and it gets translated for a foreign correspondent, President Rhee customarily will paraphrase what he has said in an appropriate statement in English, which he then considers as "official." This custom is one of the commonest sources for the contradictory or inflammatory statements which from time to time get into publication abroad.

In the spring of 1949, during eight days at the end of April, President Rhee undertook his most ambitious barnstorming tour of Korea. He set out from Seoul in a special train, which took three days for the customary twelve-hour trip to Pusan. Along the route he delivered eleven speeches the first day, ten the second, and five on the third. Some of these were major addresses to large crowds gathered in decorated town squares in the major cities along the route. Others were whistle-stop talks to crowds of farmers gathered at a crossroad. When such a crowd was spotted ahead of the train, President Rhee would order a stop, while he talked to the crowd for from ten minutes to half an hour. On one occasion, a crowd of perhaps two thousand farmers and their families had gathered behind a rice paddy fifty yards from the tracks, to wave at the president as he went by. President Rhee had the train stopped, got off, went to where the crowd had assembled and shook hands with hundreds of the people. His staff was worried for fear he would wear himself out, but upon arrival in Pusan on the third day— where a tremendous crowd had gathered for a speech—he was apparently as fresh as when he left Seoul. From Pusan he and a small party went by motor launch to Chinhae, where he held a long press conference with a dozen newsmen who had gone there by car. After that he took two days out to rest and fish, then went on by water to Moppo, at the southwest corner of the peninsula, and worked his way back by train to Seoul, talking to numerous groups along the way.

Newsmen estimated that in the eight days occupied by this trip President Rhee addressed between three and four million people.

In these talks President Rhee devoted himself to explaining the pattern of Korean-American co-operation and the communist threat. "Without American aid," he told the crowds, "we never could hope to revive our blasted and divided economy. United States military aid is helping us to build the army that already has subdued the communist guerrillas on Cheju Island, in the Chiri Mountains, and around Taegu. American technicians are helping us to organize the coal mining and electricity generating programs upon which our hope of industrialism is based. American fertilizers are providing the basis for the best crop year in our history." He would then drive home the corollary point that the aid program could only be effective if the Korean people co-operated properly with it. "American money can accomplish very little," he told the crowds, "unless it is matched by Korean labor and patriotic devotion. Don't dream of heaven on earth," he admonished them, "but work for the practical realities. We shall have to work longer hours, may have to eat less, and do without everything but the bare necessities. It is the future of our nation we are building, to make a better life for our children. If we should selfishly concentrate upon getting a better life for ourselves today, the whole future of our land may be imperiled."

This theme of building for the future has marked every phase of President Rhee's administration. During the period of aid for Korea supplied through the Economic Co-operation Administration he often was in disagreement with the officials who wanted to concentrate on bringing in consumers goods, in order to deflate the high prices, whereas Rhee insisted the Koreans were willing and able to tighten their belts for the sake of devoting all available funds to the construction of long-range factories, transportation facilities, and mining developments. In his first inaugural address he sounded this keynote: "The final destination toward which we are bound lies yet far ahead, at the end of a road that may be both long and rough. . . . This is no time to relax and take our ease. Rather than to brood upon the past, or to rejoice in the present, we must plan and work for the future." In a letter written during his first weeks in the presidency, he said: "The United States did not start out in marble halls, but in log cabins. That is the choice we must make."

In the middle of December, 1948, Paul Hoffman, director of ECA, visited Korea, and on December 14 Dr. Rhee wrote: "Hoffman was here for a day—came late Wednesday and left at 8:00 A.M. Friday. He stressed the importance of 'co-operation' between America and Korea . . . He fully agreed that Korea is ready for democracy and thinks it should be helped, etc." When Hoffman returned to the United States from this trip, he created a new watchword by telling a press conference that, "Korea is the bastion of democracy in Asia." This proved to be an astute forecast.

In these two themes: economic recovery and the establishment of a sound democracy that would be a bastion against communism, President Rhee confronted the major problems with which he had to deal. The other problems were multiple (such as the procurement of capable personnel, development of education, re-establishment of the Korean language —which the Japanese had tried hard to displace, etc.) but in general they were means of accomplishing the two great ends. As a matter of fact, the two goals are more easily separated in a narrative account than they could be in governmental policy-making and administration.

Reform of the farm tenure system, for example, was necessary economically, since the farmers had somehow to be rescued from their dire poverty, and it was also a necessity if democracy was to be given any substantial meaning to the mass of the people. Because of its far-reaching importance (with 75% of Koreans living on farms, and almost half of them being tenants), farm-tenantry—or land reform—offers a key to the fundamental nature of President Rhee's administration.

Although he was elected president of the republic, with powers defined more broadly than those of an American president, he still was far from having a free hand. American economic and military aid were essential to Korean survival, and both U. S. policy and American public opinion favored immediate and sweeping land reform for South Korea. The Military Government had sold the farm lands which had been taken over from former Japanese owners and thus set a precedent for granting ownership of the farms to their tillers. The "land reform" of the communists in North Korea was loudly and widely heralded by Owen Lattimore and the Committee for a Democratic Far Eastern Policy (which influenced many Americans before it was placed on the attorney general's subversive list). Actually the seven and a half per cent of the North Korean population which was classed as "landlords" was liquidated—jailed, exiled, or executed—and the land was placed at the disposal of communist committees in every *myun,* who were charged with the responsibility of allocating it to farmers who were dependably loyal to the regime.

In South Korea President Rhee had no intention of liquidating landlords. The problem he did confront was complex. Those who owned rental farm property, he felt, should be forced to sell it—but they should be paid a fair price. On the other hand, the tenants had no money with which to purchase the land. And the landlords must be given some chance to make other investments which would preserve their capitalist status—for Rhee was and is committed to a free enterprise society. Another complication existed in the fact that the landlords did not wish to sell their lands, and they were heavily represented in the new National Assembly, both by the Democratic Party members and by many of the Independents. Since the Korean landlords had traditionally been the most influential segment of the population, it was wholly natural that many of them had won election to the Assembly. These men had a very important vested interest in maintaining their land ownership. What President Rhee needed to do, and what he immediately set about doing, was to devise some means of making land reform acceptable to them. The solution which he devised was to offer the landowners certificates in payment for their farm properties which could be used to purchase factories that had been expropriated from former Japanese owners by the Military Government and then turned over to the government of the republic. In Rhee's view, the transfer of title to these properties from governmental to private ownership was fully as important as the solution of the farm tenantry problem, for only when that was done could the republic become a genuinely free enterprise society.

Because of a vast amount of misinformed discussion in the foreign press, the nature of the land tenure question in South Korea has been widely misunderstood. The real problem was the shortage of land, which was only sufficient to allow an average of two and a half acres per farm family, rather than the concentration of ownership in a few hands. Figures on land ownership are revealing. Only 272 landlords owned as much as 245 acres. Tracts of from 12.5 to 24.5 acres were owned by 5,488 landlords. Rental properties of from 2.5 acres to 4.9 acres were owned by 45,692 landlords, and 213,453 families owned less than 2.45 acres of land. What was bad about the farm tenure system was not the concentration of large acreages in a few hands, but excessively high rentals, which normally amounted to one-third of the annual crop. Farmers, who under the best of available circumstances were barely able to make a living for their families, were subjected to the heavy drain of losing one bushel out of every three of the rice they could grow. They had to be rescued from this burden and President Rhee placed land reform at the top of his agenda.

A land reform bill was one of the first pieces of legislation to be introduced into the National Assembly. It was referred to the Agricultural Committee, where hearings and special study consumed about eight months. On June 21, 1949, a land reform bill was passed, but because of objectionable features in it, it was vetoed by President Rhee. Finally, on March 25, 1950, he signed a new bill which had been drafted with his aid, with the advice of American agricultural economists, and which met the political requirements of the National Assembly. By April 15 arrangements were completed for the sale under this law of 1,709,320 acres of farm rental lands to 1,236,558 former farm tenants. The price charged for the farms was one-third of the annual crop (the same as the former rental charge), payable each year for a term of three years. This payment in kind was to be made to the government, which in turn paid to the former owners the equivalent value in certificates of 150% of one average annual crop. The communist attack disrupted this program, but in spite of the ravages of the onslaught (which carried the invading armies all the way to the Pusan perimeter), by March 1, 1951, more than a million acres had been transferred to the new ownership. President Rhee takes great pride in this achievement, which he considers the most sweeping land reform program ever put into effect by a sovereign democratic nation.

The problem of establishing a sound democracy which would safeguard the rights of the people and help them achieve substantial benefits was extremely complex. The Korean people had no background of democratic traditions. As President Rhee said in a press conference on March 2, 1952: "Many of the Korean people are used to the monarchial form of government and do not know fully yet how they should rule their nation, now that it is a republic. They have to learn how to exercise their rights through their established agencies, especially when the latter choose to ignore their constituents and pursue only their own ends . . . Just as the monarch of old had absolute power to enforce his will and change the law to suit his personal convenience, the people in a republic today have power to see to it that their representatives respect their will and so are able to keep the government from falling into the hands of a few—whether they be in the government or the Assembly or both. The real ruler of a modern, democratic nation is the people; they have the inherent right to restrain or remove their agents should they oppose the express will of the people, especially when a serious national issue threatens to endanger the democratic form of government."

In any fledgling government, the severest test of its basic nature comes when the first election is held, after its establishment, to determine the successor to its founders. President Rhee could talk democracy—and frequently did—but how would he act when the time came to stand for re-election and risk the loss of office? Many foreign observers felt that President Rhee failed this test, for in 1952, when under the Constitution the Assembly was to elect a president for another term—and when the Assembly made it evident that it did not intend to re-elect Rhee—he insisted upon an amendment to the Constitution to transfer the power of electing the president from the Assembly to the people themselves.

In November, 1951, President Rhee first presented to the Assembly a request for the amendment. He was advised to call in the Assembly leaders and find out what kind of favors (patronage and other privileges) they would demand as the price of voting away their own power to choose the chief executive. It was pointed out to him that this procedure is standard in older democracies (including the United States) and that he could not expect the Assembly to yield such power unless the members got something they desired in return. He scorned the suggestion. He said that the amendment was democratically sound and that if the Assembly rejected it, the people would insist upon its adoption. The result was an overwhelming rejection by the Assembly, followed by a series of actions by President Rhee which brought down upon his head official protests from Trygve Lie, secretary general of the U. N., President Truman, and the heads of state of Canada, Australia and Great Britain, as well as a veritable storm of denunciation in the world's press. What he did was to declare martial law in the Pusan area (which he said had nothing to do with the dispute with the Assembly, but was necessitated by communist guerrilla activities in the hills around Pusan, in which several American soldiers as well as a score of Koreans were killed), and to arrest four members of the Assembly. One of the members arrested had murdered a man in a café brawl; the others were accused of taking bribes to vote for a president who would favor a coalition with the North Korean communists.

What President Rhee very deliberately set out to accomplish was to create such a storm in Pusan that the Korean people in even the most remote districts would hear about it. When they did, they would ask what it was all about and would learn that President Rhee wanted the people to have the right to elect their own president; whereas the National Assembly insisted on retaining the right of election. As soon as the Korean population understood the issue, the national response was overwhelming. Every provincial legislature and over 1,400 local councils adopted resolutions supporting the amendment. Many localities sent representatives to Pusan bearing copies of their resolutions and these representatives crowded around the Assembly hall demanding passage of the amendment. On one occasion they held the assemblymen in the hall for four hours before the national police took charge and cleared an exit.

The chief concern of foreign governments was whether Rhee would disrupt the war effort against the communists by withdrawing some of the Korean troops from the front-lines to assign them to martial law duty in Pusan. This he did not do. The chief concern of many individual supporters of the republic abroad was lest democracy was being destroyed to entrench Rhee as a personal dictator. Great Britain sent Minister of State Selwyn Lloyd to Korea to investigate the situation, and Lloyd reported back to the foreign ministry, "Rhee is clearly most astute, and, in spite of his age, is head and shoulders above any of his compatriots whom I have met." Some critics abroad charged that Rhee was violating the constitution. He replied that instead he was trying to amend it. On July 4 the Assembly concluded a marathon session of two days and two nights by adopting the amendment by a vote of 163—0, with three abstentions.

On election day, August 5, with 8,218,100 citizens registered, and with four presidential candidates (including Hugh Heung-woo Cynn, an old prison mate of Rhee's, and Cho Bong-am, a former communist and presumed coalitionist), Dr. Rhee was re-elected by a vote of 5,238,769, out of the 7,033,633 votes cast (86% of the total registration). The comment by the United Nations Commission, which observed the election, was: "The chief criticism which could be made of the elections was the short time between the date when nominations closed (July 26) and polling day (August 5). . . . The Commission's teams found that, especially in the rural areas, very little was known about the personality, record, or platform of any candidate except Mr. Syngman Rhee. As to the charge of police interference, there undoubtedly was some interference, but it did not make any significant difference as far as the choice of the president was concerned."

President Rhee's own commentary was incorporated in

his second inaugural address, presented on August 15, 1952, in which he said: "The recent 'political disturbances in Pusan' so widely publicized throughout the world as a terrific crisis were in fact a tempest in a teapot. The truth is that some of our foreign friends and press correspondents unfortunately listened to what my political enemies were telling them and believed the fantastic story that I was trying to dissolve our National Assembly and eliminate democracy by armed force. Most of my friends, however, who know my life and the principles that I stand for, laughed at them and some were even indignant. However, with the solid support of my fellow citizens we have won the fight against our adversaries. As a result, our democratic institutions and principles have been strengthened immeasurably by permitting the people, at long last, to have the right to elect their president by direct, popular ballot, instead of permitting that power to remain in the hands of the National Assembly."

There are three "behind-the-scenes" additions to this story which require telling. The first is that President Rhee, throughout the fall of 1951, was honestly and fully convinced that he would not run for re-election. He was desperately tired and had begun to feel the weight of his years. He felt that by withdrawing into private life, he could still influence Korean policies, particularly in the realm of international relations, without having to bear the burdens of day-by-day administration. When he told me several times that he had decided not to run, I was not certain that he really understood his own feelings enough to insure the reliability of his conclusion. However, Mrs. Rhee, who surely understands the depths and nuances of her husband's mind better than any other person, assured me that she knew beyond any doubt that Dr. Rhee had decided firmly upon retirement. Why, then, did he change his mind? The reasons are doubtless complex. Foreign influence was unquestionably being used to affect the choice of the Assembly. The storm of denunciation from abroad aroused fully Dr. Rhee's fighting instincts and persuaded him that he must show his critics he was not defeated by their clamor. And finally, the resistance of the Assembly to the popular will convinced him that democracy in Korea was not yet sufficiently established to insure its persistence without the sheltering protection of an executive who was dedicated to it.

Another story relates to the aftermath. In the fall of 1952 when I spent two weeks in Korea, I referred to that political struggle, and President Rhee's whole body sagged and his face showed the full marks of his years. In a flat and heavy voice, he replied, "You will never know what the fight cost me."

Still a third sidelight on the event was presented in a talk I had with Colonel Harry L. Mayfield, commander of the Seoul Civil Assistance Team of the U. S. Eighth Army. "When President Rhee was forcing through the amendment," Mayfield said, "we were all against him. But we have changed our minds. We admire him for the courage and skill with which he won his fight. Moreover, we have had time for a second thought about what would have happened if he had yielded to the foreign pressures and had dropped his plan for the amendment. The National Assembly would have elected someone besides Rhee—whom, we don't know— and the people would have been divided and embittered. The whole of South Korea would probably have fallen into chaos. That would have been the end of democracy in Korea, and it would have made an impossible situation for our troops. We've got to admit the old man was right."

As has been evident, Dr. Rhee's chief concern has always been to safeguard the national independence of Korea against foreign encroachment. All other considerations, he feels, are secondary and in a sense derivative. A thoroughly independent Korean government will be able to concentrate attention upon the progressive improvement of the lot of its citizenry. On the contrary, any foreign government which has influence on the peninsula will use that influence primarily for its own ends. Thus, Russia in North Korea has behaved much as Japan did when it possessed all Korea: first, exploitation of the area, then utilization of it as a base and an avenue for further conquest. Trusteeship, or military government, or any other step short of independence, in the judgment of Syngman Rhee, would merely be a means of keeping the Korean people under foreign exploitation. In his thinking about foreign encroachments, he is even more deeply concerned about the Japanese than about the communist threat. The Soviet Union and Red China have important but not essential interests in Korea, he feels. On the other hand, Japan cannot subsist on its own island resources —and has no other outlet except in and through Korea. Hence, not because he suspects the Japanese of being inherently evil but because he understands and sympathizes with their dilemma of possessing a rapidly expanding population on land that is too small and too barren to supply a livelihood, he is convinced that necessity will impel Japan toward another adventure of conquest in Korea. Accordingly, much of his thinking about foreign policy is concerned with devising means of holding off this Japanese threat.

Dr. Rhee has devoted a great deal of energy and thought to convincing his people that their own immediate welfare is of less importance than the long-term welfare of their country. "Tighten your belts, sacrifice, and work for the future," is a recurring theme in his speeches. He thinks it more realistic to emphasize the responsibilities than the privileges of citizenship. He was not favorably impressed by New Dealism in the United States and has not tried to incorporate it into his government in Korea. A continuing dispute which he has had with his cabinet and the Assembly is over salaries paid to government employees—with Rhee arguing that Korea's disrupted situation requires that the salaries be kept low and that patriotism should be the primary inducement to government service. On one theme, however, he has strongly emphasized the immediate values of citizenship: he has never missed opportunities to urge the people to assert themselves and demand their fundamental right to govern their own destinies. Many a time he has mused (sadly, or resignedly, or angrily) half to himself and half aloud to a companion, "The trouble with these people is that they don't know their own power," or "How can they be aroused to stand up for their own rights?"

On the vital question of civil rights, President Rhee is fully aware that the Koreans under his administration have been restricted more than are Americans or Britishers. But, he points out, the position of Korea is so dangerously exposed that some rights must be restricted for the protection of the whole people. Korean newspapers have been restrained from publishing articles favoring a coalition with the communists, for example. Yet those who charge Rhee with throttling freedom of the press fail to keep track of what is printed in the ninety-odd Korean newspapers. A great many of them (on some questions more than half) are outspokenly in opposition to his policies. A favorite theme of their editorials is to denounce some of his appointments to cabinet offices. Similarly, the popular belief among foreigners far from the Korean scene that President Rhee dominates and terrorizes the National Assembly fails to take account of the fact that the Assembly has from the first opposed many of his programs and devotes many of its sessions to listening to its members denounce his administration. Rhee makes no secret of his feeling that the Assembly members are immature in political judgment and often are more concerned in protecting the interests of the well-to-do than in working for the uplift of the masses. Rather than attempting to find some means of strengthening his rapport with the Assembly, he seems almost to welcome its outspoken opposition, in the belief that this actually serves as a reminder to the great majority of the voters that he is their principal advocate and friend.

The presumed arbitrariness and alleged cruelty of the police has been another favorite target of foreign criticism. Rhee points out to those who discuss the question with him that the police force was organized and trained during its first three years by the American Military Government, and that all during his administration it has had three or more American advisers, appointed upon the recommendation of American officials. The Korean prisons are always open to inspection and newspapermen and humanitarian visitors to Korea are prone to visit them often and without advance notice. Trials of indicted persons are held publicly and in important cases the courtrooms are always attended by foreign observers. In particular, the U. N. Commission in Korea has always kept a close eye upon the judicial and police activities, as well as upon all other matters having to do with the progressive development of democracy. In its 1953 Report, the Commission observed: "In reviewing the political situation in the past year, it should be recalled that the Republic of Korea, since its birth in 1948, has held itself open to international observation of the development of representative government. . . . Despite certain trends and practices noted in previous reports which it is hoped are of a transitory nature largely resulting from war conditions, the basic constitutional structure of the Republic of Korea remains representative and democratic."

Education has made steady advances, both in its quality and in the number of students enrolled; the level of health and welfare has been raised despite the ravages of the war; the government, regardless of the newness of its institutions, the lack of democratic traditions, and the inexperience of its officials, has continued to function and to maintain its general services, in the face of the severe disruptions of invasion, bombing, and widespread destruction. Above all, the unity, cohesiveness, and sense of loyal devotion of the Korean people to their chosen government and to its general policies have never been shaken, but continue to be strengthened. In the spring of 1949, U. S. Ambassador John J. Muccio observed (preparatory to the withdrawal of the United States troops, which occurred in July of that year): "If President Rhee loses the support of his people, as Chiang did in China, we will have to abandon him." The most pertinent commentary on this warning is the conclusion expressed in the 1953 report of the U. N. Commission on Korea: "The government has furnished a strong and independent leadership. The president's prestige with the people of the Republic of Korea appears to have increased during the period under review, as a result of the stand he took in connection with the armistice and the release of prisoners. Perhaps the growing confidence of the government in its own abilities is the most significant trend of the past year. The government has convincingly demonstrated its will to insist on the recognition of what it considers the basic interests of the republic."

Chapter XV

BEHIND
THE WAR IN KOREA

THE EXTERNAL EVENTS and general development of the war in Korea have been widely reported in the press and have formed the subject matter for a score of books. The U. S. State Department and the U. N. have issued many official statements of their policies. It is to be hoped that historians of the future may somehow gain access to memoirs and official documents which will clarify the ambitions, roles and inter-relationships of the various communist participants. Meanwhile, another gap which can now be filled in is a view of the war as seen by President Rhee.

In 1949 President Rhee quietly commenced a movement to initiate a Pacific area anticommunist pact which would match the NATO alliance in Europe. In furtherance of this idea he wrote to President Quirino of the Philippines, asking him to be its public sponsor, and he invited Chiang Kai-shek to visit him at Chinhae, where they discussed the idea. On May 16, 1949, Rhee issued a press statement in which he said, "What I am advocating as a solution to the grave threat against Korea and all Asia by the aggressive forces of communism is adoption of one of the following three things: 1) The formation of a Pacific Pact similar to the Atlantic Pact; or 2) An agreement between the United States and Korea alone, or with some other nations, for mutual defense against any aggressor nations; or 3) A public declaration by the United States of a pledge to defend a reunited, democratic, independent Korea, in accordance with the policy of President Truman respecting communist aggression." This movement for a Pacific Pact gained sufficient impetus for Quirino to call a conference at Baguio to discuss it. In view of Premier Nehru's opposition to working with South Korea, Rhee and Quirino reached an understanding that the Republic of Korea should not be invited, and accordingly the conference was called to consider the safeguarding of southeastern Asia. Even this limited concept was opposed by India, and the idea of a Pacific Pact was sidetracked with a comment by Secretary of State Dean Acheson that it was "premature."

In May, 1949, Ambassador Muccio, on instructions from Washington, told President Rhee that the United States troops which still remained in south Korea (about 15,000 strong) were to be withdrawn, and asked him to issue a statement concurring in the plan for the withdrawal—in order, as Muccio said, that the communists should not be encouraged to think a split had developed between the Republic of Korea and the United States. Rhee told him, "Whether the American soldiers go or stay does not matter very much. What is important is the policy of the United States toward the security of Korea. What I want is a statement by President Truman that the United States would consider an attack against South Korea to be the same as an attack against itself. If that is done, we won't need the soldiers." This request by President Rhee was the subject of considerable discussion between the two governments, but no such statement was issued. On June 24 President Rhee wrote: "The American forces will be out of Korea by the end of this month. What do we have for our defense? Most of our army men are without rifles and so is our police and navy. Our defense minister reports that we have munitions which will last for only three days of actual fighting . . . It is highly probable that if we explain this situation in some judicious and convincing manner, the American people may understand what we need and help us get it. As I said before, it is not my place to raise my voice at this juncture but there should be many ways of explaining this pathetic situation."

On September 30, 1949, President Rhee wrote a letter in which he expressed cogently his views of the stalemate situation existing in Korea and around the world. "The longer we drag along, the harder it will be," he wrote. "The Soviets' cold war is always a winning war. First, they give the communist agitators money, weapons and propaganda literature to stir up the people to fight among themselves. Then, later, they form the communist converts into gangs of terrorists, assassins and robbers who, by killing and burning, make human society in the area a hell. By so doing the communists are strengthening themselves and spreading wider and digging deeper all the time. The more robbery they commit, the more money they get. With the money they finance their burning and killing activities. But the nationalists everywhere have no one to count on for help. They have to use every means of their own to defend themselves, and this sort of thing goes on year in and year out. The nationalists cannot keep on fighting indefinitely. They are forced sooner or later to give in. That is what happened in China and what is happening in many other places. What the Americans are doing now in the so-called cold war is a losing battle. If we continue in this losing battle by sitting still and merely warding off these gangsters, no human flesh and nerve can hold on very long."

The letter expressed feelings that were sharpened by the fact that during this period communist attacks across the 38th parallel occurred almost daily. As a requirement for receiving the small arms furnished to the Korean constabulary by the United States, the South Koreans were required to stay back at least three miles from that dividing line. This meant, for example, that in the city of Kaesong the defending forces could not dig in north of that key defensive position, but were restricted to a camp in the center of the city itself—since the 38th parallel lay just three miles to the north. In March, 1949, a communist force struck against the city, pounded it with mortar fire, and sent a column of infantry against it. In order to flank and turn back this attacking force, the Republic of Korea soldiers moved northward along a ridge running up toward the fateful parallel, and turned them back. The next day, Ambassador Muccio called on President Rhee to launch a strong protest because South Korean troops had violated the three mile neutral strip south of the parallel! In the early fall of 1949 strong communist forces, with troops numbering up to 4,000 men, attacked south of the 38th parallel on the Ongjin peninsula, a barren area above Inchon on the west coast. General Roberts, who commanded the 500-man military advisory force of U. S. troops (known as KMAG), serving in Korea, advised President Rhee to withdraw from the peninsula and let the communists have it, since it was without strategic significance. President Rhee scornfully refused and wondered publicly whether the United States ever believed communism could be defeated by retreating before its onslaughts.

On November 20, President Rhee responded to an invitation to write a brief statement for the *Korean Clipper,* a periodical circulated among former Korean missionaries who were in the United States, with the following: "The main resource of Korea in these troublesome times must be the faith of our people in their own integrity and in the principle that the right will triumph. You who have contributed to that faith deserve our humble thanks. The armies of our nation's enemy are lined up along our border—the threat of destruction hangs over our heads. Yet there is something that communist totalitarianism has not been able to understand. Free men will not surrender. Men of integrity cannot be over-awed. We are fortified by the conviction that whoever serves the cause of freedom is marching in the army of God."

On January 12, 1950, came the statement by Secretary of State Dean Acheson, before the National Press Club in Washington, that Korea lay outside of the United States defense perimeter in Asia. Shortly after that, instructions were circulated to American diplomatic personnel in Asia asking them to prepare to explain to the public the anticipated fall of Formosa to the Chinese Reds. On March 8, President Rhee wrote a lengthy memorandum, of which the following is a significant extract:

You can gain some appreciation of our position if you consider that we are sitting here in Seoul, knowing that the enemy in the north can sweep down on us at any moment with more arms, more planes, more of everything than we can muster against them. We have no antiaircraft guns, no planes we can put in the air at the present time, not even any ammunition. The present program of military aid will only provide ammunition, spare parts, and the other little things which are necessary to keep the machinery operating. I say "little" because they are only small parts which won't build anything. It is unbelievable how much these things cost, but they add nothing to our air and coastal defenses. It is only the determination of the Korean people not to compromise with communism and my determined stand against it which so far has prevented Moscow from giving the North Koreans the "green light" to invade the south. They have been better prepared at all times, and have guns and rifles with a longer range than ours . . .

To summarize this whole military problem, we are not after a large army, a large air force, or a large anything. We only want to obtain forces in each branch of the military service which will be adequate for our defense. Even a start on an air corps and a navy would have a great psychological effect on the Korean people and on our enemies in the north. However, to accomplish this means that the State Department must revise its present interpretation of the American perimeter so that it includes Korea. . . .

Two weeks later, on March 24, President Rhee answered a question about the Pacific Pact, in his weekly press conference, by saying: "If there is to be any pact at all, the main idea is to check the communist expansion; to check it by 'cold war' will not be effective. We have seen enough of it and some military approach is absolutely necessary, I believe. What worries us at the present time is the fact that some people seem to worry about our preparation for military and police forces in the national defense. I think that is entirely the wrong view. Unless our friends would like to see the communists completely successful in Korea—how can they criticize us for military and police expansion? Whatever forces we have been using for our defense are necessary. If anybody wants us to stop this military preparation for national defense then he doesn't take an interest in our security."

There, in a nutshell, is the ironic summary of the situation which confronted President Rhee on the eve of the communist attack. The danger was clear and was underlined by frequent communist raids across the 38th parallel. Intelligence reports from the north indicated beyond any doubt a large enemy build-up. The statements by Dean Acheson about the defense perimeter and about Formosa weakened the position of the republic by suggesting that it would not be supported in the event it were attacked. Meanwhile, both the United States and the United Nations were less concerned about the danger of a communist attack than they were lest President Rhee might do something to touch off a conflict. Accordingly, the United States restricted its military aid to South Korea to ten million dollars for the fiscal year and then limited this sum to expenditures only for light arms for a constabulary force. When President Rhee asked

General Roberts for tanks, he was told brusquely, "There is not a tank in all Asia!" Despite earnest and persistent requests by Rhee and his minister of National Defense, no provision was made for gunboats, fighting planes, artillery or other requirements for heavy fighting. The military instruction offered by the KMAG was limited to maneuvers for small groups, typically in company strength, not in the battle array of divisions and corps. The military status of the Republic of Korea was designed to fit it to deal with guerrilla uprisings within South Korea and nothing else.

As a matter of fact, a team of military observers was appointed to assist the U. N. Commission in the spring of 1950, and it arrived on the scene and conducted its first field survey just a week before the communist attack was launched. The purpose of this team was to insure that "neither side" was arrayed in a military posture threatening to the other. Of course the team was not allowed to observe north of the 38th parallel, but on June 24 (just about 18 hours before the attack was launched) it completed a report showing that the troops of the Republic of Korea were dispersed all through the south, and were not in the vicinity of the dividing line, except at small observation outposts. This was fitting and proper; this was the way Syngman Rhee was supposed to behave. This, presumably, was the way to have peace with the communist empire—by displaying such weakness that it would have no fear and hence would not feel impelled to make a "defensive attack." As has been indicated in the quotations from Rhee's letters of this period, he deeply and even bitterly disagreed; but his hands were effectively tied.

The first communist troops moved across the 38th parallel just east of Kaesong at 4:00 A.M. on Sunday morning, June 25, 1950. It was not clear immediately whether this was simply another border raid in force or a major attack; but by

6:30 A.M. news was brought to Kyung Mu Dai that what looked like an invasion in full force was commencing.

Without hesitation, President Rhee sent word to his defense minister, Shin Sung Mo, to resist with full force and at any cost. It was a decision freighted with heavy responsibilities. There was no precedent which might lead President Rhee to anticipate that help from the United States or the United Nations could possibly arrive in time, even if help should be proffered at all. He could well recall the similar situation of Poland on another Sunday morning, September 1, 1939, when the invasion by Germany did lead England to declare war, but did not result in any help being sent to the Poles. What had happened to Poland thereafter was not encouraging. Moreover, Poland had been assured in advance of a guarantee of support; whereas, the world had been informed that Korea lay outside the defense perimeter of the United States. The United Nations was directly involved, through having its Commission in Korea, but the history of international organizations seemed to preclude possibilities of any quick or decisive action. Neither Ambassador Muccio in Seoul nor General MacArthur in Tokyo could give President Rhee any assurance of American aid, for no such decision was reached in Washington until about twenty-four hours later. On the other hand, Rhee could recall that both Czechoslovakia and China had received at least temporarily lenient treatment when they surrendered. With no real armed force in South Korea and with no legitimate hope of substantial help from abroad, the prospect of defeating the invading army seemed so slim as to be hopeless. Yet Rhee ordered not surrender but resistance.

It was a crucial decision—perhaps the key turning point of the cold war between the Soviet Union and the free world led by the United States. A surrender by Rhee would have made the occupation of all Korea by the communists an accomplished fact and resistance after that fact would have been impossible. Endangered peoples around the periphery of Soviet territory would have been still further disheartened. At the same time, it is beyond question that the quick and easy conquest of Korea would have been followed instantly by assurances from the Kremlin that the communists had "no further territorial ambitions." Stalin surely would have made every effort available to him to lull the Allies and to persuade them to continue the "economy drive" which President Truman and Secretary of War Louis Johnson had inaugurated in the United States (and which also marked the policies of the western Europeans). "Peace" was the strange device inscribed on the communist banner, and it may be fairly assumed that the occupation without resistance of South Korea (an area which Americans contemplated with distaste, at best) would not have led many to question the reliability of this claim. Czechoslovakia fell without arousing any strong reaction by the democratic world. The fall of China did not precipitate any active movement toward rearmament. Had Korea followed this same pattern, could the reaction have been any different? The Kremlin strategists, on the basis of the statement in January by Dean Acheson, and similar later statements by President Truman and Senator Tom Connally, chairman of the Senate Foreign Relations Committee, had no reason to anticipate foreign intervention. The patent military weakness of the Republic of Korea indicated that even if it did try to resist, the effort would be futile. The plan seemed safe enough—safe except for the sentiment President Rhee had expressed in his letter of the preceding November to the *Korean Clipper:* "There is something that communist totalitarianism has not been able to understand. Free men will not surrender."

President Rhee's policies and actions in dealing with communist aggression have been subjected to much harsh criticism. Yet assuredly here is something that his worst critics must ponder: his decision to stand and fight on that lonely

Sunday morning on June 25, 1950, made the essential difference in alerting and inspiring the free world to rise up and stop the advancing tide of Russian imperialism. Korea would have to pay the price; but the world of freedom would reap the benefit of learning the necessity and buying the time to prepare to resist.

The next several days were crowded with anguish. Korean soldiers from all over the peninsula were rushed to the front by train, truck and afoot and were fed piecemeal against the invaders. The light bazookas which constituted their strongest artillery fired shells which bounced off the communist tanks like pingpong balls. Uijongbu, a crossroads town halfway between Seoul and the 38th parallel, was quickly captured. Then, miraculously, the republic's troops swarmed in and retook the city. Molotov cocktails—bottles of flaming gasoline—were thrown against the sides of tanks. Carbines sprayed back their answer to the northern artillery and long-range rifles. Fifty per cent of the ROK force of 93,600 men fell as casualties in the first few days of the fighting. After that organized resistance collapsed. In Seoul Ambassador Muccio mobilized all possible transportation and shipped every American out to safety. President Rhee ordered the Seoul radio station to transmit assurances to the population that the communist invaders were being held, and (after Truman's decision to intervene) that American help was on the way. On Tuesday, June 27, MacArthur received orders to give all possible support to the Korean forces. But the occupation troops in Japan were not ready for emergency action and help was slow in coming.

The saga of the long retreat to the Pusan perimeter was a succession of stories of individual and unit heroism, with a strong undertone of tragedy, confusion and divided decisions. Unused to this kind of warfare, General Walker, who commanded the newly arriving American forces, kept his men in the valleys where their motorized equipment could follow the roads, while the communists swarmed around them along the ridge tops. President Rhee urged that the remnants of the Republic of Korea troops be integrated with American units, but in the haste and fluidity of the situation General Walker refused to risk what he feared would be a disruptive influence. With tragically inadequate forces, undermanned, underarmed, and without real liaison between the ROKS and the U. S. troops, the heroic withdrawal went on.

On June 29, the fifth day of the war, President Rhee and Ambassador Muccio, in two light observation planes, flew up from Taejon, where the temporary capital had just been established, to meet General MacArthur at Suwon. On their way a Yak fighter plane tried to attack them, and was avoided only by the pilots maneuvering their planes back and forth through the valleys at tree-top height. David Duncan, a photographer for *Life*, was at Suwon when the planes landed, and gives this touching account of the arrival: "I thought to myself that President Rhee was a rather energetic individual for a man of his advanced years. When I learned what he had just endured I could feel only profound admiration for his composure at such a naked moment in his life, but more than that I shall always remember the way he looked down at our booted feet as we stood in the field alongside the [air] strip. With an expression of tenderness he looked up from the earth and said, 'But the young soybean sprouts. Our feet are crushing them.'" Much was being crushed in Korea; but much endured.

From the midst of the successive blows that were falling that summer, President Rhee wrote several letters expressing his feelings and views. On July 29, for example, he wrote:

So far we have been following wrong tactics. Instead of arousing the fighting spirit of the nation, we have been trying to keep the people ignorant of the facts by telling them that the U. N.

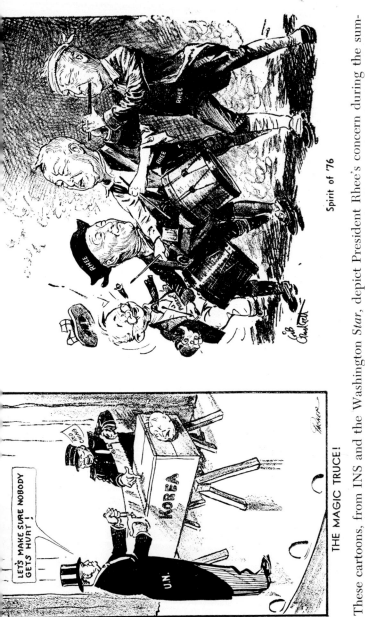

THE MAGIC TRUCE!

LET'S MAKE SURE NOBODY GETS HURT!

Spirit of '76

These cartoons, from INS and the Washington *Star*, depict President Rhee's concern during the summer of 1953 over the truce leaving Korea divided and his Fourth of July appeal to the historic spirit of American independence.

army will start an all-out combat as soon as the reinforcements of men and material have arrived within two or three days. The people, confident of their security, do not think of preparing for their own defense.

The cities and towns were captured one by one without any resistance on the part of the people themselves. Now we have come to the last city, Taegu, which is only a short distance from Pusan. The other day some 60 Red guerrillas entered Hadong and soon they increased the number to 300 men. General Chai (the chief of staff of the Republic of Korean Army) was shot to death when he entered with a small group of his men yesterday morning. It was reported this morning that they are moving toward Taegu. A group of American soldiers and Korean police have gone out there to fight them back, but so far we have no report from them. Meanwhile, another group of enemies occupied Hamyang, a little way to the north of Taegu. This city is profoundly stirred up and asked us what to do. I am telling them to get up and arm themselves with sticks, bamboo spears or any kind of homemade bombs and get ready to fight. I tell them not to run away from their homes, for there is nowhere to go when this city falls. We must stand together in defense of our homes and our city and our friends will do all they can to assist us on land and in the air. If we manage to hold this city for several days until the ships from America bring in the reinforcements, we will have nothing to worry about. Now the youth groups are marching in from all directions, singing songs of cheer. Their fighting spirit is thoroughly stirred and they are preparing for resistance . . .

On August 2 he wrote:

I hold myself responsible for the Taejon disaster. Had I known in time how the American army and the Korean army were to hold separate fields of action, I would have advised against it. The Americans just arriving in Korea, comparatively few in number, rushed to the battle front to face a preponderant enemy force, without any knowledge of the country or the people, whose language they do not understand. Either the Korean troops or the Korean police should have been in the front serving as guides or interpreters. These Americans held the western sector, which is mostly plain rice fields, while the Korean army took charge of the high, rough mountain region between Taejon and the eastern sea coasts. The enemies concentrated most of their men and machines on the Taejon front and General Dean would not back down. This disaster forms a sad story on the pages of history. Utilizing this sad experience, the Korean and American armies should march shoulder to shoulder and the result will be entirely different.

A new phase of the war commenced after the successful landing of the U. N. armies at Inchon, on September 15, followed by the sweep northward across the 38th parallel, as authorized by the U. N. General Assembly resolution of October 7. Everywhere the North Korean communist armies were broken and dispersed. The civilian population welcomed the advancing armies as liberators with every manifestation of joy. Against the advice of the Unified Command, which feared he might be assassinated, President Rhee went north and spoke to throngs of tens of thousands at Wonsan and at Pyengyang. Every evidence indicated that the reunification of Korea would present no problem, so far as the feelings of the people themselves were concerned.

The urge to bring the divided nation together as quickly as possible was uppermost in President Rhee's thinking, even before the communist southward surge was checked. On July 19 he sent a long cablegram on the subject to President Truman, of which the following are the most significant passages: "It would be utter folly to attempt to restore the *status quo ante,* and then to await the enemy's pleasure for further attack when he had time to regroup, retrain and re-equip . . . The people of North Korea are the same as the people of South Korea. All are loyal to the land of their birth with the very minor exceptions of foreign-trained and foreign-directed communists. This war is not a conflict between north and south; it is a conflict between the few who are communists, and who by an accident got control of half of our country, and the overwhelming mass of the citizens of Korea, wherever they may live . . . For anything less than reunification to come out of these great sacrifices of Koreans and their powerful allies would be unthinkable."

What President Rhee did to help accomplish reunification is indicated in a memorandum, written in the third person, which he sent out to a few friends on October 19. In part, it reads: "When General MacArthur was here on September 29th and had a talk with the president in regard to the 38th parallel, the general wanted to wait 2-3 weeks and get all the supplies ready and march on. It was the directive from the higher-ups not to cross the parallel but to wait for the U. N. decision and act accordingly. The president told him that it will be perfectly all right for the Americans to stay behind the 38th parallel, but the Koreans will move on and nobody can stop them. If they get the air support, they can make it. The president knew that the backbone of the enemy was broken and any delay would only give them time to regroup and reinforce and it would be that much more difficult to fight them . . . MacArthur finally agreed . . ."

While the war in North Korea was going well, new trouble developed between President Rhee and the United Nations. The U. N. directed that the authority of the Republic of Korea should be restricted to the south, and indicated that when order was restored in the north, a new election would be held there under U. N. auspices. President Rhee insisted that the constitution of the Republic of Korea extended over the entire nation, and that the U. N. had never questioned that fact. He said the Unified Command was not prepared to administer North Korea, and would have no means of distinguishing between the loyal citizens and the communists. And he pointed out that the Soviet Union had been telling the North Koreans the war had been instigated by the United States, in order that American troops might take over the rule of all Korea. "Now," he said, "if American soldiers do move into the cities and villages and try to govern them, this Soviet propaganda will seem to be true and the people of the north will feel that they must fight to defend their nation against foreign imperialism." President Rhee's arguments were not well received, and U. S. Army officers moved into the areas directly behind the advancing troops, to set up a new military government.

The dispute quickly became academic, for the Chinese Reds poured across the Yalu River to aid the North Korean communists, and on November 28 General MacArthur announced that "an entirely new war" had started. President Truman announced that "under no conditions" would the war be expanded into China, and General MacArthur declared that—forbidden to bomb the Yalu River bridges on which the enemy was crossing or to bomb the bases from which they were coming—he was forced to fight under handicaps without precedent in military history. According to press reports, the U. S. Joint Chiefs of Staff were seriously considering withdrawing all U. N. forces from Korea rather than risk an all-out war with Red China.

President Rhee expressed his own feelings in a lengthy communication dated December 16: "Every day both the Chinese and the North Korean communist forces are moving southward, destroying lives and property, looting, murdering, and raping everywhere they reach, striking the entire population of the north with terror. Thousands of men are being killed on both sides every day. Refugees by hundreds of thousands are pouring to the south, exposed to snow, ice and freezing air, night and day. The Red hordes are slowly moving on without meeting any serious resistance. No one knows what the U. N. may decide to do. All this time the U. N. forces are in a state of suspense, since the decision has not been made as to whether they shall stay and fight or withdraw ... What are the countries that compose the U. N.? Some of them are struggling between the anticommunist and the procommunist elements in their own country. Some are trying to appease the Soviets, hoping to save their own necks. If they continue compromising and appeasing, their procommunist elements will multiply and their governments will begin to crumble."

In another note on December 24 he added: "General Walker's sudden death is a great blow to us all. He was not only a brave soldier but a true friend of Korea. ... The most important thing our friends can do at the present time is to make the American people realize that the situation in Korea is not as gloomy as some of the defeatist press reporters seem to make of it. We are in a hundred per cent stronger position than we have ever been. And we have full confidence. We can take care of the Chinese Communist invaders."

The exuberant confidence expressed in these last sentences was in part the result of General Ridgway's calm announcement upon his arrival to replace Walker, "I am here to stay." Rhee's every effort was designed to counteract the very heavy pall of pessimism which was being spread on every side as the Red Chinese poured in and the U. N. nervously tried to make up its mind what to do. In part, his sentiments reflect the natural expectations that the war with the Red Chinese would inevitably follow the same pattern as that of the war with the North Koreans: initial successes for the invaders, but a resounding reversal as soon as the great Western powers assembled their strength for a counterblow. Where he misconstrued the facts was in his conclusion that the democracies really had no choice except to turn and fight the enemy that was pouring in its soldiers against them. In Rhee's view, it was perfectly clear that the Soviet Union was testing the will to self-defense of the free world, and that if timidity or hesitation were shown, the Kremlin would proceed with its plans for world conquest. So believing, he took it for granted that either Allied prescience or else the sheer force of events would soon arouse the principal U. N. powers to the simple necessity of fighting to win. The loss of the local war in Korea, in Rhee's view, would simply be a prelude to a world war.

Although the leading Western statesmen did not accept this conclusion, and decided instead to work for a compromise and a stalemate in Korea, Rhee has never weakened in his own belief in the soundness of his analysis. This is why he opposed the truce, when it was first initiated. It is why he released the anticommunist prisoners of war, in an attempt to force a reconsideration of the truce proposals, when it was evident the communists were ready to sign. And it is the basis for his present efforts to induce the U. N. to confront the fact that the communists have not abided by the truce terms, and that no solution has yet been reached. Stalemate, Rhee believes, is not so much postponement as it is an invitation to disaster. History will have to be the arbiter.

During the war President Rhee shared the hardships imposed on his people and despite his years he found the strength to make a trip to some forward unit of Korean troops almost every week. General James A. Van Fleet, paying high tribute to Syngman Rhee as "one of the greatest thinkers, scholars, statesmen and patriots of our times," wrote in *Life* how, "For almost two years he went out with me to the front lines and to training areas on an average of about once a week, under all kinds of conditions. When we had to travel by jeep in cold weather, he would shrug away my apologies and smile at my expressions of concern. Then he would climb up into the jeep, and ride there with his fine face and his fringe of white hair standing up out of his parka like a sun shining from above a dark cloud."

These trips, in the summer heat, in the heavy seasonal

rains of June and July, or in the biting continental cold of the Korean winter, were made under the rigorous conditions of war. On one of them on which I accompanied him in the late fall of 1951, we left his Pusan home by car and drove through the traffic-clogged streets of Pusan. At one point his car was stopped by a halted motorcade of military trucks, and a crowd of curious Koreans soon gathered around—containing no one knew how many refugees from the communist north. At the Pusan airfield, we boarded a two-motor plane and flew to a landing field improvised in a valley in east central Korea, just below the 38th parallel. Then we transferred to small planes, each with barely room for a single passenger crowded behind a pilot, in an open fuselage. In this manner we flew through the valleys, almost literally touching the treetops, for another twelve miles to the north. There President Rhee alighted to be greeted by the commanding officers of three ROK Divisions which were destined the following day to enter the battle of Heartbreak Ridge. President Rhee reviewed these troops, and spoke to them for about fifteen minutes. The theme of this and others of his talks to the frontline soldiers is well summarized in the legend he wrote to be inscribed over the entrance of the first Korean military academy: *Sang-mu-dal*, which may be translated as, "Hail to the spirit of the honorable soldier." Many a participant in these forward area gatherings has testified to the great boost which these visits by President Rhee have given the morale of the troops. President Rhee always thought of them as a two-way exchange, for he never failed to return from the front without his own spirits and his own determination heightened.

On this particular trip, our return to Pusan found the airfield closed in with heavy weather, and the pilot was ordered to go back to Taegu. By the time of our arrival there, however, the clouds had closed in there also. The gas supply was too low for the flight to Seoul, and the only available strip was a small jet fighter base at Pohang on the near-by east coast. Fortunately our plane was able to land there, although just in time to beat the lowering clouds. Our party, which besides President Rhee included Ambassador John J. Muccio, General John B. Coulter, and Admiral Sohn Won Il of the Korean Navy, was not expected, and half an hour passed on the drafty field before several jeeps came out from the barracks. By this time it was 7:30 P.M. and the only available food was some warmed up left-overs from the soldiers' mess. After this meal we all sat around in the cramped quarters of the major, who was base commander, until after 11:00 P.M., when several jeeps took us through a driving rainstorm to an adjacent spur of rail line on which a car had finally arrived to carry the president back to Pusan. All in all it had been a day that might have tried the strength and nerves of a vigorous youth, but to the very end President Rhee was laughing, jesting, and giving every appearance of being a host who was having a good time himself and wanted his guests to enjoy themselves. As a matter of fact, even though many of these front-line trips were tiring, and many came at inconvenient times, on the whole President Rhee enjoyed them and found them a welcome relief from the pedestrian duties of day-long conferences and paper work.

In Pusan President and Mrs. Rhee lived in a weathered and somewhat dilapidated old brick residence on a hillside above the harbor. On the lower floor the president had a study ten feet square and a conference room ten by eighteen feet in size, besides which there were two work-rooms for the secretarial staff. Upstairs were a small bedroom, and a five-by-seven-foot office for Mrs. Rhee on a glassed-in porch. Their meals were served commonly in President Rhee's study. The house was heated by an oil stove which stood in one of the secretarial offices, and from which a certain amount of warmth circulated through the remainder of the house. The only other heat came from passages built under the *ondol* floor of Dr. Rhee's study. It was useless for anyone to suggest more comfortable quarters for the president, for in wartime Pusan these accommodations were about as good as could be found. Some solicitous American officials did on one occasion suggest that perhaps he should have a private plane for his trips around the country, but he replied emphatically, "If I had an airplane, I'd want it to be used for carrying bombs to the enemy."

The grounds of the Pusan home amounted merely to a few square feet on each of three of its sides. About a quarter of this space was devoted to the raising of vegetables for the Rhees' table. Under a small tree in the back yard he had a table placed and during the summer months preferred to hold his conferences and do his paper work there. In an area about fifteen by twenty-five feet in size several shrubs and a plot of scraggly lawn were growing. This was the locale to which Dr. Rhee was restricted during the war years for his beloved outdoor exercise. Understandably, in the early summer of 1953 he was eager to return to Seoul, and actually did move back up to Kyung Mu Dai two months before space was found in that badly damaged city for the transfer of the general governmental offices.

There he found not relaxation from the tensions of the war or relief from his labors, but the hardest struggles of his life as he fought stubbornly to try to unsnarl what he felt were the unworkable tangles of the truce. Walter S. Robertson was sent by President Eisenhower as his special representative to work out a means of co-operation between the American and Korean governments. Robertson found Rhee a tough negotiator, but when he got back to Washington he told the Congressional committees which requested his report, "You hear lots of things said about President Rhee but what it all adds up to is that he insists on fighting communism. We'd have less trouble around the world if all our allies had his spirit."

In the talks with Mr. Robertson, President Rhee explained that he opposed a truce because in his view it constituted a surrender to communist aggression, which would be a heavy blow to the prestige of the free world, a danger to the future of peace, and a veritable death-blow to the independence of Korea. So long as Korea is divided, he declared, it cannot be self-sustaining economically and will always have to maintain a huge military establishment with American aid. The time will come when the American Congress no longer will vote funds for such a purpose and then Korea will slip helplessly into communist control. Even before such a time might arrive, the people of Korea and of all Asia would lose faith in the determination of the Western Allies, thus opening the door to communist subversion. In view of the unquestionable truth of these views, Mr. Robertson agreed with President Rhee that one of the necessities for safeguarding even the half of Korea which remained free (for which so much sacrifice had been made) would be the negotiation of a Mutual Defense Treaty between the United States and Korea.

During the period of the talks, which lasted for three weeks, President Rhee made several public statements frankly appealing for the support of American public opinion, including an eloquent Fourth of July broadcast likening the Koreans to Patrick Henry and the American Revolutionists. The response came in the form of thousands of commendatory letters from individual Americans and resolutions of support adopted by scores of state and national organizations. The Hearst and Scripps-Howard Press, David Lawrence and other influential publicists gave President Rhee strong approval. The usually non-committal Roscoe Drummond, Chief of the Washington Bureau of the *Christian Science Monitor,* summed up what many felt in his dispatch of June 15, after Rhee's agreement "not to obstruct" the truce: "Mr. Rhee has not been conquered, and he deserves never to be conquered. He is the leader of the strongest, best-equipped, highest moraled anticommunist forces in the Far East today. The will to resist communist tyranny to the very end is universal and militant among the Korean people. I think it would be accurate to say that there is no more anticommunist population on earth at the moment than in South Korea. Korea needs the West and the West needs Korea. Nothing should be allowed to separate us." President Rhee ended the talks with this conclusion: "I have opposed the signing of the truce because of my conviction that it will prove to be the prelude to more war, not less; to more suffering and ruin; to further communist advances by war and by subversion. Now that it is signed, I pray that my judgment of its effects may turn out to be wrong . . ."

Secretary of State John Foster Dulles went to Seoul in July to negotiate the text of the proposed treaty. Rhee and Dulles had been acquainted in Washington, and Dulles had visited Korea just a week before the communist attack in 1950—at which time he assured the National Assembly that Korea would never be left to face an invasion alone. With this background, the talks between the two men during the four days of Dulles' visit were friendly and understanding. Nevertheless, it could not be said that there was a genuine meeting of minds. Secretary Dulles told Rhee that the signing of a truce did not mean the United Nations was surrendering to the aggressors. The aim of reunifying Korea as a free and democratic nation was still retained; the only difference was the U. N. wanted to achieve it by negotiation, rather than by fighting. President Rhee replied to this assurance: "I am in full agreement with your views. No country has suffered so much from the war as Korea has and if our goal can be achieved in peace no people will be happier than ours. The only question I want to ask is this: if you cannot accomplish our joint purpose by peaceful negotiation, what then?" This question formed the nub of the four-day conference. Rhee would not leave it unanswered, and Dulles would not (could not) answer it.

The result is that the talks ended with a certain amount of uncertainty which was sure to lead to future misunderstandings. In Dulles' view, the United States was committed only to assisting the Republic of Korea militarily in case it should once more be openly attacked by the communist armies. In Rhee's view, the U. N. and the U. S. were committed to a struggle with communist aggression which was left unsettled and in which the repeatedly stated aims of the democracies had not been attained. It followed, then, that they must either be prepared to admit defeat—which in President Rhee's judgment would simply signal the beginning of another period of sweeping communist advances around the world—or else they would have to find some way of bringing sufficient pressure on the Red Chinese to induce them to withdraw across the Yalu River and permit the goal of reunification for Korea to be achieved. In Rhee's view, arguments that the U. N. had "succeeded" in the war because "aggression across the 38th parallel had been repelled" were simply shallow verbalisms. He pointed out that Korea was a united nation for thousands of years before it was divided by foreign agreement—that the U. N. and the U. S. have repeatedly promised that the nation would be reunited under a free democratic government of its own choice—and that this has not been achieved. Wherein, then, has there been success? Moreover, the U. N. armies at one point occupied most of North Korea (having advanced across the 38th parallel in accordance with the resolution adopted by the U. N. General Assembly on October 7, 1950) and after that were beaten back by as much as 200 and 300 miles. Is that success? Finally, in North Korea a million Red Chinese troops have settled down as a foreign army of occupation, where there had been none at all when the war started. In the opinion of Syngman Rhee, these common-sense factors indicate beyond any reasonable question that the war in Korea was lost by the Allies—when he was certain that with resolution it could have been won, and for the sake of the future of freedom in Asia it had to be won.

But his was the voice not heard. His was the policy not adopted. His was the country left dismembered by allies who still hoped that concession was a road to world peace. His was the policy rejected. And his was the voice raised in foreboding prophecy, warning the free world it had paid far too high a price for a booby trap spuriously labeled "peace." Whether his fear that compromise in Korea will cost the democratic nations far more in the future than would have been required for a decisive victory there, remains for the future to unveil. But no one can doubt that he was eminently right in his assessment that the truce in Korea was a resounding defeat for the Korean people and nation. Time will have to demonstrate whether that loss will eventually be retrieved. And for Syngman Rhee (and in a sense for his people also) time is running out.

Chapter XVI

WHAT MANNER
OF MAN

Syngman Rhee's long life has been distinguished by a remarkable consistency of principles and by an unusual record of success in foreseeing and foretelling the course of events. He has won and held the devotion of his people as no other man has ever done in Korea and as few have done in any country. He has suffered physical tortures and the long maddening misery of condemnation and rejection of his views by the major statesmen of the world. When the sharpest crisis in the struggle between communism and the free world was precipitated, he was on the spot and was equipped with the courage to confront it and make the only decision which could serve the fundamental welfare of free people everywhere. He has been often condemned—usually for upholding policies which events have lost little time in justifying. He is near the end of his life, but he fights on with the strength of enduring convictions.

In some more tranquil time to come, after the burning issues of this day are resolved and have become merely data upon which historians may ponder and moralize, a final judgment will be rendered concerning the justice and wisdom of the course he has pursued. It is not, however, too early now to state with assurance that he has carved for himself a lasting niche in the heroic chronicles of the men

318

who fight against disheartening odds for the good of their people and for the principles in which they deeply believe. The name of Syngman Rhee will be long remembered.

But although his name is widely known, the nature of the man himself remains obscure. It is easy to say that Rhee is often misunderstood. But why should he suffer more than other public men from prejudiced, or misinformed or ill-natured reporting? The question is a fair one and the answer is not hard to find. Rhee has been associated with a cause, the establishment and defense of Korean independence, which has long been and still remains unpopular. He advocated freedom for Korea while it was under Japanese rule and we were at peace with Japan. He denounced communism and warned against Russian treachery while the free world was allied with the Soviet Union. He opposed methods and policies of the American Military Government in Korea. He was against the policy of "waiting for the dust to settle in the Far East." He has warned against errors and has forecast disaster. When his judgment was vindicated by the communist attack on Korea, the U. S. and the U. N. were drawn into the Korean war and nobody liked either the war itself or the limitations under which it was fought. The general public distaste with involvement in the Korean war came into focus against Syngman Rhee—the highly vocal leader who stood out boldly calling for stronger measures and more determination.

Of his character and personality, his temperament and habits, his methods and his goals—little is known; and that which is known is reported out of context in scattered newspaper stories. The name of Syngman Rhee, then, stands not so much for a real man as it does for a distorted and misleading myth. What has long been needed is a factual and detailed record of the real Syngman Rhee, with the myth and the prejudice stripped away.

Among the newspaper readers in this turbulent period

President Rhee is most widely known for his adroit capacity
to set the world by its ears. He is also known, in some
quarters with admiration, in others with dismay, as one of
the most influential men of our time. A contemporary of
Winston Churchill, Rhee matches him fully in the length
and in the drama of his public career. Seven years older
than Franklin D. Roosevelt, Rhee was in prison with a distinguished record of political liberalism and leadership
already behind him while Roosevelt was an undergraduate
student in Harvard. Twelve years older than Chiang Kai-
shek, Rhee has both learned much from and taught much to
his compeer in the anticommunist struggle in North Asia.
He is fourteen years older than Nehru, between whom and
Rhee there flows a current of biting personal animosity, and
six years younger than Gandhi, with whom he had much in
common, though they never met. Rhee was a student and
a disciple of Woodrow Wilson, and his life was significantly
interwoven with the careers of Theodore Roosevelt and
William Howard Taft. In his youth he resisted the encroachments of Czar Nicholas II of Russia and in later life the
imperialist ambitions of Lenin, Stalin and Malenkov. He was
one of the first to expose the continental designs of Japan
and remained one of the sharpest critics of Japanese mili-
taristic and territorial ambitions.

Rhee had reached the age of customary retirement before
the start of World War II, yet his period of most influential
leadership came a full decade later. He was editor of Korea's
first daily newspaper in 1895 and a member of the Emperor's
Privy Council in 1897. Yet almost sixty years later he was
the pivotal figure around whom revolved the questions of
war or peace in the crucial struggle between the communist
and democratic worlds. Few men have played so significant
a role in the twentieth century as has Syngman Rhee. Yet
among all the important figures of our era, he is perhaps the
least known.

It is the destiny of Syngman Rhee that he stood at the crossroads of Korean history in a period when Korea has been a focal center of the global power struggle. He has had the clarifying gift of being able to see the essential simplicity of issues which have confused other national leaders because of their seeming complexity. In the history of Korea his name will stand out as by far the greatest statesman yet produced by that prolific land. But in this era of the inter-relationship of peoples, Syngman Rhee belongs to America and to the entire free world, as well.

It is not because of Dr. Rhee's education and forty-year residence in the United States that he has become a part of American history. Nor is it because his political and social thinking became Americanized—though in the long perspective his success in planting the roots of genuine democracy on the continent of Asia may prove the most significant turning point in the relationship of the two hemispheres. His significance for us arises only in part from the fact that he identified himself so closely with the United States that he has not been able to avoid looking at problems largely from an American point of view, nor has he at any time since 1904 thought of world or of Korean problems except in relation to official policies and public opinion in our country.

His basic connection with America's destiny in the Pacific is that he offered guidance for our Far Eastern policies which, to our cost, we ignored, and through his unswerving resistance to the communization of Asia he provided the United States and the United Nations with an opportunity for bringing to a halt the long forward sweep of Soviet aggression. If the Pacific basin continues to grow in world significance, as it seems certain to do, historians of the future will devote increasing attention to the role played by Syngman Rhee in the westernization, the modernization, and the democratization of that half of the world.

Great statesmen are not the exclusive products of large

and powerful states. Small peoples may produce great leaders. Syngman Rhee is a great man. He combines the shrewdness of the organizer, the strength of the leader and the vision of the prophet. He has long and persistently been ignored, but he could not be erased. He has been denied, but he could not be dismissed. He has been repeatedly condemned, only to have his judgment and policies repeatedly exonerated. He has been often shunted aside, but the logic of events he foretold has cast him directly back into the center of the world's affairs.

This, then, is the story of Syngman Rhee: founder of the new Korea! Syngman Rhee: a catalyst of democracy in Asia! Syngman Rhee: the man who has done much to save the values Americans cherish in the Far East, even at times against our will. The story of his life is one of the most dramatic and sensational chronicles of this century. It is also one of the most enlightening and suggestive life stories of our time; for he has lived in and through successive crises which for seventy-five years have jarred and shaken the tenuous relationship between the West and the East.

It is a curious anomaly that Rhee has been commonly rated even higher by his critics than by his friends. In an orgy of denunciation (chiefly emanating from officials and publicists who favored reaching an accommodation with Asian communism) he has been credited with powers almost supernatural and indicted with a bevy of contradictions. The communist propaganda line charges that he is an "American puppet, propped up and held in power by American bayonets." Andrei Vishinsky, in the October, 1952, session of the General Assembly of the United Nations, described him as "notoriously pro-American and pro-Japanese." The *Christian Science Monitor* called him "the problem child of the United Nations." Owen Lattimore labeled him "a little Chiang Kai-shek." The Washington *Post* has depicted him as the *egregious* or the *unspeakable* or the *despicable* Dr. Rhee.

The *Nation,* the *Christian Century,* the Manchester *Guardian* and the London *Times* have denounced him as dictatorial, ambitious, reactionary, irresponsible, and even bloody-handed. Sir Winston Churchill has insisted that England would never fight "to conquer North Korea for Syngman Rhee." At times when his policies and those of the United States have happily been in concurrence, critics have charged that he is "leading the United States around by the nose," and "forcing the United States to ride on his coattails."

He has been caricatured in numerous cartoons as an impish, mischievous or irresponsible disrupter of the farsighted plans of the world's true statesmen. He has been the recipient of some of the sharpest notes ever dispatched to the head of a friendly state by two presidents of the United States, two prime ministers of Great Britain, the officials of Australia, India and Canada, and by two secretaries-general of the United Nations. He has long been a favorite whipping boy of the press in the Western nations and has concurrently been a chief target for vituperation in the communist press. He has received thousands of friendly letters and has been the subject of hundreds of resolutions of support by organizations in countries whose inhabitants would ordinarily have paid no more attention to Korea than they do to Timbuktu or Uruguay. Like Washington, Jefferson and Lincoln in their times, he has had the capacity of arousing virulent denunciations and astonishingly zealous devotion and loyalty. He has become one of the epicenters of his age—a symbol, a magnet, a target; and also a prophet and a statesman as well.

The truly amazing vitality of Rhee after he became president of the new Republic of Korea in his midseventies has led to an unnatural concentration of attention on his age. Drew Pearson, who knew Rhee casually in Washington, wrote a column about him upon his return to Korea in October, 1945, declaring that he was at that time at least eighty.

Every successive year, as his birthday rolls around and another year is tallied, perplexed observers ask doubtfully, "Can it be true that he is *only* seventy-eight?" (or whatever his current age might then be). News correspondents find it difficult to write about him without reference to his advanced age. Yet this very concentration upon his age arises from the amazed perception that he can outwork, outwalk, outtalk, outhope and outplan men also notable for special abilities who have no more than two-thirds his years.

By his critics even more than by his friends, "this old man" is credited with abilities and energy truly beyond human endurance. He is often charged with being an absolute dictator who dominates every cabinet post in the Korean government, who makes every decision of state, who personally passes upon every passport application and every contract for supplies, who supervises the arrest, trial and conviction of every alleged enemy of the state, who not only shapes the foreign policy of Korea but also determines everything that is said about it by every one of its spokesmen abroad, and who (it is admitted) in addition to this still has time to work out expansive and detailed plans for the future development of his nation. *Time* credits him with an appointment schedule of thirty visitors a day—an exaggeration, but wholly in line with the widely held theory of his omniscient grasp of every phase of Korean life. Aside from these exaggerations, it is true that most of the great number of people he does see go out from their conferences with him amazed by his detailed knowledge of the special project they have come to discuss.

No less notable than Rhee's presumed comprehensiveness of power and knowledge is the contradictoriness of the views confidently ascribed to him—again, more vehemently by his critics than by his friends. The newspaper and magazine discussions of Rhee are replete with claims that he was "raised to power in Korea by the American Military Government," but also that "his unco-operativeness and anti-Americanism were the chief causes of the failure of the American Military Government in South Korea." He has been damned as being allegedly both reactionary and socialistic. His hatred of Japan has been denounced concurrently with strictures upon his presumed leadership of the pro-Japanese Korean collaborators. He has been reviled not only for supposedly heading an unholy coalition of landlords and wealthy oppressors of the poor, but also for demagogically organizing the masses of Korea into a political machine. He has been described as having the Messianic delusion that the Korean people will follow blindly wherever he may choose to lead them, and also with perfecting a tight political organization that reaches down into every *myun* and *goon.* He is said to be a terroristic dictator who will brook no slightest show of opposition—and this is said to be proved by the very existence of a highly articulate opposition in the National Assembly, among some of the Korean newspapers, and by some of the Western-educated politicians and businessmen. It is claimed that he appoints no one to office except his own abject supporters, who dare not think a thought or utter a syllable except at his behest; and at the same time it is pointed out that he is continually in the midst of quarrels and disputes with his cabinet officers and other officials of the republic.

Those who hate Rhee (without knowing him) spare no lengths in their vilification. If it were not for the unparalleled loyalty and affection of the people of Korea for him and the high praise from notable men who know him well, it might be thought that Rhee has a talent for inspiring dislike. But to General James A. Van Fleet, who worked closely with him in the Korean war for two years, he is "worth his weight in diamonds," and "one of the greatest statesmen who ever lived." To his long-time Methodist pastor and chaplain of the U. S. Senate, Reverend Frederick

Brown Harris, Rhee is "one of the gentlest and truest Christian gentlemen I have ever known." U. S. Secretary of State John Foster Dulles is proud to refer to him frequently as "my friend" and as a "genuine statesman." He has been highly admired and indeed loved by men as diverse as Woodrow Wilson and Douglas MacArthur. His worst critics have paid tribute to his selfless patriotism and to the tenacity with which he stands by his principles. Those who denounce his policies most unsparingly are usually willing to admit that he has been right in the past, though they hasten to add that he is tragically wrong in terms of whatever present issue they are concerned with.

The truth about Syngman Rhee is that he is that rare being, an *original*, who follows his own convictions even though they lead him into the teeth of direct opposition by world opinion and by the policies of the strongest states. As one of his severest English newspaper critics, Robert Guillain, wrote in the Manchester *Guardian* during the truce talks in September, 1951: "Syngman Rhee, with a blindness to facts equaled only by his ambition, intends that South Korea—and ultimately, of course, all Korea—shall be no one's satellite." Satellite indeed! In all his life Rhee never has swerved from adherence to what he is convinced is right. What "everybody believes" has not influenced him, for he is no opportunistic seeker after popularity. Once his mind is made up as to what is the fundamentally right course of action, he doesn't argue with himself and is impatient with those who argue with him. He simply forges ahead on what he believes implicitly to be the path of history and waits for the laggards to catch up.

If the events of the past three-quarters of a century had proved him to be wrong, he would require no iota of our interest, but would be relegated to oblivion among the countless mistaken doctrinaire thinkers. But since the course of twentieth-century history can be pretty well traced in terms of the causes for which he has fought, he has become a major influence in our time, and must be numbered among the great political prophets of history.

In his youth in a hermit kingdom just emerging from medievalism, he foresaw the inevitability and the desirability of modernization and democratic reform—and was subjected to seven years of torturous imprisonment for being a generation ahead of his times. While English and American policy combined to assist the onrush of Japan to a position of power, he foresaw and warned against the imperialism that was to lead through Korea, Manchuria, China and southeast Asia to Pearl Harbor. When power politics evolved the plan of inviting Czarist Russia into Asian competition with Japan to maintain an equipoise of power in North Asia, he warned fruitlessly that the only hope of maintaining peace in that part of the world was through support for Korean independence as a buffer among contending states. While Western statesmen were trying to negotiate an agreement with communist Russia based on "final concessions," he insisted that the status quo represented by a divided Europe and a divided Asia is too great an imbalance to persist. And after war broke out in Korea in 1950 because his pleas and warnings went unheeded, he urged that the only salvation for democracy, security and a lasting peace lay in a policy of beating the aggression back across the Yalu River whence it had come—an appeal in which he was overruled, with the results yet to come.

For all his achievements as a prophet whose vision has not been distorted by his struggles with power politics, Syngman Rhee is a humble and simple man. He neither drinks nor smokes, yet is not at all an ascetic. He enjoys good food, good books, good talk and such pleasant diversions as fishing, tennis, working in his garden, playing with his dogs, and writing Chinese calligraphy. He chuckles with solid enjoyment over good stories and mercifully forgets them so quickly that his appreciation extends through several re-tellings. He has a great capacity for enjoying the companion-ship of friends and is fortunate in possessing the essential quality of being able to relax and forget the care and responsibilities of office when his day's work is done. More basically, despite his alleged involvement in every minutia of his government, in actuality he holds himself aloof from the detailed operations of his administration and is thus enabled to keep his attention concentrated on the underlying principles and over-all policies.

When one has finished cataloguing what Syngman Rhee does and how he does it, the fact remains that he possesses the undefinable and rare quality of personal magnetism which distinguishes true leaders. No one can associate with him for long without coming to the conviction that he is a truly great man, who lives on a somewhat higher and un-questionably different plane from most people. Genius has never yielded to analysis, though many (including some undoubted geniuses) have tried to define it. Thomas Edi-son's often-quoted explanation that "Genius is ninety-eight per cent perspiration and two per cent inspiration" is sup-ported by the indomitable industry of Rhee. Napoleon is said to have declared that the leader is one who dreams great dreams and then sets out to make them come true. This, again, is an apt statement of the course of Dr. Rhee's life. On the other hand, Buffon's belief that genius is "a great aptitude for patience" finds no support from an examination of the life of Syngman Rhee, for he has made a virtue of impatience—even if he has been forced by circumstances to wait and postpone and try and try again before he ever has been able to carry forward any of his major programs. Those critics who have tried to explain Rhee's pre-eminence with-out being willing to concede to him any special abilities have been prone to call him a symbol. But this label in itself wholly fails to explain why or how Rhee early became for his own people a transcendent figure in whom they long centered their hopes and to whom their loyalties have been dedicated during a grievously heartbreaking period of devastation. The dynamism of Syngman Rhee can be expressed adequately only in the term *leader*. He has known where he was going and he has known how to rally his own people to follow this course. If he has not been equally successful in carrying the great nations with him, it at least is true that he has exercised a far greater influence over the major powers than could ever have been expected from the head of a small and weak nation. Moreover, it has often proved to be true that the major statesmen refused to follow his counsel to their own cost and that of the free world.

Rhee is not a man who gains dignity from his executive position, but rather he is one who imparts meaning and significance to whatever he may do or wherever he may be. This quality is not alone apparent to his intimates but is instantly transmitted to great crowds when he speaks to them or officiates in public ceremonies. His very presence radiates the calm conviction of command, the assurance of knowing what he is about, the consciousness of being a leader—and this he does with no strutting, no pomposity, no pretense. He is inwardly serene, both because he feels himself to be in the right and because he never doubts that both his own people and history are with him. He must be interpreted as a humble man who claims no special credit for what he does but keeps intently and single-mindedly at his work.

Syngman Rhee's basic humility derives from his deep spirituality. From his earliest manhood he has been convinced of the eternal justice and compassion of God and has found his greatest source of strength in prayer. For many years he has accompanied his breakfasts with his wife by reading aloud one or more chapters from the Bible.

Frequent solitary prayer has been for him not so much a solace as an unfailing stimulus to hopeful reaffirmation of his faith. No matter how harshly his course may be criticized or denounced, he has subjected his own policies to the test of prayerful meditation and if they stand that test he remains sure they will eventually succeed. Since his return to Korea in 1945 he has not customarily attended church services and there are few references in his speeches to divinity or religious symbolism. Yet among all the national leaders of our time, there are few others who rest as solidly as does Rhee upon a bedrock of religious faith.

Finally, in assessing his unique position of world-wide influence, there must be noted his native intellectual capacity and excellent education. In his youth he attained the highest levels of achievement in mastery of the old Chinese classics. He earned three degrees from three of America's best universities after he had undergone a period of leadership and trial which provided for him an unusual maturity of judgment to guide his studies. In this college work he majored in international relations, specializing in United States policies of neutrality in dealing with the Far East. He is one of the very few men who ever rose to the presidency of a nation after earning the Ph. D. degree. He did not spring to fame as did England's William Pitt, who became prime minister at twenty-two. He did not climb to political power through demagogic ability as did Adolf Hitler. He did not patiently work his way up the political ladder to eventual top-ranking success as did Franklin D. Roosevelt and Winston Churchill. He combined in his own person the best education of the East and the West; he devoted himself unselfishly to the determined pursuit of a great ideal; and when the time came he was ready not only to lead his own people but also to serve the needs, in a time and place of great crisis, of all the free peoples of the world.

BIBLIOGRAPHICAL NOTE

THIS LIFE of Syngman Rhee is based almost entirely upon original, unpublished sources. In part it derives from two trunks full of personal papers which I was granted the privilege of examining in the storage attic of *Kyung Mu Dai* in Seoul in May, 1949. Just over thirteen months later Seoul was captured by the communists in a sudden attack, and within two weeks after that date Andrei Vishinsky, the Soviet Ambassador to the United Nations, claimed to be quoting from some of those papers in a debate in the General Assembly. This valuable source collection, which was accumulated by President and Mrs. Rhee, and which is partly in English and partly in Korean, is now scattered or lost or held in the archives of the communists—probably in Moscow.

Another principal documentary source for this book is the correspondence which I have had with Dr. and Mrs. Rhee over a period of some ten years and which since 1947 has normally consisted of an exchange of letters each week. Included in this correspondence are copies of various unofficial memoranda, which reveal the background of Rhee's thinking on particular issues as well as clarify the general tenor of his policies, and which define clearly the nature of the problems he has confronted. He has, further, given me access to a large filing cabinet full of correspondence and records covering his activities on behalf of Korean independence between 1919 and 1945. These papers are not now accessible to public examination; but it is to be hoped that at least a generous selection from among them may be published— as a contribution to better understanding both of Korean history and of the operations of some phases of American foreign policy during this period.

Newspaper files, including especially the *Star-Bulletin* and the *Advertiser* in Honolulu, the Washington *Post* and *Star*, *The New York Times*, the *Christian Science Monitor*, the Los Angeles *Times*, and others referred to in this biography, are of value principally in tracing the consistency both of Rhee's policies and of his methods. The files of *The Korean Repository* (1895-98), *The Korean Review* (1901-06 and 1919-22), and *The Korean Pacific Weekly* (1915 to date) contain little about Rhee's personal life but much about the conditions and the issues with which he dealt. *The Voice of Korea*, published in Washington by Youngjeung Kim, of The Korean Affairs Institute, since 1942, contains consistently unsympathetic criticisms of Rhee's policies and actions. So does *The Korean Independence*, a newspaper published in Los Angeles by a Korean group which regularly supports policies for Korea that seem closely parallel to those advocated by the Soviet Union.

An unpublished doctoral dissertation by S. M. Vinocour, entitled *Syngman Rhee: Spokesman for Korea* (Pennsylvania State University, 1953) presents a detailed analysis of Rhee's policies, problems, and methods of leadership during the period of political crisis between June 23, 1951 and October 8, 1952. *American Military Government in Korea*, by E. Grant Meade, King's Crown Press, Columbia University, 1951; *The Epic of Korea*, by A. Wigfall Green, Public Affairs Press, Washington, 1950; *Korea Today*, by George M. McCune, Harvard University Press, 1950; *The Russians Came to Korea*, by Henry Chung, Korean Pacific Press, 1947; and *Korea—My Country*, by Yung Tai Pyun, Korean Pacific Press, 1953 all give valuable interpretations of the situation in and affecting Korea during the period of American Military Government, 1945-48.

Among the books most valuable for interpreting the conditions in Korea during the Japanese rule (1910-1945) are: *The Annual Report on the Administration of Chosen* (in English) compiled by the Government-General of Chosen, 1923-24 to 1937-38; *The Annual Report on Reforms and Progress in Chosen (Korea)* (in English), compiled by H. I. J. M.'s Residency General for 1908-1909, and compiled by Government-General of Chosen, 1909-1910 to 1921-22; *Korea: Forgotten Nation* by Robert T. Oliver, Public Affairs Press, Washington, 1944; *Now Welcome Summer* by Francis Herlihy, the Hawthorne Press, Melbourne, Australia, 1946; *Korea of the Japanese,* by H. B. Drake, Dodd, Mead, 1930; *My Forty Year Fight for Korea* by Louise Yim, A. A. Wyn, 1951; *The Case of Korea* by Henry Chung, Fleming H. Revell, 1921; *The Rebirth of Korea* by Hugh Heung-woo Cynn, Abingdon Press, 1920; *Korea's Fight for Freedom* by F. A. McKenzie, Fleming H. Revell, 1920; *The Tragedy of Korea* by F. A. McKenzie, E. P. Dutton, n. d.; *The Song of Ariran* by Kim San and Nym Wales, John Day, 1941; and *Modern Korea* by Andrew J. Grajdanzev, John Day, 1944. The Japanese case for annexation of Korea is presented by Kiyoshi K. Kawakami in *American Japanese Relations,* Fleming H. Revell, 1912; by Durham White Stevens in "China and Japan in Korea," *North American Review,* Vol. 159 (1894) pp. 308-316; and by George T. Ladd in *In Korea with Marquis Ito,* Scribner's, 1908.

The turbulent conditions in the Korea of Rhee's youth (1875-1905) are best described in *The Passing of Korea* by Homer B. Hulbert, Doubleday, Page, 1906; *God, Mammon and the Japanese* by Fred Harvey Harrington, University of Wisconsin Press, 1944; *Americans in Eastern Asia* by Tyler Dennett, Barnes and Noble, 1941; *The Coming Struggle in Eastern Asia* by B. L. Putnam Weale, Macmillan, Ltd., London, 1908; *America's Finest Gift to Korea—The Life of Philip Jaisohn* by Channing Liem, William-Frederick Press, 1952; "A Chronological Index," in *Korea: Fact and Fancy* by

Horace N. Allen, Methodist Publishing House, Seoul, 1904; *Korea* by Angus Hamilton, Scribner's, 1904; *The Grass Roof* by Younghill Kang, Scribner's, 1932; and *Undiplomatic Memories* by William Franklin Sands, Whittlesey House, 1930.

The nature of life in Korea as the country was emerging from medievalism to modernization (1882-1900) is well depicted in *Chosen, The Land of Morning Calm* by Percival Lowell, Ticknor, Boston, 1886; *Life in Corea* by W. R. Carles, Macmillan, 1888; *Korea and the Sacred White Mountain* by A. E. J. Cavendish, George Philip and Son, London, 1894; *Korea and Her Neighbors* by Isabella Bird Bishop, Fleming H. Revell, 1898; *Fifteen Years Among the Top-Knots* by L. H. Underwood, American Tract Society, 1904; *Korea in Transition* by James A. Gale, Board of Foreign Missions of the Presbyterian Church, New York, 1909; *A Forbidden Land: Voyages to the Corea* by Ernest Oppert, Putnam's, 1880; *Histoire de L'Eglise de Corée,* two volumes, by Ch. Dallet, Victor Palmé, Paris, 1874; *Religions of Old Korea* by Charles Allen Clark, Fleming H. Revell, 1932; and *Korean Games* by Steward Culin, University of Pennsylvania, 1895.

An over-view of life in Korea in recent years (1920-1953) is presented in *Why War Came in Korea* by Robert T. Oliver, Fordham University Press, 1950; *Verdict in Korea* by Robert T. Oliver, Bald Eagle Press, State College, Penna., 1952; *The Korea Story* by John C. Caldwell in collaboration with Lesley Frost, Henry Regnery, Chicago, 1952; *I Married a Korean* by Agnes Davis Kim, John Day, 1953; *The Koreans and Their Culture* by Cornelius Osgood, Ronald Press, 1951; *The Reds Take a City* by John W. Riley, Jr., and Wilbur Schramm, Rutgers University Press, New Brunswick, 1951; *Cry Korea* by Reginald Thompson, MacDonald, London, 1952; *Mission to Korea* by Edgar S. Kennedy, Derek Verschoyle, London, 1952; *In Korean Wilds and Villages* by Sten Bergman, John Gifford, London, 1938; and *Pictorial Korea,* two volumes, by International Publicity League, Seoul, 1950, 1952.

The long history of Korea, out of which came the first formative influences in shaping the mind and character of Syngman Rhee, has been only inadequately presented in western languages, but the best histories are: *Korea and the Old Orders in Eastern Asia* by M. Frederick Nelson, Louisiana State University Press, Baton Rouge, 1946; *History of Corea, Ancient and Modern* by John Ross, Elliot Stock, London, 1891; *The Story of Korea* by Joseph H. Longford, Fisher Unwin, London, 1911; *Corea, The Hermit Nation* by William Elliott Griffis, Scribner's, 1897; *The History of Korea,* two volumes, by Homer B. Hulbert, Methodist Publishing House, Seoul, 1905; and the valuable historical studies published in *The Transactions* of the Korea Branch of the Royal Asiatic Society, issued periodically from 1900 to 1941.

The cultural history of Korea is represented by *A History of Korean Art* by Andreas Eckhardt, translated by J. M. Kindersley, Edward Goldston, London, and Karl W. Hiersemann, Leipzig, 1929; *The Culture of Korea* ed. Changsoon Kim, Korean-American Cultural Ass'n., Honolulu, 1945; *Corean Pottery* by W. B. Honey, Van Nostrand Co., 1948; by various works on Korean architecture, archeology, and ceramics in the Japanese language, by various collections of Korean folk tales and poetry, such as those by Horace Allen, Y. T. Pyun, Frances Carpenter, James A. Gale, and Berta Metzger, who dedicated her *Tales Told in Korea* (Stokes, 1932) "to Dr. Syngman Rhee, from the garden of whose memory came many of these stories"; and by occasional articles in the monthly magazine, *The Korean Survey,* published by The Korean Pacific Press, Washington, D. C. A good bibliography of Korean literature is that prepared by Bishop M. Trollope, "Corean Books and their Authors," *Transactions,* Korean Branch, Royal Asiatic Society, Vol. 16 (1932) pp. 1-105.

The best bibliographies on Korea are: *Bibliographie Coréenne* by Maurice A. L. M. Courant, E. Leroux, Paris, 1894-

96 and 1901; *A Partial Bibliography of Occidental Literature on Korea* by Horace Underwood, *Transactions* of the Korea Branch of the Royal Asiatic Society, volume XX, Seoul, 1931 —with a Supplement prepared by E. Gompertz and published in the *Transactions,* volume XXIV, 1936; *Korea—An Annotated Bibliography of Publications in Western Languages* compiled by Helen D. Jones and Robin L. Winkler, Library of Congress, 1950; *Korea—An Annotated Bibliography of Publications in Far Eastern Languages* compiled by Edwin G. Beal, Jr. and Robin L. Winkler, Library of Congress, 1950; and *Korea—An Annotated Bibliography of Publications in the Russian Language* compiled by Albert Parry, John T. Dorash, and Elizabeth G. Dorash, Library of Congress, 1950. Current bibliographies on Korea are included periodically in *The Far Eastern Quarterly,* published for The Far Eastern Association by The Science Press, Lancaster, Penna. Shorter selected bibliographies have been issued by The Institute of Pacific Relations; by Shannon McCune, Colgate University; and by The Korean Pacific Press, Washington.

Poem composed, in Chinese, by Dr. Rhee at the Carlton Hotel, Washington, on February 19, 1947. Text of his own translation:

> My heart lies with my thirty million fellow countrymen, to weld them together into one nation.
> Then my work will be done and I will retire to the beauty of the mountainside to live out my life in quiet and peace.

APPENDIX

Supplementary Documentation

Chapter I:

The genealogical records of the family of Syngman Rhee are preserved in the Royal Archives in Seoul, under the supervision of Dr. Yun Hong Sup, the Administrator of the Royal Palace. Rhee's paternal line extends from Prince Yang Yung's fifth son, Yi Keun, down through Yi Soon, Yi Yun-in, Yi Kui-dang, Yi Won-yak, Yi Kyung-cho, Yi In-hoo, Yi Yu-won, Yi Ching-ha, Yi O, Yi Chui-kwon, Yi Hwang, and Yi Chang-nok to Rhee's father, Yi Kyung-sun.

Chapter II:

The general significance of the Independence Club in the context of the situation then existing in Korea is described by H. B. Hulbert in Chapter X of *The Passing of Korea.*

The story of the fascinating Horace Allen is told by F. H. Harrington in *God, Mammon and the Japanese;* the Horace Allen Manuscript Collection is in the New York City Library.

Among the Korean reformers of the 1890-97 period were Kim Ok-kiun, Kim Hong-jip, Pak Yung-hyo, Su Kwang-gum, Kim Pyung-si, Yun Chi-ho, Pak Chong-yang and Yi Wan-yong—along with Syngman Rhee, Philip Jaisohn, Prince Min and General Hahn. Leading opponents of reform included Min Yong-ik (who started as a reformer, then changed sides),

Kim Yung-jun, Yi Yong-ik, Kim Hong-nyuk, and Taiwunkun.

Homer B. Hulbert, *The Passing of Korea*, tells in detail the story of the Russian intrigues for control of the Emperor. Valuable historical analyses of Russia's role in Korea are presented by Henry Chung, *The Russians Came to Korea*, Korean Pacific Press, 1947; Edward Henry Zabriskie, *American-Russian Rivalry in the Far East, A Study in Diplomacy and Power Politics, 1895-1914*, University of Pennsylvania Press, 1946; William Appleman Williams, *American-Russian Relations, 1781-1947*, Rinehart, 1952; and David Dallin, *Soviet Russia and the Far East*, Yale University Press, 1948.

The biography of Henry G. Appenzeller, founder of the Pai Jai School, is told by William E. Griffis, in *A Modern Pioneer in Korea*, Fleming H. Revell, 1912. He describes the school building in which Rhee studied as, "a long, low, one-storied edifice, the first brick building in the country. Of necessity, it could not be lofty, for anything high was feared in the palace. All ideas of Korean propriety would have been violated had it been higher than the squatty native structures in use from king to coolie." Pp. 208-209.

The extent of the changes taking place in the Korea of Rhee's youth is well indicated in Griffis's story of an incident that occurred during the digging of the foundations for the Pai Jai School. The laborers, he said, "were in abject fear of the ghosts and spirits that lurked in the soil. A foreign tree, fir or elm, said to have been planted during the Japanese invasion of 1592, which had stood on the site of the school was blown down in 1885. As a powerful spirit lived in this tree, no one dared to take away or burn the wood; but after A(ppenzeller) bought the ground the ghost left. . . . A(ppenzeller)'s smile and wit quieted their fears, and succeeding days and years helped to improve the climate of belief, as prosperity followed. In a word, ghosts and demons alike made way for truth and education." P. 239.

Leaders of the Peddler's Guild in the attacks against the

reformers were two court politicians named Hong Jong-woo and Kil Yung-soo.

Chapter III:

The autobiographical sketch of which a portion is quoted was written by Rhee with the assistance of the scholar-missionary James A. Gale following Rhee's release from prison in 1905. Rhee rewrote it in a hotel room in Seattle, Washington, in March, 1912 while on his way to Minneapolis. Earlier portions of the sketch provide a basis for some of the events presented in Chapter I.

Details of Rhee's life in prison were related to me in 1949 by Hugh Heung-woo Cynn, who was one of Rhee's childhood friends and a fellow prisoner. In the prison school which the inmates organized, Chinese calligraphy was taught by Yang Kwee Chang (later known as Yang Kee Pak), arithmetic and geography by Hugh Cynn, the Japanese language by Kong Won Dal (who had studied at the Tokyo Imperial University), and history by a nephew of the famous Ahn Kyung Soo.

The Spirit of Independence consists of forty-seven chapters and an appendix on "Essential Conditions of Independence." Since the book has never been translated into English, there may be interest in the titles of the first thirty-four chapters, which were written in prison and which comprised the first edition of the book:

1. Preface
2. Each Man Ought to Know His Own Responsibility
3. Without Performance of Duty, Nothing Can be Expected But Disaster
4. If the People Work Together, Independence Will Be Accomplished
5. The Foundations of True Loyalty
6. Be Sure to Have Independence in your Heart
7. The International Complications Confronting Korea

In a note covering the origin and nature of this book, President Rhee said: "It should be remembered that I wrote this book in prison, with very few reference materials, and that I addressed it in very simple terms to the Korean people, most of whom were uneducated and without any earlier knowledge of the Western world."

Among other prison inmates with whom Rhee was intimate were Yi Sang Choi, Yi Wong Kung, Kim Sang Ok, and Lee Hi Chun.

Chapter IV:

In the Confucian system, China was the Middle Kingdom, surrounded by a "family" of other independent nations which were in the relation of younger brothers to the big brother, China. This relationship is fully analyzed in *Korea and the Old Orders in Eastern Asia* by M. Frederick Nelson—who, however, was handicapped in his analysis by his inability to use Korean language sources. The "family of nations" concept was loosely similar to that of the British Commonwealth, without the unifying influence of a common monarch. In a yet truer sense it was an early Oriental fore-runner of the internationalism which led to formation of the League of Nations, the World Court, and the United Nations. Korea was wholly independent, yet was "related" to China, with a sense of mutual responsibility existing between them. This pattern of familial relationships in the Far East preserved the peace in a way never achieved in the Western world. After Japan's seizure of Korea in 1910, the Japanese Shintoists invented a myth that the sister of their Sun-goddess, Amaterasu, had come to earth at a spot near Chunchon, in central Korea—thus hoping to persuade the Koreans to consider themselves a part of the new order of the Japanese Co-Prosperity Sphere.

The efforts of the Korean Emperor to prevent Japan's seizure of Korea are related by F. A. McKenzie in *Korea's Fight for Freedom,* Chapter V, and in the Appendix to *The Unveiled East;* and by Henry Chung in Chapter II of *The Case of Korea.* Hulbert's *The Passing of Korea* is the most comprehensive account of the situation, but it is reminiscent rather than analytical. Tyler Dennett's *Roosevelt and the Russo-Japanese War,* 1925, and Edward Zabriskie's *American-Russian Rivalry in the Far East* are dependable sources for questions involving Roosevelt's policies toward Korea and its neighbors in that period. Y. S. Kuno's *Japanese Expansion on the Asiatic Continent,* University of California Press, 1937-40, is a frank discussion by a Japanese scholar of his country's aggression in Korea. George Vernadsky's *Political and Diplomatic History of Russia,* 1936, tells the story of Czarist intervention in Korea from Russian sources.

Chapter V:

Mrs. Ethel Boyer Kamp has kindly supplied a lengthy account of her memories of Syngman Rhee at Ocean Grove, of which the following are extracts:

One day a slightly built, very aristocratic looking young man, probably five feet five inches tall, wearing a summer weight immaculate black alpaca suit and white shirt with a black tie—and also wearing sun glasses—came out the side door of the house facing ours and sat down looking toward our porch.

He sat intently watching us, but being used to scrutiny (as is every professor's family) we thought nothing of it. The next afternoon Mr. Rhee (for it was he) again took up his post of observation. On the third afternoon Edwin came from the beach holding tightly to the hand of our new neighbor. Being the housekeeper of the family, I at once got him a chair. He told us he was attending George Washington University, so the talk ran of schools and the usual chatter of young people the world over.

We liked Mr. Rhee very much and when he rose to go a few moments later, Mother asked him to come again. This he did a few days later, in company with my small brother, and with a kite in his hand. He asked me if I would like to go down to the beach to watch him fly a kite, since kite-flying was quite a pastime in his country. The day was almost windless and the two men (he always treated Edwin gravely, as if he were a full grown person) had some trouble getting it aloft, even after running swiftly along the beach.

How Mr. Rhee's eyes shone when it finally took the air! It

was a very graceful thing, oblong, white in background, with a round red ball in its center, part of which was cut out to allow the wind to pass through. There were guy strings from the four corners to the guide string held by the kite-flyer. Later I discovered it was modelled on the Korean flag.

The boardwalk was practically deserted when they began to lift the kite into the sky, but soon a crowd gathered. Mr. Rhee, sensing my embarrassment at the stares of the spectators, suggested we take a walk up the boardwalk. Even there he attracted attention, people constantly turning to look at him, for he had a trick of holding his head very, very high and thrown back, as if he would catch every morsel of air in its passing. Once when I asked him about this posture he startled me by saying that he had spent seven years in jail and was indeed breathing in all the air of freedom he could capture. . . .

Mr. Rhee spent his entire time, with the exception of his walks to the post office or along the boardwalk, studying. He was very alert to every word I said, frequently asking of some phrase, "Is that what you call slang?" I would then elucidate the exact meaning and if he did not understand it, would use other words with which he was familiar.

Syngman Rhee attended church faithfully every Sunday alone, tastefully attired in a cream colored silk suit and wearing a panama hat. . . . At the age of twenty-nine he was a dynamic, forceful personality who had one goal in life—the independence of his people, which goal he combined with a deep concern for their individual material welfare. His innate dignity communicated itself to everyone, friend or stranger, so that he was always spoken of, as well as to, as Mister Rhee. Never loquacious himself, he had a way of putting people at ease in his company, while his quiet reserve forbade undue impertinence from strangers. . . .

He had the coveted power of shrewdly evaluating character, plus the ability of reading the unspoken thoughts of those with whom he came into contact. . . .

One day he joined us while we were window-shopping along the walk, with a very radiant face. "What has happened to make you so happy?" I asked. "Letters from home," was the answer.

When we did not see him for several more days, he admitted he was answering them at once, since they took such a long time crossing the ocean. He used to speak often of his mother. Once he mentioned her jewelry and told us his family was considered to be well off financially in his country. . . .

I asked Mr. Rhee about his name and he explained that in Korea surnames are stated first, then one's given name. I asked him what Syngman meant, to which he replied that he did not know. Then I asked who named him, and he said, "My mother." "You must have been a happy baby to be called Sing Man," I jested. He replied, "I do not know about that, but my people are a happy race."

A letter from Rev. Merritt Earl, who was Rhee's classmate at George Washington, casts some additional light on Rhee's personality during these years. Written on December 2, 1949, the letter reads, in part:

Mrs. Earl (formerly Miss Winfred King) and I attended Foundry Methodist Church and it was there that we became friends with President Rhee. I was President of the Bolgiano [Sunday School] Class and Mr. Rhee was a member. . . .

Mr. Rhee visited us at various of our appointments later. One time he came to Waverly Methodist Church Parsonage, Baltimore, Md., and we all took a trip to Annapolis, taking our four children with us. What a trip it was in his big machine! He was attired in a white suit, for it was warm weather, and when he stopped on the way and got out to get some fruit we were objects of interest to all on the road. That's one time when we felt quite important and favored.

When he visited Miss King at her home he showed a special interest in their colored care-taker, named Jim Colson, and one day he missed Jim; then Miss King told him Jim was in the hospital. Mr. Rhee sent flowers or fruit, and visited him there, showing that he did not harbor race prejudice.

He evidently distrusted cats, for he was always uncomfortable when "Skeets," the family cat, was around. He said: "You can't trust them, they are so treacherous."

In the collection of Horace Allen papers in the New York City Library is a note in Allen's handwriting, dated May 13, 1905, Seoul, copying a portion of a letter Allen had written to Hugh A. Dinsmore. It reads: "I refused to give Ye Sung Mahn a letter to a single person in America and tried my best to keep him from going." No reason is given.

A news story in *The New York Times* for August 20, 1949, reveals that George Washington University received a check for $1,100 from President Rhee to be used in furnishing a room in the University's hospital, in memory of the late Dean William Allen Wilbur. In the preceding June Commencement, the University had awarded President Rhee its annual Alumni Achievement Award.

In an interview with Rhee in the Newark, N. J., *Morning Star* for July 25, 1907, is a paragraph in which Rhee's views of Russian and Japanese methods of imperialism are presented: "The Japanese idea of absorbing the whole of Asia is not a bit different from that of Russia, but the method they use is different. Russia, too big-headed, didn't care much about the outside criticism during the hostilities with Japan (1904-05), but the Japs, realizing the necessity of good appearance, at least tried to cover their wolf nature with the sheepskin of Western civilization. Therefore, the former's blows sounded louder, hence hurt the public ear only, while the latter's gun shoots to the heart without noise. . . ."

Chapter VI:

One of Rhee's students at Chong-No Academy was Ben C. Limb, whom Rhee encouraged to come to America for study, and for whom a scholarship was secured at Mt. Hermon School in Northfield, Mass. Following further study at Ohio State College, Limb became Rhee's secretary at the Korean Commission, and later Foreign Minister and Ambassador for the Republic of Korea to the United Nations.

The "Christian Conspiracy Case" is described in detail by Henry Chung in Chapter IX of *The Case of Korea,* and by F. A. McKenzie in Chapter XIII of *Korea's Fight for Freedom.* The case is also discussed in the *Annual Report on Reforms and Progress in Chosen (Korea),* for 1912-13, compiled by the Government-General of Chosen, on pp. 56-59. This report notes that of 121 arrested, 16 were dismissed for lack of evidence and 105 were found guilty of plotting the assassination of Count Masakataka Terauchi. After this judgment was rendered on September 28, 1912, an appeal was heard in the Seoul Court of Appeals, and on March 20, 1913, 99 of the convicted men were found innocent and released, while the terms of imprisonment of the remaining six were reduced. In still another hearing of the case by the Taegu Court of Appeals, the sentence of one of the prisoners was increased by two years and the other sentences were re-affirmed. In a concluding paragraph, "the absurd rumors spread abroad" about the torture used against the prisoners is denied: "As if such imputations could be sustained for one moment when the modern regime ruling in Japan is considered!"

According to Merritt Earl, Dr. Rhee was the first foreign delegate ever to attend officially one of the quadrennial conferences of the Methodist Church.

The Korean Compound School in Honolulu was located on Punchbowl Street, between S. Beretonia and Hotel Streets. Mrs. Loofborrow and Mrs. Zurbruchen were two American teachers in the school; their long presence on the staff helped Dr. Rhee establish his thesis that he was not furthering a "racist" program by segregrating Korean students, but was rather trying to preserve Korean culture and the nationalist spirit.

Walter Jhung, one of the students in the Christian Institute (who became the Executive Assistant to the Prime Minister of the Republic of Korea) recalls that Dr. Rhee spoke frequently in the daily chapel services. The boys sat on one side of the central aisle, the girls on the other, and strict decorum was always observed.

In 1916 Rhee opened his school on upper Liliha Street and in 1918 moved it to more commodious quarters on Waialae Avenue, between Sixth and Seventh Avenues. Mrs. Nodie Kim Sohn became Principal in 1920 and was later succeeded by Mrs. Won Soon Lee. In 1924 the school was moved to a still larger location in Kalihi Valley, where it remained until, in 1932, it was converted into a home for orphans and abandoned children. The school property rose in value to over $100,000. In 1952 it was sold, along with the Liliha Street Church properties, which brought over $200,-000. The combined sum, at Dr. Rhee's request, was used to start an International University at Inchon, Korea.

Many of the Heunsadang members (including Chough Pyung-ok, W. P. Kim, John Myun Chang, Myo Mook Lee, etc.) were appointed by President Rhee to the cabinet of the Republic, after 1948, and to other high posts in the Government, in an effort to end the old feud and create a new spirit of unity. The factional division, however, has never been healed.

Chapter VII:

Gandhi used passive resistance as a political weapon in South Africa prior to 1919, but his famous bloodless revolution against England in India began two months after the Mansei demonstrations in Korea.

For an account of the background of the Mansei revolution among the Korean patriots in Hawaii, see, "Korean Independence Activities of Overseas Koreans" by Walter Jhung, in *The Korean Survey,* Vol. I (December, 1952) pp. 7-10. For vivid portrayals of the preparation and conduct of the revolution inside Korea, see *The Grass Roof* by Young-hill Kang (Scribner's, 1932); *My Forty Year Fight for Korea* by Louise Yim (A. A. Wyn, 1951); and the excellent historical analyses by Chung, Cynn and McKenzie.

The Chuntokyo Cult is described in *The Culture of Korea* by Changsoon Kim and *Religions of Old Korea* by Charles A. Clark.

The Bright Moon Café in Seoul was not damaged in the successive sieges of the city in 1950-51.

Valentine McClatchy was the publisher of the Sacramento *Bee* who wrote an eye-witness account of the Japanese brutalities against the demonstrators.

Another eye-witness account was written by Sidney Greenbie, "Korea Asserts Herself," for *Asia*, September, 1919.

The letter by the anonymous American is given in full in F. A. McKenzie's, *Korea's Fight for Freedom*, which in Chapter XV offers considerable substantiating evidence of Japanese atrocities against the passive patriots.

In the *Annual Report on the Reforms and Progress in Chosen (1918-21)*, the "Independence Agitation" is described (pp. 157-160) in vastly different terms. It was limited to half a million agitators, according to this report by the Japanese Governor-General, most of whom were misled by a few leaders, and the Japanese reacted with force only when "the mobs assumed a more defiant attitude toward those in authority."

"In discussing the uprising of 1919," the report states, "it must be repeated again that it was planned by some Koreans at home and abroad who felt discontent at the Government. They were blind not only to the general trend of the world, but to the cast of world thought, and following the doctrine of self-determination of nations, which they could not fully comprehend, eagerly looked for the occurrence of some great political change. . . . For a time it seemed as if the populace were really responding to their cry, but the hold they gained was only fleeting, for the majority joining the movement scarcely knew what it was all about. . . .

"While the uprising was still in full swing most of the more thoughtful Koreans, though fully convinced of the folly of the Independence Movement, were compelled by force of intimidation to appear tacitly in favor of it. . . . Furthermore, on all the facts of the Korean situation being more clearly made known to the world on the conclusion of the peace treaty at Paris, the utter futility of the movement became apparent to even the most ardent upholder of it, with the result that outside assistance almost completely ceased. Though there are still some rebellious Koreans secretly trying to mislead the people by scattering wild rumors or seditious writings, their efforts are foredoomed to failure, for the people are in no mind to be led astray by them . . ."

In that same *Annual Report*, on page 232, it is noted that 831,667 Koreans (out of a population at that time of 17,288,-989) were arrested—as contrasted with 61,444 persons arrested in 1917.

The story of the Mansei demonstrations was told by Korean participants in three pamphlets, *Korean Independence Movement*, Shanghai, 1920; *Independence for Korea*, issued by the Bureau and League of Friends for Korea, Philadelphia, 1920; and *Japanese Diplomacy and Force in Korea*, issued by the Korean National Association, San Francisco, May 1, 1919. A fuller account was written by Carlton W. Kendall, *The Truth About Korea*, published by the Korean National Association, San Francisco, 1919.

Koreans elected to the National Assembly of the Republic in Exile were: Mansik Lee, Yong-kiu Lee, Hun Kang, You Kim, Jun-ku Choi, Lai-soo Lee, Shik You, Myung-sun Kim, Syk Ki, Taik Kim, Hang-yung Park, Jong-wook Lee, Kun Lyu, Yik Ju, Ryun-jun Kim, Jang-ho Park, Ki-hun Song, Ji-hyung Kang, Sung-wok Hong, Dam-kio Jung, Yong-joon Lee, Dong-wook Lee, Sung Jang, Jooi Chang and Taik Park.

Members of the first cabinet were: President—Syngman Rhee; Premier—Dong-whi Lee; Minister of Foreign Affairs—

Youngman Park; Minister of War—Pak-lin Low; Minister of Law—Liu-sin Shin; Minister of Communications—Chang Pum Moon; Chief of Staff—Dong-ul Lew; Vice Chiefs of Staff—Nam-soo Han and Sei-yung Lee; Minister of Interior —Dong-yung Lee; Minister of Treasury—Si-yung Lee; Minister of Education—J. Kiusic Kimm; and Minister of Labor— Chang Ho Ahn. (Note: all these names are listed in the Western rather than Oriental style, with the surname last. Cabinet members are listed in order of precedence.)

The local chapters of the League of the Friends of Korea, together with their Presidents, were as follows:

Alliance, Ohio	Dr. T. W. Bryan
Ann Arbor, Michigan	Dr. W. C. Rufus
Mansfield, Ohio	Rev. R. E. Tuloos
Newberg, Oregon	Dr. Charles F. Gibson
Chicago, Illinois	Senator J. S. Barbour
Parksville, Missouri	Senator Selden P. Spencer
Fostoria, Ohio	Dr. F. A. Wilbur
Kansas City, Missouri	Dr. Grant A. Robbins
Washington, D. C.	Admiral J. C. Watson
Lima, Ohio	Rev. T. R. Hamilton
Findlay, Ohio	Dr. W. W. Geyer
Boston, Mass.	Dr. L. N. Murlin
New York City	Dr. Charles J. Smith
Columbus, Ohio	Dr. William Houston
Philadelphia, Pa.	Dr. Floyd W. Tomkins
Reading, Pa.	Mr. Frank S. Livengood
San Francisco, Cal.	Dr. L. A. McAfee
Upper Perkiomen Valley, Pa.	Rev. Colvin M. Delong

Youngman Park was assassinated in Peking in 1921.

During this period every effort was made by Dr. Rhee to engage all possible help. An example is a letter which he wrote on September 3, 1921 to Mr. Young Han Choo, a poor but ardent partisan, who from that time devoted himself wholly to the cause of restoring the Korean nation. In 1948

Mr. Choo was named Consul General for the Republic of Korea at San Francisco. The letter follows:

"Your good letter of August 29 was received the other day and I was glad to hear from you.

"As you have said in your letter, there are certain elements in Peking, Hawaii and even in America who are trying to overthrow or at least to undermine the Government which was established and has been maintained at the sacrifice of the blood of our compatriots. This is the time when all patriotic people of Korea should do their part in defending and supporting the Government.

"You who have been always true and loyal to me as your friend and as a leader of your people must cooperate with many others in their patriotic activities, for you cannot make your influence felt anywhere in any big undertaking unless you work with others. I want you to take part in the movement which our people in Hawaii and America and also in the Far East are launching now. Some may do it openly and publicly and some may do it quietly on a small scale, yet there are many activities going on in different parts of the world at this time, because the situation demands such an organized effort on the part of the good citizens of our Republic.

"I have no money to send you anywhere or to support you while engaged in any part of the movement. Thousands of our compatriots at home are doing things for their country without having someone to support them or finance them. You will have to finance yourself while opening your way to such a place where your service will be most needed.

"The people in Hawaii are talking about you and want someone like yourself. They cannot send you your travelling expenses and promise you a certain sum of money for your support or anything like that. But if you go there, I know they will do all they can to use you and to work with you until you can make room for yourself and get a living and an opportunity to serve your country.

"There are several things you can do in this country and you will find many who feel just as you do. I have no time to enumerate them but you have some ideas of your own.

"With no motive other than my desire to serve the Cause to my best ability, I appeal to your patriotism to take up some work which will help me and our common Cause.

Yours affectionately,
(signed) S. Rhee"

The credentials wired to President Rhee from the Shanghai Government, on September 21, 1921, read as follows:

"Be it known that the Provisional Government of the Republic of Korea at its special session duly called and held on the 29th day of September, 1921, passed and enacted the following resolution, to wit:

"Whereas, Syngman Rhee, the President of the Republic, has duly constituted and appointed a Commission with full plenary powers to appear before and make representations to and participate in the Disarmament Conference, to be convened at Washington, District of Columbia, United States of America, on the eleventh of November, 1921, with the following personnel:

> Syngman Rhee, *ex officio*, chairman
> Philip Jaisohn, vice-chairman
> Henry Chung, secretary
> Fred A. Dolph, counsellor

with full and complete power in the persons named to add an additional member so that the full membership of the commission shall be five;

"Now, therefore, be it resolved that this Congress undertakes to entrust and empower fully and completely the aforementioned Commission to the Conference to present the case of Korea at the Conference and to negotiate and contract any and all agreements, protocols, treaties and covenants arising therefrom, for and on behalf of the Republic of Korea."

Dr. Syngman Rhee photographed in Washington, D.C., in March, 1947. (*G. F. Wooten*)

The following note was written by President Rhee on January 8, 1954:

"*J. J. WILLIAMS:* I met him first in his office on Pennsylvania Avenue in April, 1919. It was the time when telegrams were being received from Shanghai, Paris, Honolulu and elsewhere, reporting the continuation of the demonstrations and of the terrible massacres by the Japanese gendarmes. I went upstairs to the office and introduced myself to him and showed him a couple of these messages. He at once pulled out his typewriter and wrote an article. The next morning the story was out in many papers. After that time I took all such messages to him and slowly and surely the stories spread all over the country. How fortunate I was to find a friend who could lay before the American public the story no pro-Japanese in America or anywhere would dare publish.

"Williams was the Hearst paper correspondent in Paris after the Paris Conference finished in 1919 and was returned to Washington. Since that time his interest in Korean independence remained, even while every other newsman, or any other man for that matter, cared nothing for the dead issue of Korean independence. From then on he did everything to bring the Korean question before Americans and was a champion for the cause of weak nations. His never waning interest won my deep gratitude and friendship, which remains even now."

President Rhee wrote the following explanation of his election to the presidency of the exiled government, in a note dated January 8, 1954:

"The Declaration of Independence was read on March 1st in the public squares of every large city and the Japanese started out to arrest and torture and commit wholesale murder. Boys in the street, dressed like newspaper boys went around and distributed the mimeographed copies of the *Independence News*. The Japanese searched all over the city and finally found the place where the mimeographed copies had been made but found all had been moved away. The Japanese continued to look everywhere but the new paper continued to appear consistently and the Japanese were helpless.

"In the meantime, another group of patriotic leaders met secretly and organized a Provisional Government. A Constitution was drawn up and printed, setting out the organization and the general principles of the Government and the duties of the people, tax payments, laws, etc. This was distributed simultaneously throughout the country. Missionaries and other foreigners marvelled at the set-up and the Japanese police were perplexed. The representatives elected Syngman Rhee as *Jib Jung Kwan Chong Choi* (Chief Executive). Most of the Cabinet members were chosen from those who were abroad with the exception of a few deputies and vice-ministers then in Korea and these immediately fled to Shanghai, secretly escaping the Japanese police. At that time Ahn Chang Ho was in San Francisco and he at once left America for Shanghai. I remained in America, knowing that Mr. Ahn was to establish the Provisional Government in Shanghai. Together with the Cabinet members, many Koreans came out from Korea and with the leading agitators from America and Siberia gathered in Shanghai. They set about electing the members of the upper and lower house for the Korean Congress. There they tried to elect Mr. Ahn as President, but the Seoul election was reported in newspapers all over the world and the people naturally attached more importance to the Seoul set-up than to that of any other organization outside of Seoul. The Congress in Shanghai debated for a long time on the question of whether they should ignore the Seoul set-up and organize another Cabinet or simply change the names of the Seoul Cabinet and follow that program. Finally the latter plan was approved and in order to make Shanghai the place of birth of our Government, Rhee was elected as President and not as *Jib Jung Kwan Chong Choi* because if they recognized the earlier title they would also have to acknowledge the earlier election.

"In the meantime another group in Siberia held a conference and organized a Government with my name as President and Lee Dong Whi as Prime Minister, but when they received the news from Seoul they gave up and joined the Shanghai group. That is how Shanghai became the seat of the Provisional Government, acknowledged by all Koreans both in and outside Korea.

"Later, when the Japanese succeeded in keeping the revolution under control and the money from Korea stopped flowing out to Shanghai, all the politicians began to quarrel over their positions and titles and kept on quarrelling without end. Then the communist elements came into the Government by offering the members some funds, and it was interesting to notice in the Government Bulletins during the years 1944 and 1945 that the Cabinet included some Rightists, some Leftists and one Anarchist."

The following note was written by President Rhee on January 8, 1954:

"*FREDERIC A. DOLPH:* He was one of the outstanding lawyers and as a partner of a large law firm in Chicago was a well-to-do attorney-at-law. His legal briefs were generally short and convincing. During the influenza epidemic he lost all his family and he himself lost his voice and could no longer serve as a lawyer. I do not remember how I got to know him, but through friends he was introduced to me and he told me that the Korean question gave him new spirit. He asked to take up our cause as legal advisor with no compensation, as he knew we were not in a position to pay him any fees for his services. Thus he became legal advisor to the Korean Commission. He prepared many documents, the most outstanding of all being the official brief he presented at the Disarmament Conference in 1921.

"His early acquaintance with Secretary Hughes, Chairman of the Disarmament Conference, made it possible for him to present to Mr. Hughes, together with the Korean petition, a small pamphlet printed secretly in Korea which contained the signatures of some three hundred of the most prominent leaders in Korea, representing every walk of life, petitioning the Disarmament Conference to give a sympathetic hearing to the appeal made by the Korean Commission. When this pamphlet was presented to Secretary Hughes he was asked not to reveal the names on the petition to the Japanese. Mr. Hughes called the Japanese delegates while Mr. Dolph was in the next room and they told Mr. Hughes that he should pay no attention to the signatures as the Koreans were very clever at forging such papers. Mr. Hughes requested the Japanese not to punish those whose names appeared on the petition and they promised not to do so. Then Mr. Hughes called Mr. Dolph into the room and produced the signatures. Dolph testified that the petition was secretly brought to him and was authentic. However, the Japanese ruled that the petition could not be presented to the Conference and it was never presented.

"One evening, somebody knocked at the door of the small Oxford hotel on Pennsylvania Avenue where Dolph was living and as he opened the door the Japanese Ambassador introduced himself and asked if he might come in. He told Dolph that he appreciated his interest in Korea but he was making a mistake by taking up the hopeless case of Korea and that he would more wisely be associated with the Japanese Embassy and help Korea through that channel. Dolph refused to accept this offer.

"Dolph never severed his connection with the Korean Commission until he died in that small hotel. I owe him an everlasting debt of gratitude."

During the early exciting days of the Mansei movement it was reported in Shanghai foreign newspapers that the Japanese Government had set a price on Rhee's head. His return from China was more difficult than his trip to Shanghai, because all the boats plying between the Orient and America made a call at one of the Japanese ports and there was not a ship travelling directly from Shanghai to America. To be safe he could not visit any of the Japanese ports.

Rhee consulted with an old friend, Dr. George Fitch, who asked Rhee if he could get into Honolulu without difficulty. Rhee told him he could and a couple of days later he bought a first class passage on the S. S. *Columbia* going to Manila from Shanghai, without stopping at Yokohama. He told Rhee not to say anything on the boat and to land in Manila and wait until the boat had sailed.

The second day Rhee was on the S. S. *Columbia* he noticed a dignified looking American, whose name he later learned was Bergzole, who had been the U. S. Consul General in Seoul. He was so openly sympathetic with the Koreans during the 1919 revolution that the Japanese had requested the U. S. State Department to remove him from Korea, and he was travelling from Washington with his mother on his way to Canton, where he would serve as U. S. Consul General. Evidently he got on the same boat with Rhee at Shanghai but, of course, they did not know each other. The day after the departure, he met Rhee on the upper deck and said, "Are you not a Korean?" Rhee answered yes and then Bergzole asked his name and he said his name was Rhee. "Are you Dr. Syngman Rhee?" he asked. Rhee told him quietly that he was travelling incognito. He was so excited that he went back to his stateroom, calling his mother, saying that President Yi Seungman was on the boat. His mother, an elderly lady, came out to shake hands with Rhee and they talked of many things.

Finally the boat docked at the Manila pier and Rhee waited until all the passengers who were to land there had been checked by the Immigration Officer. Then Rhee went to him and told him quietly that he was a Korean and he wanted to see the city of Manila. He asked for Rhee's passport and Rhee told him that he had none. The official said he would have to stay on the ship. Mr. Bergzole stepped forward, showing his official credentials, told him Rhee was his friend and would go back to the United States after a short visit in Manila. Rhee was allowed to stay in the Manila Hotel with the understanding that he would appear before the Immigration Chief the following morning. There the Episcopal Bishop did all he could to help him remain for a few days.

Chapter VIII:

This chapter is based largely upon diaries kept by Dr. and Mrs. Rhee, which I examined in Seoul in the Spring of 1949.

Some of the activities of Dr. Rhee during this period are indicated in the pamphlets, *Korea Must Be Free*, issued by the Korean Commission to America and Europe, Washington, 1930; *Korean Liberty Conference*, issued by the United Korean Committee in America, Los Angeles and Honolulu, 1942; *The New Korea*, issued by the Korean National Association, Los Angeles, 1938; and in the book, *Korea: Forgotten Nation* by Robert T. Oliver, Public Affairs Press, Washington, 1944.

The data on Dr. Rhee's activities in Geneva are taken from his diary notes covering that period.

In passing through Denver on his way home to Hawaii from Geneva, Dr. Rhee was interviewed by Francis Wayne, who wrote a long story for the September 12, 1933 issue of the Denver *Post,* which fore-tells with considerable accuracy the price the Western nations would have to pay for their acquiescence in the Japanese seizure of Manchuria.

On April 24, 1938 the Koreans in Hawaii dedicated their new Church, a replica of Seoul's ancient and famous South Gate, on Liliha Street. Dr. Rhee, as Chairman of the Board of Directors, conducted the campaign for funds for the new building.

Speaking in Honolulu, on June 27, 1938, Dr. Rhee said: "In the interests of world peace, and particularly the peace of the Pacific, the people of the United States and the great democracies must become aware of Japan's true motives."

The May 20, 1939 issue of *The Senator*, a weekly hotel magazine, quotes Dr. Rhee as saying: "Maybe this time I can get help for Korea. Anyway, I hope so. But I shall never stop fighting."

For a fuller account of the mistreatment of Koreans in Japan at the time of the Tokyo earthquake of 1923, see Oliver's *Korea: Forgotten Nation*. The *Annual Report on Administration of Chosen, 1923-24*, compiled by the Government-General of Chosen, makes no reference to the events in Japan, but under the sub-title, "Protection of Koreans Abroad," it makes this interesting observation: "Among the Korean residents in Siberia, China, Hawaii, and the United States are found not a few who fled the country because of political discontent or despair at the time of annexation, and these cajoled or extorted money from their honest, hardworking nationals under the plausible pretext of raising funds for the independence movement. But neither their deception nor coercion appears to have influence any longer with the Koreans in general, who are already awakened to the utter futility of their movement, while the so-called Korean Provisional Government established at Shanghai in the spring of 1919 was recently compelled to disband by the French authorities. Though its members still continue their secret activity with Bolshevik backing, they have entirely lost credit with their own people and even among themselves are bitterly divided because of the lack of funds and the difference in views. It is believed that sooner or later they will disperse and be buried in oblivion." Page 147.

In summarizing the guerrilla activities sponsored by the Provisional Government, the *Annual Report* says: "Of late the Korean migration to Manchuria has been induced by the greater difficulty in gaining a living at home due to the high cost of daily necessities. *[Sic]* Among these settlers is a sprinkling of political outlaws, and these men, under the guise of patriotism, instigate or intimidate their peacefully-inclined compatriots into rioting, and plan nefarious actions in conjunction with the professional agitators in Shanghai and Vladivostok, taking advantage of being beyond the reach of the Japanese police. At times malcontents from across the Tumen and Yalu have invaded the frontier regions in armed groups and killed men and cattle, looted and damaged houses, and carried off hostages for ransom. Moreover, they have frequently sent secret emissaries into the country to carry out some desperate designs. In September and October of 1920 a mixed band of some 400 Korean malcontents, Chinese bandits, and Russian Bolsheviki made descents upon Hunchun near Chientao, and destroyed the Japanese Consulate and other buildings, looted them, and massacred many inhabitants, and these sinister incidents became the incentive to further offensive activity by disaffected Koreans in different parts of Chientao. The situation at last obliged Japan and China to send punitive forces to the disturbed regions. After a campaign of a few weeks the expedition succeeded in sweeping brigandage from the scene, and seeing quiet fully restored Japan withdrew all her troops from the district in April of the following year." Pages 146-147.

A Korean account of this same "campaign of a few weeks" is presented by General Lee Bum Suk (who became the first Prime Minister of the Republic of Korea, in 1948), under the title, "The Battle of Ching-Shan-Li," in *The Korean Survey*, Vol. I (October and November, 1952) pp. 7-10 and 8-10. General Lee gives a vivid account, based on his own experiences, of how 2,800 Korean guerrillas harassed and decimated a Japanese force of 90,000 men before the Koreans were finally driven into the hills and dispersed.

Chapter IX:

Dr. Rhee's letter to Cordell Hull reads as follows:

"You are familiar, I assume, with the many efforts I have made, as the representative of the Provisional Government of the Republic of Korea, to bring to the attention of the Government of the United States, especially since December 7, 1941, the desire of the Korean people to be as active as are any of the participants in the war against Japan.

"I feel I can address you, my dear Mr. Secretary, as a contemporary who has, as you have done, both dedicated and devoted his life to the cause of Democracy.

"There have been times in the past when a representative

of Korea could ask and be granted a hearing by the highest diplomatic officer of the United States, as Secretary of State Gresham, in the administration of President Cleveland, addressed on behalf of the President of this great Democracy, a sharp note of protest to the even-then menacing Japanese. He did this when the Korean Minister, invoking the Treaty of 1882 between our two nations, sought, under its terms, the intercession of the powerful Republic which had persuaded Korea to forsake isolation and to permit trade and diplomatic relations to exist between our two countries. That Treaty has never been abrogated.

"You are aware of the long and bitter fight of the Korean people to regain their liberty; you are aware of the revolution of 1919 against the Japanese and the continuous struggle since then of a government-in-exile, the oldest government-in-exile in the world, to keep aflame the light of Democracy for 23 million people who have ever willingly continued to give their life's blood in its defense.

"We have, Mr. Secretary, a national existence of more than 40 centuries and we are compelled to supplicate the world's greatest Democracy and to receive in nearly fifteen months of war against a common enemy no word of encouragement, no deed of assistance, no sign that America, save for one fleeting reference by President Roosevelt, was aware of our existence, sympathized with us, wished to help us, or even cared to receive our offers of assistance.

"I wish in this letter to go on record that, with the publication of reported Russian aims to establish a Soviet Republic of Korea, your Department, more than a year ago, was warned, both by me and by American friends of Korea, in visits and talks with your aides that the inevitable consequence of the rejection of the Government of the Republic of Korea—a government conceived in the ideals of Democracy—would result in the creation of a communist state.

"May I not beseech you again, my dear Mr. Hull, for the opportunity to come by and talk to you personally?"

On March 6, 1942, three of Dr. Rhee's closest friends, Reverend Frederick Brown Harris, Chaplain of the United States Senate, Mr. John Wesley Staggers, a Washington attorney, and Mr. Jay Jerome Williams, Washington correspondent for the International News Service, wrote to President Franklin D. Roosevelt, setting forth a detailed plan which they had worked out with Dr. Rhee for the integration of Korea into the Allied war plans. Their letter follows:

"Mr. President, despite all the onerous cares which beset you, we beseech you to give personal consideration to this matter. As American citizens, we feel it involves the honor of our country of 130 million people, and we know it involves the fate of the Korean nation of 23 million people.

"May we state, with deep appreciation, that our efforts in behalf of the Korean people already have evoked a sympathetic and a realistic response from gentlemen high in your council.

"We wish to register with you, sir, our thanks to Col. William J. Donovan, the Coordinator of Information, to whom we first presented the Korean cause; the Hon. Frank Knox, Secretary of the Navy; the Hon. Henry L. Stimson, Secretary of War; and your assistant, the Hon. Lauchlin Currie.

"The immediate utilization of the Korean situation may be accomplished by:

1. Recognition of the Provisional Government of the Republic of Korea, request for said recognition having unofficially been in the hands of the Department of State since prior to December 7, 1941, and officially since February 7, 1942.

2. Designation of the American military mission now in Chungking, China, to collaborate with Korean and Chinese military authorities in the further development of the Korean National Army in China.

3. Designation of an existing agency, such as that of the Office of the Coordinator of Information, to collaborate with the Korean Commission here in Washington, to:

A. Send to Chungking, accompanied by one or more Korean nations chosen by Dr. Rhee, experts in the use of explosives and the art of incendiarism;

B. These emissaries to train Koreans for infiltration and instruction of patriots in the homeland; and

C. Utilize to the full the short-wave radio both here in the United States and powerful standard wavelengths of certain Chinese stations to broadcast direct to the Korean people the patriotic and preparatory messages of Dr. Rhee, Kim Koo and other leaders. (One such message, requested of Dr. Rhee by the Office of the Coordinator of Information, has, after six weeks of deliberation by the Department of State, failed to win the approval of that Department, we have been advised by the COI. The COI now asks if Dr. Rhee would be willing to prepare an address, for broadcast to both the Filipino and Japanese peoples on the Japanese rule of terrorism over the people of Korea.). . .

"Specifically, the ingredients offered the United States are as follows:

"1,000 Koreans for infiltration purposes.

"Three divisions of Koreans, or approximately 40,000-45,000 men who constitute the Korean National Army.

"Another 250,000 Koreans impressed into the military service of Japan for duty in Eastern China primarily. These represent fertile ground for mutiny, desertion and sabotage.

"Another 450,000 Koreans in conscript labor battalions throughout occupied China, Manchuria and Korea proper, representing additional manpower for desertion and sabotage.

"Dr. Rhee assures us of the intense collaboration of the Chinese General Staff in all Korean espionage efforts.

"The foregoing figures do not take into account the hundreds of young men who, hearing of the existence of a Korean National Army in China, are leaving their homeland by stealth and are begging for the opportunity of military service against the Japanese. Nor do the foregoing figures apply to increments from the 2,000,000 or more Koreans resident in Manchuria, Siberia and occupied China.

"In addition, Koreans now know what war industries and supplies have been moved to their country and Manchuria by the Japanese, to avoid bombing damage in Japan proper.

"Thus the pattern of revolution which Dr. Rhee has entrusted us to deliver to you.

"Here [is] the opportunity to provide literally a blazing backfire in Japan's backyard.

"Here [is] the inspiration to develop the Korean National Army to a force of more than 500,000 men who, with arms and munitions, will redeem their nation and drive the Japanese from it.

"Here [is] the moment for a tremendously effective political offensive, for who are better able to refute Japan's [claim of establishing a] new order in Asia than that order's first victims, the Korean people?

"Finally, here is the one chance for the Government of the United States to prove the American people's belief in the inviolability of treaties, to right the wrong we have done the Korean nation and to demonstrate forever to the people of Asia that the leadership we now enjoy is consistently just and consistently honorable. Let not the lofty ideals expressed in the Atlantic Charter be inert. Let them march before and inspire our brave men in battle.

"The undersigned, trustees of the American-Korean Council, are American citizens who, for more than a quarter of a century, have been interested in the Korean people, serving without compensation and no hope of pecuniary gain."

The Honorable Hollington K. Tong, Chinese Ambassador to Japan, assured me in August, 1953, that the Cairo pledge

of independence for Korea was inserted in the Joint Declaration issued by Roosevelt, Chiang Kai-shek and Churchill at
the suggestion of Chiang Kai-shek. Harry Hopkins is presumed to be the author of the specific wording, including
the phrase, "in due course."

Chapter X:

The Case for Korea by Robert T. Oliver, was issued by
The Korean-American Council, Washington, D. C., April,
1945.

A circumstantial account of Lyuh Woon Hyung's deal
with Governor-General Abe is presented in Chapter XV of
Louise Yim's *My Forty Year Fight for Korea.*

Chapter XI:

Dr. Rhee's 27-point program, which became the basis for
the 1948 Korean Constitution, was as follows:

NATIONAL PROGRAM OF THE REPRESENTATIVE
DEMOCRATIC COUNCIL OF SOUTH KOREA

*(Outlined by Dr. Syngman Rhee in a nationwide broadcast 6
February, 1946, and unanimously adopted by the Council 15
March, 1946)*

1. To establish an independent Korean State based on the principle of political, social, economic and educational justice
   for all.
2. To establish a permanent National Government by popular
   election as soon as possible. All men and women over 20
   years of age shall have the right to vote and those over 25
   to have the right to be elected to public offices.
3. To promulgate a progressive democratic Constitution guaranteeing freedom of speech, of assembly, of religion, of press
   and of political action.
4. To eliminate all influences of Japanese imperialism from the
   laws and institutions of Korea.

5. To confiscate all the property of the Japanese and of their collaborators whether in public or private ownership.
6. To inaugurate economic programs for rehabilitation of Korean industry and commerce and to begin speedy production of all essential consumer goods.
7. To nationalize all heavy industry, mines, forests, public utilities, banks, railways, water power, fisheries, communication and transportation systems.
8. To inaugurate state supervision of all commercial and industrial enterprises to insure fair treatment to consumers, traders, and producers alike.
9. To redistribute all confiscated agricultural lands to small farmers according to their capacity and ability to work them.
10. To break up and redistribute large private estates to small farmers in accordance with the principles stated in article 9, with equitable payments to the present owners of said large estates.
11. To permit small farmers to repay the state for the redistributed lands on a long term basis.
12. To control terms and interest rates charged by private loan agencies and to abolish private pawn shops.
13. To establish a sound and stable currency system.
14. To control the prices of all basic commodities and to insure equitable distribution of all essential foods by rationing until such controls are no longer needed.
15. To reform the tax system by reducing the tax burden on small farmers and by abolishing taxes entirely from poor laborers and peasants whose incomes are too small to afford taxable surpluses.
16. To revise inheritance and gift taxation at a high degree of progressive rate.
17. To establish a system of public-supported compulsory education.
18. To promote and encourage with public support the preservation and development of Korean culture.
19. To institute systems of Unemployment- and Social Security-insurance.
20. To promulgate Minimum-wage laws.

21. To institute State control of medicine and to provide adequate public health facilities for the benefit of all workers.
22. To prohibit employment in labor of minors under 14 years of age.
23. To establish a 6-hour day for all women workers and minors over 14; an 8-hour day for all adult male workers.
24. To provide medical assistance and social aid for expectant mothers.
25. To establish friendly relations with all freedom-loving nations, and to foster reciprocal foreign trade on the basis of equal treatment for all nations and special privileges for none.
26. To forestall and prevent any domination of Korea by any nation or any group of nations.
27. To establish an Army, a Navy and an Air Force for national defense.

Colonel Ben C. Limb's letter of November 7, 1945 to John Carter Vincent read as follows:

Pursuant to our conversation concerning the procedure for restoring self-government and independence to the people of Korea, I have communicated with Dr. Syngman Rhee, who is now working with the political leaders in Korea as well as with the United States Military Government there and [with] the Korean Provisional Government for the establishment of an independent Korean Government. Allow me to present herewith the principles collectively enunciated by the leaders of the Korean people and in which they, under the guidance of their revered spokesman, Dr. Rhee, are determined to achieve immediate self-government:

1. That the capability for self-government can be demonstrated by a nation only by the actual practice of self-government.

No one is now in a position to assert that the Koreans are unable to govern themselves because no one has any proof to support that assertion—until the Korean people have an opportunity to administer their affairs.

Therefore, it is imperative that the Government of Korea must be turned over to the people of Korea by holding a national election at once.

2. The military occupation of Korea was instituted for the purpose of facilitating the surrender of the Japanese military forces there. Now that the task has been accomplished, the military forces of Russia will best be withdrawn from Korea by a mutual arrangement between the United States and Russia.

3. Such withdrawal is essential for:

(a) The unification of the nation both economically and politically, which is manifestly impossible under the arbitrary division of the land as at present;

(b) The freedom of communication and unhampered procedure for a nation-wide election for a government.

4. The fact that Korea was under an enemy domination for thirty-five years is not a valid reason for denying her immediate self-government.

Other nations have amply proved their ability to administer themselves, as exemplified by Bulgaria after the War of 1877 and by Poland after the World War.

5. Korea has maintained an independent nationhood for over forty centuries, during which she has contributed much to the civilization of the world. She can at once resume her self-government as soon as she is given a chance to do so. Any idea calculated to apply international trusteeship over Korea is destructive to the true interests of the Korean people, for such a trusteeship by its very nature will divide up the people and country and make unity and independence impossible. Article 73 of the United Nations Charter is obviously intended for uncivilized colonial peoples. Korea, with a history of forty centuries, is one of the most highly civilized and most homogeneous and literate nations on the continent of Asia. Any trusteeship is most definitely inapplicable to Korea if the spirit of the United Nations Charter is to be honestly respected.

6. The commanders of the American occupation forces in Korea have repeatedly expressed their pleasure in having the cooperation and ability of the Koreans in the task of governing the country. The aspiration of the whole population, the thirteenth largest in the world, is definitely and unanimously for self-government for their nation.

7. The Chinese Government has always advocated immediate

independence for Korea. The President and the people of the United States have unmistakably stood for the same end. Russia also has come out for it. Korea is ready, eager and able to take up self-government. There is no reason whatsoever why self-government should not be accorded to Korea at once.

8. The sacred pledged word of the American Government to the Korean people—as exemplified in the Korean-American Treaty of 1882, the Cairo Declaration of 1943, the Potsdam Proclamation of 1945 and President Truman's declaration of September 18, 1945—must be redeemed without any delay whatsoever, so that all the peoples of Asia may not lose their faith in the integrity of international pledges and in the national conscience of the great powers.

9. The Korean people have ably governed themselves for many milleniums among great warring powers; they have determinedly fought against the rule of terrorism of the Japanese; they will never submit to any foreign rule or trusteeship; they will fight to the last to regain their absolute independence and self-government.

In the words of Generalissimo Chiang Kai-shek at Chungking, November 14, 1945, "Peace for East Asia and the world hinges upon the speedy achievement of independence for Korea. All East Asia is watching the fate of Korea."

If there is to be peace in the Far East, therefore in the world, Korea must be allowed to administer her own independent government. Any other arrangement by which Korea is prevented from attaining the paramount will of her 30,000,000 people will surely lead to another world war. Human consideration must prevail over expediency and all other considerations. Appeasement in any form and sacrifice of justice invariably lead to war. Immediate independence and peace in Korea will greatly strengthen democratic institutions and peace in the world.

Leaders of Korea's political parties adopted a resolution addressed to the Allied Powers on November 2, 1945, at Seoul, declaring that they would refuse joint trusteeship of Korea or any other measure short of complete independence.

In his foreign policy address of October 27, 1945, President

Truman pledged the United States to twelve fundamentals of foreign policy. One of these is: 'Self-government for all peoples prepared for it without any interference from any foreign source.' Korea will present an acid test of the application of this policy.

Chapter XII:

The principal Korean newspaper in Seoul, *Dong-a Ilbo*, carried on July 23, 1946, the results of a poll conducted by the Korean Public Opinion Association, which asked 6,671 passers-by on four street corners in different sections of Seoul: "Who will be the first president of Korea?" The answers were as follows:

Dr. Syngman Rhee	1,916 persons	29%
Mr. Kim Koo	702 persons	11%
Mr. Kimm Kiusic	694 persons	10%
Mr. Lynh Woon Hyung	689 persons	10%
Mr. Pak Hur Yung	84 persons	1%
Others	112 persons	2%
Don't know	2,476 persons	37%

Detailed supplementary accounts of the American Military Government in Korea are presented in Oliver's *Why War Came in Korea;* Meade's *American Military Government in Korea;* Green's *The Epic of Korea;* and McCune's *Korea Today.*

Chapter XIII:

The United Nations' official summary of the situation in Korea between September 1947 and October 1949 is presented in *Background Paper No. 62,* "The Korean Question Before the United Nations," ST/DPI/SER. A/62, issued on May 18, 1950.

The U. N. report on the elections of 1948, including the charges made by Choi Neung Chin, was issued on July 14, 1948 under the code number A/563.

Chapter XIV:

A factual and statistical summary of Korean "Governmental Procedures during Two Years of Peace and Two of War" is presented in the form of summaries prepared by each cabinet ministry, in *Korean Report, 1948-1952,* Korean Pacific Press, 1952. A detailed description of developments under the Republic is set forth in Oliver, *Verdict in Korea,* 1952.

A thorough examination of the expenditure of United States funds for the economic development of southern Korea appears in the *Hearings* before the Committee on Foreign Affairs of the House of Representatives, between June 8 and 23, 1949; and in "Aid to Korea," the Report issued by the same committee on July 1, 1949 as House Report No. 962.

Mr. Kim Koo was assassinated in the summer of 1949 by a Korean Army lieutenant with whom he had been on friendly terms, and who explained his deed by saying he felt Mr. Kim had become an enemy of his country's freedom. Kim Koo was given a state burial and the lieutenant was found guilty of murder and executed.

The detailed story of the election of 1952 is told by S. M. Vinocour in his unpublished doctoral dissertation, *Syngman Rhee: Spokesman for Korea,* Pennsylvania State University, 1953.

Chapter XV:

A comprehensive chronology and selection of official documents relating to American-Korean relations from 1943 to 1953 is Senate Document No. 74, 83rd Congress, 1st Session, entitled "The United States and the Korean Problem," issued July 30, 1953. The chief U. N. summations are contained in the successive annual reports issued by the U. N. Commission in Korea.

In a note written in December, 1953, President Rhee further explained the nature of his session with General MacArthur at Suwon: "After the briefing and a talk with me, General MacArthur bade me good-bye and made an automobile trip to the Han River. In spite of the advice of his staff officers not to do so, he went directly to the bank of the river, where the bridge had been blown up a few days before. From the riverbank he observed the war situation in Seoul, then returned to the Suwon airfield, where I was consulting with the Korean General Staff. He told me then that the enemy had lost its chance and would not succeed. At the time I did not know what he meant, but when the United States troops and material began to pour in, I understood his meaning. The enemy should have pushed on southward immediately, but instead they spent nearly a week in Seoul, giving America time to send the essential aid. The success of the Pusan Perimeter was actually determined by that vital week of delay."

INDEX

373